Objective-C for Absolute Beginners

iPhone, iPad and Mac Programming Made Easy

Stefan Kaczmarek

Brad Lees

Gary Bennett

Mitch Fisher

Apress®

Objective-C for Absolute Beginners: iPhone, iPad and Mac Programming Made Easy

Stefan Kaczmarek
Phoenix, Arizona, USA

Brad Lees
Phoenix, Arizona, USA

Gary Bennett
Scottsdale, Arizona, USA

Mitch Fisher
Glendale, Arizona, USA

ISBN-13 (pbk): 978-1-4842-3428-0
https://doi.org/10.1007/978-1-4842-3429-7

ISBN-13 (electronic): 978-1-4842-3429-7

Library of Congress Control Number: 2018937904

Managing Director, Apress Media LLC: Welmoed Spahr
Acquisitions Editor: Aaron Black
Development Editor: James Markham
Coordinating Editor: Jessica Vakili

Cover designed by eStudioCalamar

Cover image by Freepik (www.freepik.com)

Distributed to the book trade worldwide by Springer Science+Business Media New York, 233 Spring Street, 6th Floor, New York, NY 10013. Phone 1-800-SPRINGER, fax (201) 348-4505, e-mail orders-ny@springer-sbm.com, or visit www.springeronline.com. Apress Media, LLC is a California LLC and the sole member (owner) is Springer Science + Business Media Finance Inc (SSBM Finance Inc). SSBM Finance Inc is a Delaware corporation.

For information on translations, please e-mail rights@apress.com, or visit www.apress.com/rights-permissions.

Apress titles may be purchased in bulk for academic, corporate, or promotional use. eBook versions and licenses are also available for most titles. For more information, reference our Print and eBook Bulk Sales web page at www.apress.com/bulk-sales.

Any source code or other supplementary material referenced by the author in this book is available to readers on GitHub via the book's product page, located at www.apress.com/978-1-4842-3428-0. For more detailed information, please visit www.apress.com/source-code.

Printed on acid-free paper

Table of Contents

About the Authors

Stefan Kaczmarek has 20 years of software development experience specializing in mobile applications, large-scale software systems, project management, network protocols, encryption algorithms, and audio/video codecs. As chief software architect and cofounder of SKJM, LLC, Stefan developed a number of successful mobile applications including iCam (which has been featured on CNN, Good Morning America, and The Today Show, and which was chosen by Apple to be featured in the "Dog Lover" iPhone 3GS television commercial) and iSpy Cameras (which held the #1 Paid iPhone App ranking in a number of countries around the world including the United Kingdom, Ireland, Italy, Sweden, and South Korea). Stefan resides in Phoenix, Arizona, with his wife, Veronica, and their two children.

Brad Lees has more than a decade of experience in application development and server management. He specialized in creating and initiating software programs in real estate development systems and financial institutions. His career has been highlighted by his positions as information systems manager at The Lyle Anderson Company, product development manager for Smarsh, vice president of application development for iNation, and IT manager at The Orcutt/Winslow Partnership, the largest architectural firm in Arizona. A graduate of Arizona State University, Brad and his wife, Natalie, reside in Phoenix with their five children.

Gary Bennett teaches iPhone/iPad programming courses online. Gary has taught hundreds of students how to develop iPhone/iPad apps, and has several very popular apps on the iTunes App Store. Gary's students have some of the best-selling apps on the iTunes App Store. Gary also worked for 25 years in the technology and defense industries. He served 10 years in the U.S. Navy as a nuclear engineer aboard two nuclear submarines. After leaving the Navy, Gary worked for several companies as a software developer, chief information officer, and resident. As CIO, he helped take VistaCare public in 2002. Gary also co-authored *iPhone Cool Projects* for Apress. Gary lives in Scottsdale, Arizona with his wife, Stefanie, and their four children.

Mitch Fisher is a software developer in the Phoenix, Arizona area. He was introduced to PCs back in the 1980s when 64K was a lot of memory and 1 MHz was considered a fast computer. Over the last 25 years, Mitch has worked for several large and medium-sized companies in the roles of software developer and software architect, and had led several teams of developers on multi-million dollar projects. Mitch now divides his time between writing iOS applications and server-side UNIX technologies.

Introduction

Over the last two years, we've heard this countless times: "I've never programmed before, but I have a great idea for an iOS app. Can I really learn to program the iPhone or iPad?" We always answer, "Yes, but you have to believe you can." Only you are going to tell yourself you can't do it.

For the Newbie

This book assumes you may have never programmed before. It is also written for someone who may have never programmed before using object-oriented programming (OOP) languages. There are lots of Objective-C books out there, but all of those books assume you have programmed before and know OOP. We wanted to write a book that takes readers from knowing nothing about programming to being able to program in Objective-C.

Over the last nine years we have taught thousands of students at xcelMe.com to be iOS developers. We have incorporated what we have learned in our first two courses, Introduction to Object Oriented Programming and Logic along and Objective-C for iPhone/iPad developers, into this book.

For the More Experienced

There are many developers who programmed years ago or programmed in a non-OOP language and need some background in OOP and Logic before they dive into Objective-C. This book is for you. We gently walk you through OOP and how it is used in iPhone/iPad development.

Why Alice: An Innovative 3D Programming Environment

Over the years, universities have struggled with several issues with their computer science departments:

- High male-to-female ratios

- High drop-out rates

- Longer than average time to graduation

One of the biggest challenges to learning OOP languages like Java, C++, or Objective-C is the steep learning curve from the very beginning. In the past, students had to learn at once the following topics:

- Object-oriented principles

- A complex integrated development environment (IDE)

- The syntax of the programming language

- Programming logic and principles

Carnegie Mellon University received a grant from the U.S. government and developed Alice. Alice is an innovative 3D programming environment that makes it easy for new developers to create rich graphical applications. Alice is a teaching tool for students learning to program in an OOP environment. It uses 3D graphics and a drag-and-drop interface to facilitate a more engaging, less frustrating first programming experience.

Alice enables the students to focus on learning the principles of OOP without having to focus on learning a complex IDE and Objective-C principles all at once. They get to focus on each topic individually. This helps the students feel a real sense of accomplishment as they progress.

Alice removes all of the complexity of learning an IDE and programming language syntax. It is drag-and-drop programming. You'll see that it is actually fun to do, and you can develop really cool and sophisticated apps in Alice.

After the OOP topic has been introduced and readers feel comfortable with the material, we then move into Xcode, where readers get to use their new OOP knowledge to write Objective-C applications. This enables readers to focus on the Objective-C syntax and language without having to learn OOP at the same time.

How This Book Is Organized

You'll notice that we are all about successes in this book. We introduce the OOP and Logic concepts in Alice and then move those concepts into Xcode and Objective-C. Most students are visual and learn by doing. We use both of these techniques. We'll walk you through topics and concepts with visual examples and then you'll follow step-by-step examples to reinforce it all.

Often we will repeat previous topics to reinforce what you have learned and apply these skills in new ways. This enables new programmers to reapply development skills and feel a sense of accomplishment as they progress.

The Formula for Success

Learning to program is an interactive process between you and your program. Just like learning to play an instrument, you must practice. You must work through the examples and exercises in this book. Just because you understand the concept doesn't mean you will know how to apply it and use it.

You will learn a lot from this book. You will learn a lot from working through the exercises in this book. *But you will really learn when you debug your programs.* Spending time walking through your code and trying to find out why it is not working the way you want is a learning process that is unparalleled. The downside of debugging is it can be especially frustrating to the new developer. If you have never wanted to throw your computer out the window, you will now. You will question why you are doing this, and whether you are smart enough to solve the problem. Programming is very humbling, even for the most experience developer.

Like a musician, the more you practice the better you get. You can do some amazing things as a programmer. The world is your oyster. One of the most satisfying accomplishments you can have is seeing your app on the iOS App Store. However, there is a price, and that price is time spent coding.

Here is our formula for success:

- Believe you can do it. You'll be the only one who says you can't do this. So don't tell yourself that.

- Work through all the examples and exercises in this book.

- Code, code, and keeping coding. The more you code, the better you'll get.

- Be patient with yourself. If you were fortunate enough to have been a 4.0 student who can memorize material just by reading it, this will not happen with Objective-C coding. You are going to have to spend time coding.

- DON'T GIVE UP!

Required Software, Materials, and Equipment

One of the great things about Alice is that it's available on the three main operating systems used today:

- Windows

- Mac

- Linux

The other great thing about Alice is it is free! You can download Alice at `http://www.alice.org/`.

Operating System and IDE

Although you can use Alice on many platforms, the IDE that developers use to develop iOS apps is Xcode, which is free and is available from the Mac App Store.

Dual Monitors

It is highly recommended that developers have a second monitor connected to their computer. It is great to step through your code and watch your output window and iOS simulator at the same time on dual, independent monitors. Apple hardware makes this easy. Note that it is **not required** to have dual monitors. You will just have to organize your open windows to fit on your screen if you don't.

1. To access the dual-monitor set-up feature, go to **Apple System Preferences** and select **Displays**, as shown in Figure I-1.

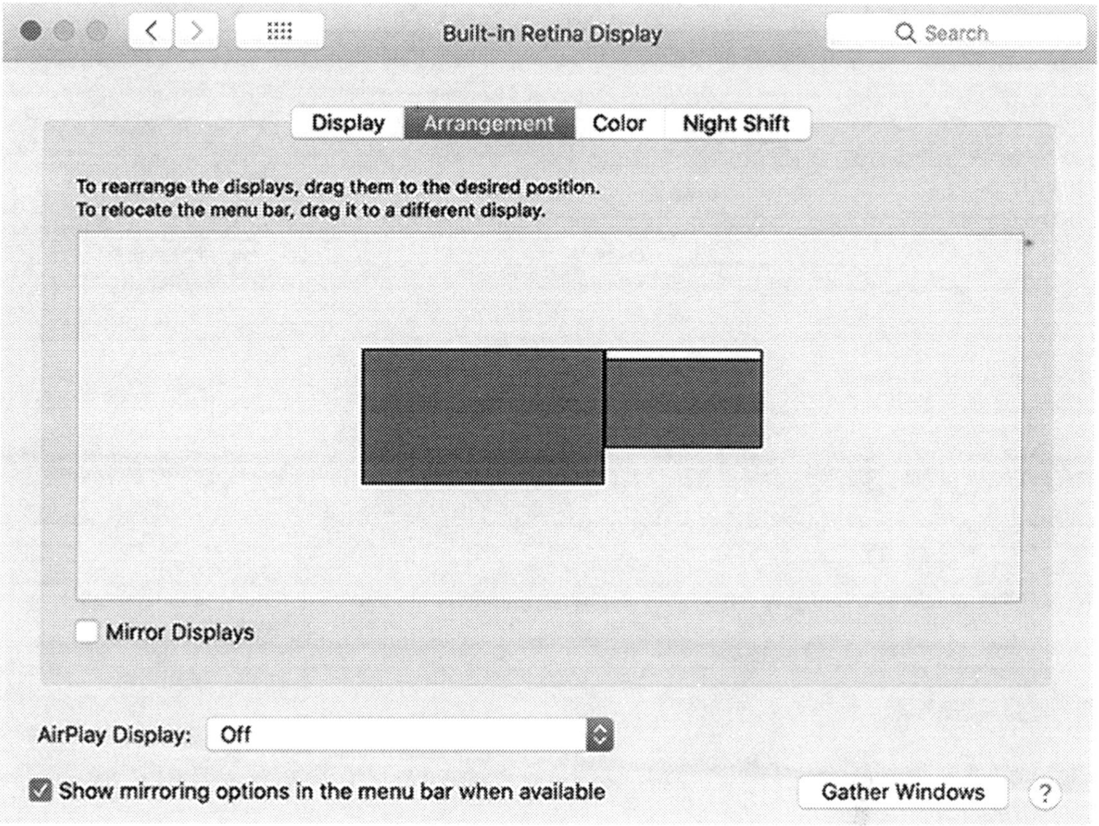

Figure I-1. *Dual monitors*

Book Forum

We developed an online forum for this book at http://forum.xcelme.com/ where readers can go to ask questions of the authors while they are learning Objective-C. See Figure I-2.

xcelMe.com
xcelMe Training Center And Interactive Developer Forum.

◇ Board index

⊕FAQ ⋈Members ✓Register ① Login

It is currently Sat Jan 27, 2018 9:18 am

FORUM	TOPICS	POSTS	LAST POST
How To Access Your Course Webinars And How To Use The Forum New students need to download the attached pdf and follow instructions to register for your webinars after you purchase the class. Additionally, there are directions and updates on how to access your course and forum, post questions, navigate the message board, watch training videos, etc. Moderator: gary.bennett	3	12	by zenith9356 ▣ Thu Mar 13, 2014 10:24 am
Book -> Swift 3.0 for Absolute Beginners: iPhone and Mac Programming Made Easy 3rd Edition This forum contains answers readers may have for each chapter as well as any corrections to the book. The forum also contains the Source Code for the book. Moderator: gary.bennett	17	22	by schurms ▣ Wed Jan 17, 2018 6:04 pm
Book -> Swift 2.0 for Absolute Beginners: iPhone and Mac Programming Made Easy 2nd Edition This forum contains answers readers may have for each chapter as well as any corrections to the book. The forum also contains the Source Code for the book. Moderator: gary.bennett	17	96	by zany76 ▣ Thu Aug 31, 2017 3:11 pm
Book -> Developing for Apple TV using tvOS and Swift This forum contains answers readers may have for each chapter as well as any corrections to the book. The forum also contains the Source Code for the book. Moderator: gary.bennett	10	12	by mdstebel ▣ Mon Jun 13, 2016 11:26 am
Book -> Objective-C for Absolute Beginners: (2nd Edition) iPhone and Mac Programming Made Easy This forum contains all the assignments and questions readers may have for each chapter. Moderator: gary.bennett	20	224	by Drago ▣ Mon Jun 16, 2014 9:27 pm
Free Live Webinars for iPhone Developers This forum lists the schedule for upcoming live webinars for iPhone developers. Webinars are live and have limited seats. Current and former students get first notifications. Seats for all others is first-come-first serve. The sessions are recorded and will be made available to current and former students on this forum. Moderator: gary.bennett	1	9	by Miptigninguaw ▣ Tue Nov 29, 2011 3:48 am

Figure I-2. *The Reader Forum for accessing answers to exercises and posting questions for authors*

CHAPTER 1

Becoming a Great Objective-C Developer

Now that you're ready to become a software developer and have read the introduction of this book, you need to become familiar with several key concepts. Your computer program will do exactly what you tell it to do—no more and no less. It will follow the programming rules that were defined by the operating system and programming language. Your program doesn't care if you are having a bad day or how many times you ask it to perform something. Often, what you think you've told your program to do and what it actually does are two different things.

Key to Success   If you haven't already, take a few minutes to read the introduction of this book. The introduction shows you where to go to access the free webinars, forums, and YouTube videos that go with each chapter. Also, you'll better understand why we are using the Alice programming environment and how to be successful in developing your apps in Objective-C.

Depending on your background, working with something absolutely black and white may be frustrating. Many times, programming students have lamented, "That's not what I wanted it to do!" As you gain experience and confidence programming, you'll begin to think like a programmer. You will understand software design and logic, and you will experience having your programs perform exactly as you want and the satisfaction associated with this.

© Stefan Kaczmarek, Brad Lees, Gary Bennett, Mitch Fisher 2018
S. Kaczmarek et al., *Objective-C for Absolute Beginners*, https://doi.org/10.1007/978-1-4842-3429-7_1

Thinking Like a Developer

Software development involves writing a computer program and then having a computer execute that program. A **computer program** is the set of instructions that you want computer to perform. Before beginning to write a computer program, it is helpful to list the steps that you want your program to perform, in the order you want them accomplished. This step-by-step process is called an **algorithm**.

If you want to write a computer program to toast a piece of bread, you first write an algorithm. This algorithm might look something like the following:

1. Take the bread out of the bag.

2. Place the bread in the toaster.

3. Press the Toast button.

4. Wait for the toast to pop up.

5. Remove the toast from the toaster.

At first glance, this algorithm seems to solve the problem. However, the algorithm leaves out many details and makes many assumptions. Here are some examples:

- What kind of toast does the user want? Does the user want white bread, wheat, or some other kind of bread?

- How does the user want the bread toasted? Light, medium, or dark?

- What does the user want on the bread after it is toasted: butter, margarine, honey, or strawberry jam?

- Does this algorithm work for all users in their cultures and languages? Some cultures may have another word for toast or not know what toast is.

Now, you might be thinking we are getting too detailed for just making a simple toast program. Over the years, software development has gained a reputation of taking too long, costing too much, and not being what the user wants. This reputation came to be because computer programmers often start writing their programs before they have really thought through their algorithms.

The key ingredients to making successful applications are the **design requirements**. Design requirements can be formal and detailed or as simple as a list on a piece of paper. Design requirements are important because they help the developer flesh out what the application should and should not do when complete. Design requirements should not be completed in a programmer's vacuum but should be produced as the result of collaboration between developers, users, and customers.

Another key ingredient to your successful app is the user interface (UI) design. Apple recommends you spend more than 50 percent of the entire development process focusing on the UI design. The design can be done using simple pencil and paper or using Xcode's storyboard feature to lay out your screen elements. Many software developers start with the UI design, and after laying out all the screen elements and having many users look at paper mock-ups, they then write the design requirements from their screen layouts.

Note   If you take anything away from this chapter, let it be the importance of considering design requirements and user interface design before starting software development. This is the most effective (and least expensive) use of time in the software development cycle. Using a pencil and eraser is a lot easier and faster than making changes to code because you didn't have others look at the designs before starting to program.

After you have done your best to flesh out all the design requirements, laid out all the user interface screens, and had the client(s) or potential customers look at your design and give you feedback, coding can begin. Once coding begins, design requirements and user interface screens can change, but the changes are typically minor and are easily accommodated by the development process. See Figures 1-1 and 1-2.

Figure 1-1 shows a mock-up of a rental report app screen prior to development. Developing mock-up screens along with design requirements forces developers to think through many of the application's usability issues before coding begins. This shortens the application development time and makes for a better user experience and better reviews on the App Store. Figure 1-2 shows how the view for the rental report app appears when completed. Notice how mock-up tools enable you to model the app to the real thing.

Figure 1-1. *This is a UI mock-up of the Log In screen for an iPhone mobile rental report app before development begins. This UI design mock-up was completed using InVision.*

Figure 1-2. *This is the completed iPhone rental report app. This app is called WalkAround.*

Completing the Development Cycle

Now that you have your design requirements and user interface designs and have written your program, what's next? After programming, you need to make sure your program matches the design requirements and user interface design and ensure that there are no errors. In programming vernacular, errors are called **bugs**. Bugs are undesired results of your programming and must be fixed before the app is released. The process of finding bugs in programs and making sure the program meets the design requirements is called **testing**. Typically, someone who is experienced in software testing methodology and who didn't write the app performs this testing. Software testing is commonly referred to as **quality assurance (QA)**.

Note   When an application is ready to be submitted to the App Store, Xcode gives the file an .app or .ipa extension, such as appName.app. That is why iPhone, iPad, and Mac applications are called **apps**. This book uses **program**, **application**, and **app** to mean the same thing.

During the testing phase, the developer will need to work with QA staff to determine why the application is not working as designed. The process is called **debugging**. It requires the developer to step through the program to find out why the application is not working as designed. Figure 1-3 shows the complete software development cycle.

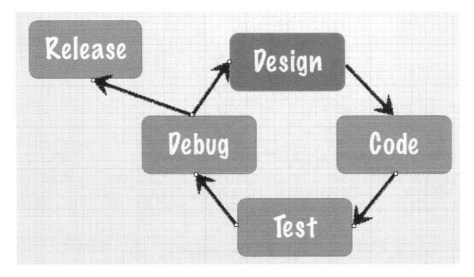

Figure 1-3. *The typical software development cycle*

Frequently during testing and debugging, changes to the requirements (design) must occur to make the application more usable for the customer. After the design requirements and user interface changes are made, the process begins over again.

At some point, the application that everyone has been working so hard on must be released. Many considerations are taken into account when this happens:

- Cost of development

- Budget

- Stability of the application

- Return on investment

There is always the give-and-take between developers and management. Developers want the app perfect and management wants to start realizing revenue from the investment as soon as possible. If the release date were left up to the developers, the app would likely never ship. Developers would continue to tweak the app forever, making it faster, more efficient, and more usable. At some point, however, the code needs to be pried from the developers' hands and released to the end users.

Introducing Object-Oriented Programming

As discussed in detail in the introduction, Alice enables you to focus on **object-oriented programming (OOP)** without having to cover all the Objective-C programming syntax and complex Xcode development environment in one big step. Instead, you can focus on learning the basic principles of OOP and using those principles quickly to write your first programs.

For decades, developers have been trying to figure out a better way to develop code that is reusable, manageable, and easily maintained over the life of a project. OOP was designed to help achieve code reuse and maintainability while reducing the cost of software development.

OOP can be viewed as a collection of objects in a program. Actions are performed on these objects to accomplish the design requirements.

An **object** is anything that can be acted on. For example, an airplane, person, or screen/view on an iPad can all be objects. You may want to act on the plane by making the plane bank. You may want the person to walk, or to change the screen color within an iPad app. Actions are all being applied to these objects; see Figure 1-4.

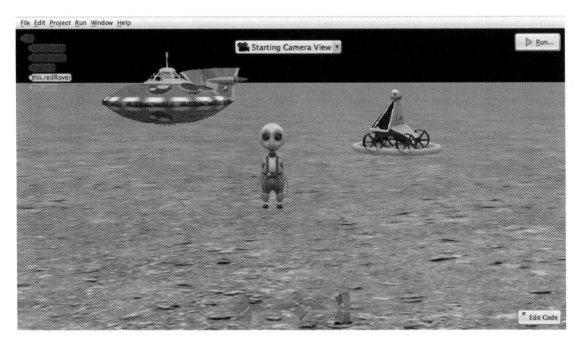

Figure 1-4. *There are three objects in this Alice application: UFO, Rover, and Alice. The UFO object can have actions applied: takeoff, landing, turn right, and turn left.*

Alice will run a program, such as the one shown in Figure 1-4, for you if you click the Run button. When you run your Alice applications, you can apply actions to the objects in your application. Similarly, Xcode is an **integrated development environment (IDE)** that enables you to run your application from within your programming environment. You can test your applications on your computers first before running them on your iOS devices by running the apps in Xcode's iOS simulator, as shown in Figure 1-5.

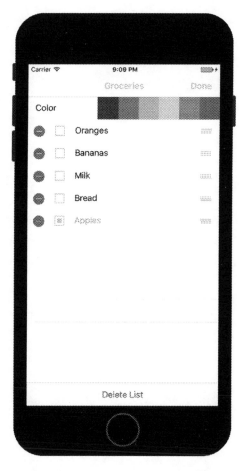

Figure 1-5. *This sample iPhone app running in the iOS Simulator contains a table object to organize a list of groceries. Actions such as "rotate left" or "user selected row 3" can be applied to this view object.*

Actions that are performed on objects are called **methods**. Methods manipulate objects to accomplish what you want your app to do. For example, for a jet object, you might have the following methods:

goUp

goDown

bankLeft

turnOnAfterburners

lowerLandingGear

The table object in Figure 1-5 is actually called UITableView when you use it in a program, and it could have the following methods:

numberOfRowsInSection

cellForRowAtIndexPath

canEditRowAtIndexPath

commitEditingStyle

didSelectRowAtIndexPath

Most objects have data that describes those objects. This data is defined as properties. Each property describes the associated object in a specific way. For example, the jet object's properties might be as follows:

altitude = 10,000 feet

heading = North

speed = 500 knots

pitch = 10 degrees

yaw = 20 degrees

latitude = 33.575776

longitude = -111.875766

For the UITableView object in Figure 1-5, the following might be the properties:

backGroundColor = Red

selectedRow = 3

animateView = No

An object's properties can be changed at any time when your program is running, when the user interacts with the app, or when the programmer designs the app to accomplish the design requirements. The values stored in the properties of an object at a specific time are collectively called the **state** of an object.

Working with the Alice Interface

Alice offers a great approach in using the concepts just discussed without all the complexity of learning Xcode and the Objective-C language at the same time. It takes only a few minutes to familiarize yourself with the Alice interface and begin writing a program.

The introduction of this book describes how to download Alice. After it's downloaded and installed, you need to open Alice. It will look like Figure 1-6.

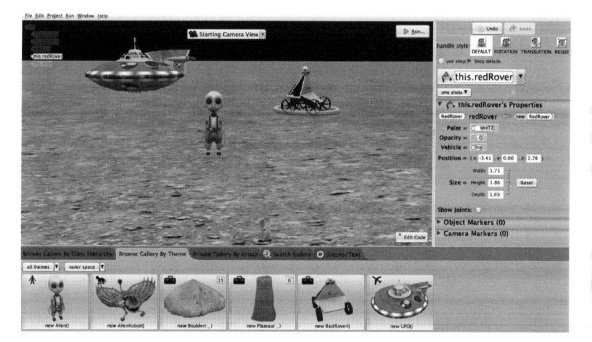

Figure 1-6. *Alice IDE running*

Technically speaking, Alice is not a true IDE like Xcode, but it is pretty close and much easier to learn than Xcode. A true IDE combines code development, user interface layout, debugging tools, documentation, and simulator/console launching for a single application; see Figure 1-7. However, Alice offers a similar look, feel, and features to Xcode. This will serve you well later when you start writing Objective-C code.

Figure 1-7. *The Xcode IDE with the iPhone simulator*

In the next chapter, you will go through the Alice interface and write your first program.

Summary

Congratulations, you have finished the first chapter of this book. It is important that you have an understanding of the following terms because they will be reinforced throughout this book:

- Computer program

- Algorithm

- Design requirements

- User interface

- Bug

- Quality assurance (QA)

- Debugging

- Object-oriented programming (OOP)

- Object

- Property

- Method

- State of an object

- Integrated development environment (IDE)

Exercises

Answer the following questions:

- Why is it so important to spend time on your user requirements?

- What is the difference between design requirements and an algorithm?

- What is the difference between a method and a property?

- What is a bug?

- What is state?

Perform the following tasks:

- Write an algorithm for how a soda machine works from the time a coin is inserted until a soda is dispensed. Assume the price of a soda is 80 cents.

- Write the design requirements for an app that will run the soda machine.

CHAPTER 2

Programming Basics

This chapter will focus on the building blocks that are necessary to become a great Objective-C programmer. This chapter will go over how to use the Alice user interface, how to write your first Alice program, and how to write your first Objective-C program. It will also explore some new OOP terms.

Note We will introduce new concepts in Alice and later, in this chapter, enable you to use these concepts in Objective-C. We have used this approach for a number of years, so we know from personal experience that this approach helps you learn the concepts quickly, without discouragement, and gives you a great foundation to build upon.

Taking a Tour with Alice

Alice's 3D programming environment makes it easy to write your first program because it applies some of the principles that you learned in Chapter 1. First, you need to learn a little more about Alice's user interface. When you first launch Alice, you are presented with a screen that looks like Figure 2-1.

© Stefan Kaczmarek, Brad Lees, Gary Bennett, Mitch Fisher 2018
S. Kaczmarek et al., *Objective-C for Absolute Beginners*, https://doi.org/10.1007/978-1-4842-3429-7_2

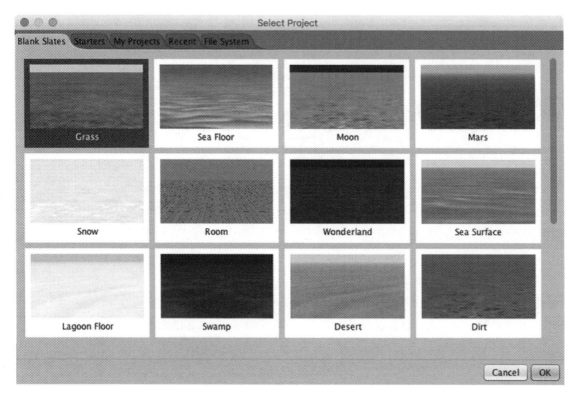

Figure 2-1. *Opening screen in Alice*

You can start with the blank Grass project or pick another Blank Slate project with a different background. Feel free to explore and have fun. This is where you will spend most of your time and write your first Alice application.

The Alice user interface is set up to help you efficiently write your applications. The user interface is similar in form and function to the Xcode integrated development environment (IDE). You will now explore the major sections of Alice.

Application Menu

The Application Menu, shown in Figure 2-2, enables you to open and close files, set your application preferences, and view scene statistics. You can also access example projects and Alice Help from the Application Menu.

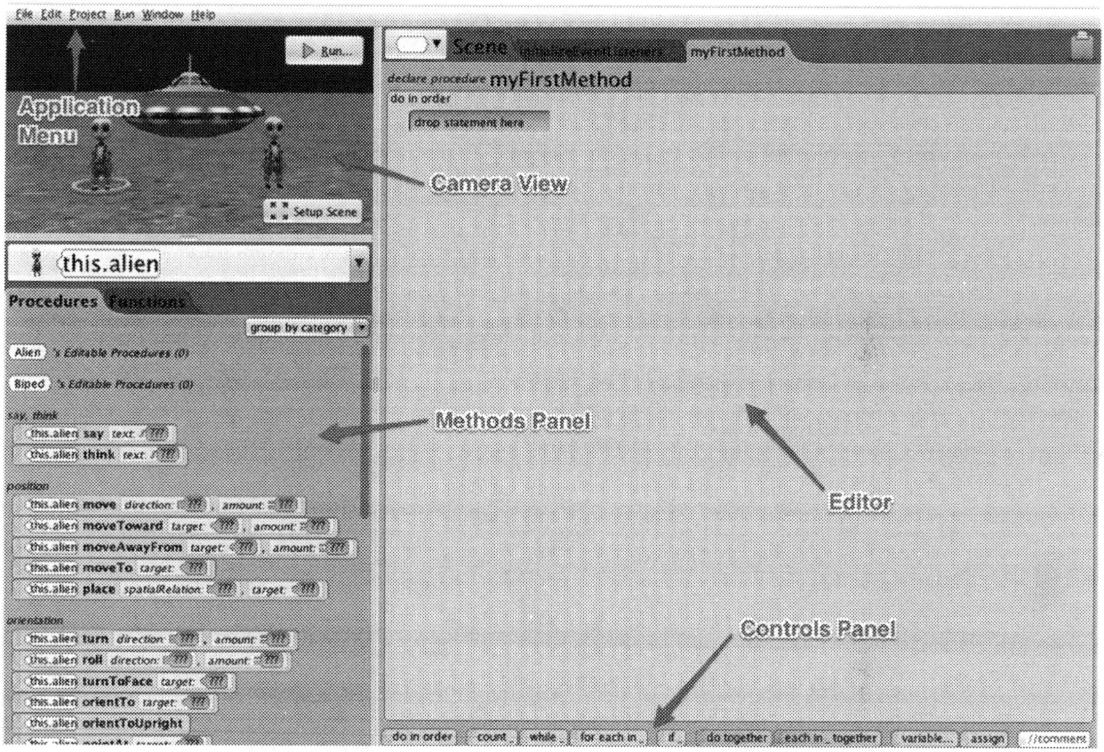

Figure 2-2. *This shows the main sections of the Alice user interface. Take some time to explore the user interface. You will see in this chapter how it compares with Xcode and how it will help you learn Objective-C.*

Note   It is important that you save your program frequently when using Alice. If Alice crashes and you haven't saved your work, you will lose all your code or changes since you last saved. Additionally, we recommend that you close Alice completely and reopen it when you want to open a new Alice project.

Editing a Scene

One of the most important Alice controls is the **Setup Scene** button (see Figure 2-3). When you click the Setup Scene button, you launch Alice's **Scene Editor**.

Figure 2-3. *The Setup Scene button will launch Alice's Scene Editor and enable you to add objects to your Alice scene*

It is important to learn how to move the camera around your scene in order to get the view you want the users to see.

By moving the camera around, you can provide the perspective you want with your app. See Figure 2-4.

Figure 2-4. *Use the Camera Controls to control the camera perspective in the Scene Editor*

Take a minute to familiarize yourself with the Scene Editor shown in Figure 2-5. The Scene Editor enables you to do the following:

- Add objects to your scene from the gallery

- Add objects to your scene from the Internet

- Position the objects in your scene

- Adjust the camera view for your scene

You will spend a lot of time adding objects and adjusting the camera in your scenes using the Scene Editor.

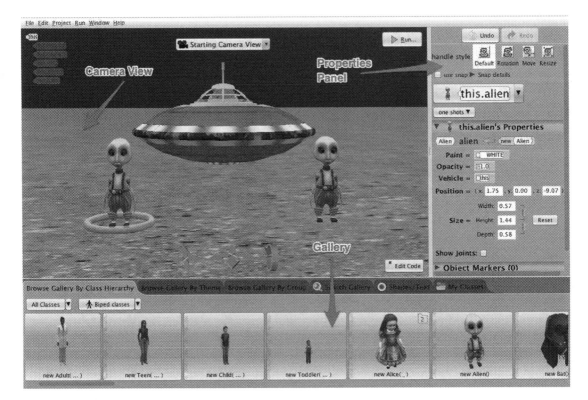

Figure 2-5. *Alice's Scene Editor*

Classes, Objects, and Instances in Alice

A group of objects with the same properties and same methods (actions) are called a **class**. For example, you could have a class called `Airplane`. In this class, you could have five objects:

```
boeing747
lockheedSR71
boeing737
citation10
f18Fighter
```

These objects are nearly identical. They are from the same `Airplane` class. They all have the same following methods:

```
land
takeOff
lowerLandingGear
raiseLandingGear
bankRight
bankLeft
```

The only things that differentiate the objects are the values of their properties. Some of the properties of the values might be as follows:

```
wingLength = 20 ft
maxThrust = 200,000 lbs
numberOfEngines = 2
```

In your scene, you may have two objects that are exactly the same. You may want two Boeing 737s in your view. Each copy of a class is called an **instance**. Adding an instance of a class to your program is called **instantiation**.

Object Tree

The **Object Tree** (see Figure 2-6) enables you to view all the objects in your Alice scene. Additionally, if the object has subparts, you can view these subparts by clicking the plus sign, and you can collapse the subparts by clicking the minus sign.

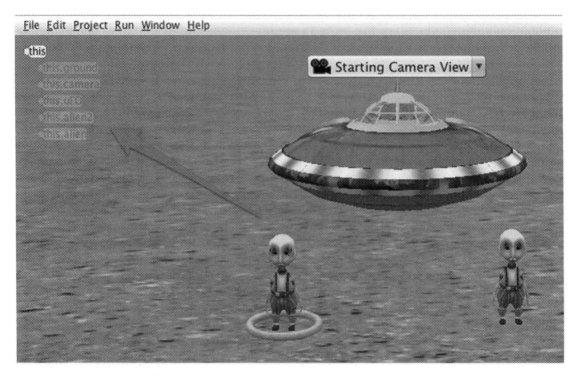

Figure 2-6. *The Object Tree*

Many of the Alice projects come with several built-in objects that you will need for your apps. The project in Figure 2-6 comes with the **camera** and **ground** objects.

Editor

The **Editor**, the largest area of the Code Editor, is where you write your code. With Alice, you don't have to actually type code; you can drag and drop your code to manipulate your objects and properties.

Note   Don't forget the bottom of the Controls Panel. The panel contains a row of control and logic tiles for looping, branching, and other logical structures that you can use to control the behavior of your objects.

Methods Panel

The **Methods Panel** of the Alice Code Editor contains the tabs for procedures and functions related to the object instance selected in the Object Tree. Refer back to Figure 2-2.

- Procedures are methods that perform actions upon the object (such as takeoff and land).

- Functions are methods that either ask a question or return a value.

Creating an Alice App: To the Moon, Alice

You just learned some new terms and concepts, and now it is time to do what programmers do: write code. It is customary for new developers to write a **Hello World** app as their first program. You will do something similar, but Alice makes it more interesting. You will then follow up your first Alice app with your first Objective-C app.

This Alice app will have three objects on the screen: the UFO object and two Aliens. One Alien will say, "The Eagle has landed." The other Alien will say, "That's one small step for man, one giant leap for mankind."

Alice really makes apps like this easy and fun to do. Make sure you follow these steps:

1. Click **File** and then **New**.

2. Click the **Blank Slates** tab.

3.   Choose the **Moon project**, and click the OK button. See Figure 2-7.

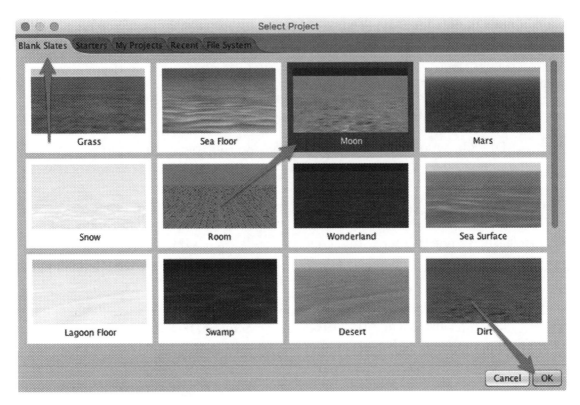

Figure 2-7. *Select the Moon project*

4.   Now, you need to add your objects. Click **Setup Scene**. It was the
important button in the Code Editor shown in Figure 2-3.

5. In the Object Gallery, select a new **UFO** from **All Classes ➤ Transport classes ➤ Aircraft classes**. See Figure 2-8.

Figure 2-8. *Viewing and adding objects to your scene*

6. Click OK to add the UFO object to your scene. You can also drag and drop objects from the gallery to place them within a scene.

Note   You can see in this example why an instance is a copy of an object. You are making a copy of the object and putting it in your scene. *Instantiation* is a big word for the process of making a copy of and initializing your object.

---

7. Next, add two **Aliens** from the **Biped classes** to your scene. See Figure 2-9.

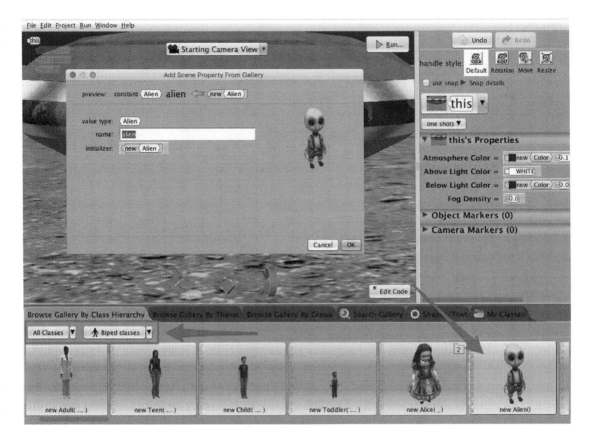

Figure 2-9. *Adding two Aliens to your scene*

8. Use the **Camera Controls**, shown in Figure 2-10, to achieve the look and perspective you desire.

Tip   Sometimes when you add two objects, Alice places one object over the other. Drag the top Alien to the side of the other Alien if this occurs. Your world should look like Figure 2-10.

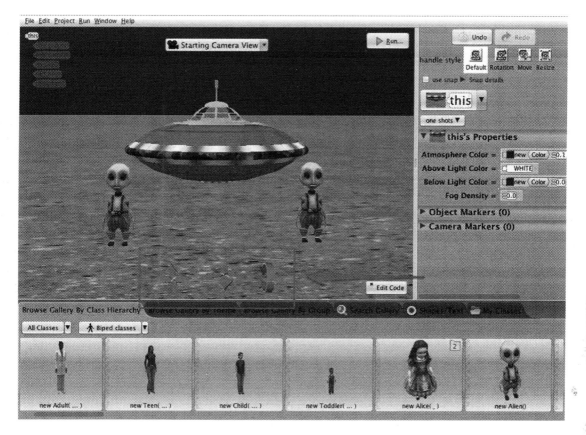

Figure 2-10. *Use the Camera Controls to adjust the user perspective of the scene*

9. Near the top-right corner of the window in the Properties Panel are the **Handle Styles**. Hover the mouse over each tile to discover what each handle style will do to the object.

10. Notice the Object Tree in the top-left corner of the Camera View in Figure 2-10. The ground, UFO, camera, alien, and alien2 objects are in the Object Tree.

11. Click the **Edit Code** button located near the bottom-right corner of the Camera View. This will return you to the Code Editor.

12.   Click the left alien in the Camera View. Make sure the **Procedures tab** is selected in the Methods Panel. See Figure 2-11.

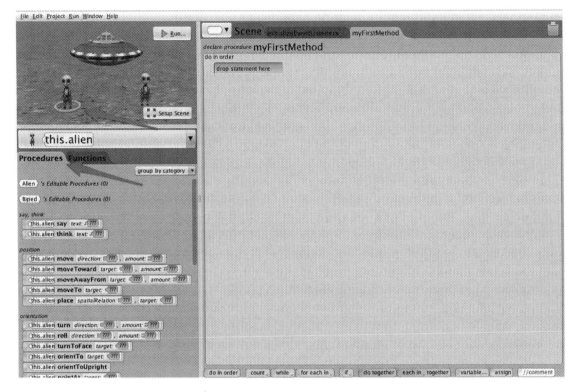

Figure 2-11. *Select the left Alien and the Procedures tab*

13. You are now going to make your Aliens say something. Remember, to apply actions on an object, you need to use methods or procedures. From the Procedures tab, drag the **this.alien|turn** tile from the Methods Panel to your Editor area. Select **LEFT**, with an amount of **0.25** from the parameter lists. See Figure 2-12. When you run your app, the left Alien will turn to the left one-quarter of a rotation and face the other Alien.

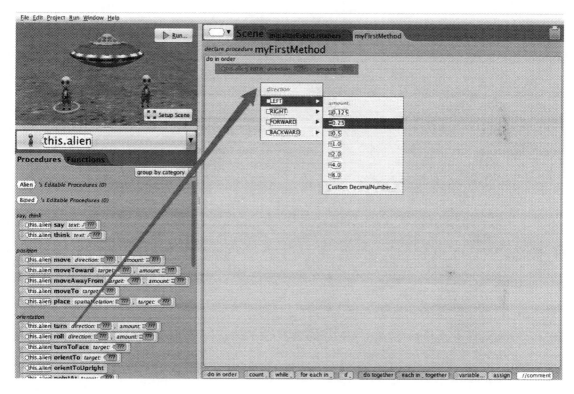

Figure 2-12. *Adding a method instructing the alien to turn to the left*

14. Let's do the same thing for the other Alien. Click the right Alien. Drag the **this.alien2|turn** tile from the Methods Panel to the Editor. Select a **RIGHT** turn with a **0.25** rotation amount from the parameter lists. See Figure 2-13.

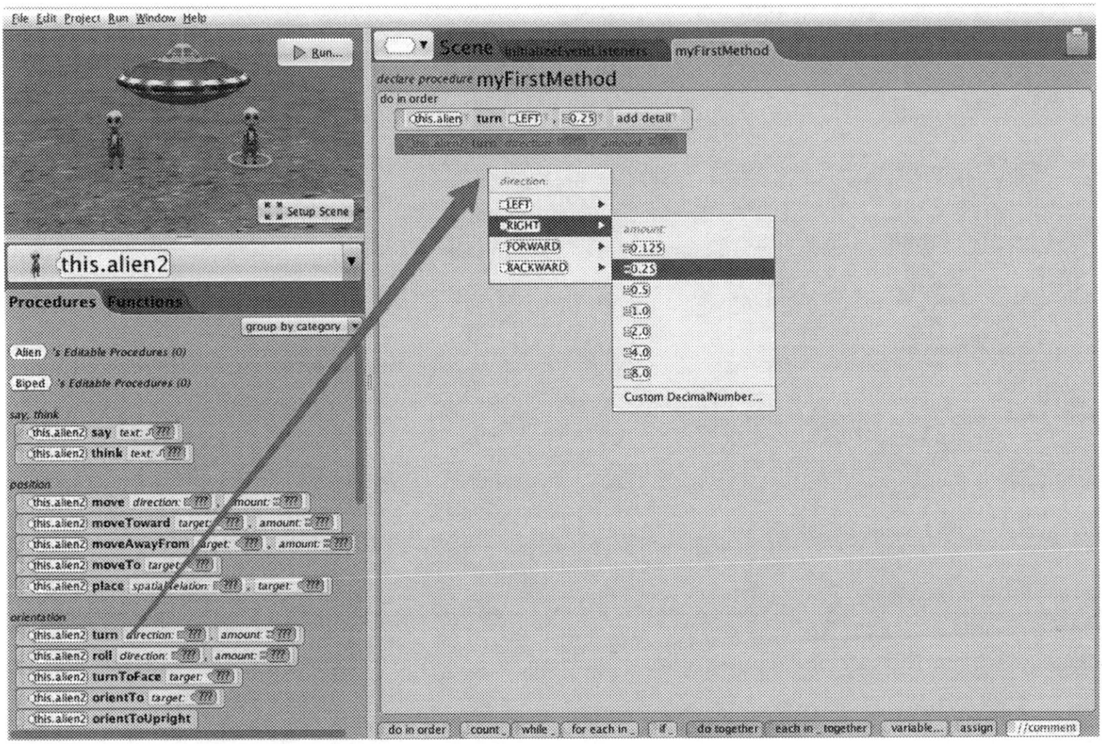

Figure 2-13. *Adding a method instructing the second alien to turn to the right*

15. A **parameter** is the information a method needs to act upon the object. Some methods may require more than one parameter.

16. Click the left Alien, drag the **this.alien|say** tile to the Editor, select **Custom TextString**, and then type **The Eagle has landed.** Place the tile between the other two tiles.

17. Click the right Alien, drag the **this.alien2|say** tile to the Editor area, select **Custom TextString**, and then type **That's one small step for man, one giant leap for mankind**. Your app should look like Figure 2-14.

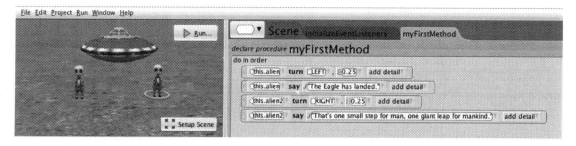

Figure 2-14. *Your Editor should contain these methods along with the associated parameters*

18. Run your first program by clicking the Run button. If you have completed everything correctly, your app should look like Figure 2-15 when it runs. If not, you have some debugging to do.

Figure 2-15. *From the top portion of Run window, you can play, pause, and restart your program. You can also speed up or slow down the playback, depending on how slow or fast your program is running.*

19.   From the main Alice window, select **File ➤ Save As** to save the app as `toTheMoonAlice.a3p`. You will be using this app later.

Your First Objective-C Program

Now that you have learned a little about OOP and you have your first Alice program completed, it's time to write your first Objective-C program and begin to understand the Objective-C language, Xcode, and syntax. First, you must install Xcode. Xcode is the IDE that you use when developing Objective-C apps. It is equivalent to Alice's interface.

Launching and Using Xcode

Xcode is available for download from the Mac App Store for free. See Figure 2-16.

Xcode
Create great apps
for Mac, iPhone, and iPad.

Xcode 4+

(Essentials)

Xcode includes everything developers need to create great applications for Mac, iPhone, iPad, Apple TV, and Apple Watch. Xcode provides developers a unified workflow for user interface design, coding, testing, and debugging. The Xcode IDE combined with the Swift programming language make developing apps easier and more fun than ever before.

...More

What's New in Version 9.1
Xcode 9.1 includes Swift 4 and SDKs for iOS 11, watchOS 4, tvOS 11, and macOS High Sierra 10.13

...More

Figure 2-16. *Xcode is available for download from the Mac App Store for free*

Note This package has everything you need to write Objective-C iOS, tvOS, watchOS, and macOS apps. To submit apps to the App Store and to gain access to the frequent beta OS and software releases, you will need to apply for the Apple Developer Program and pay $99 per year. See Figure 2-17.

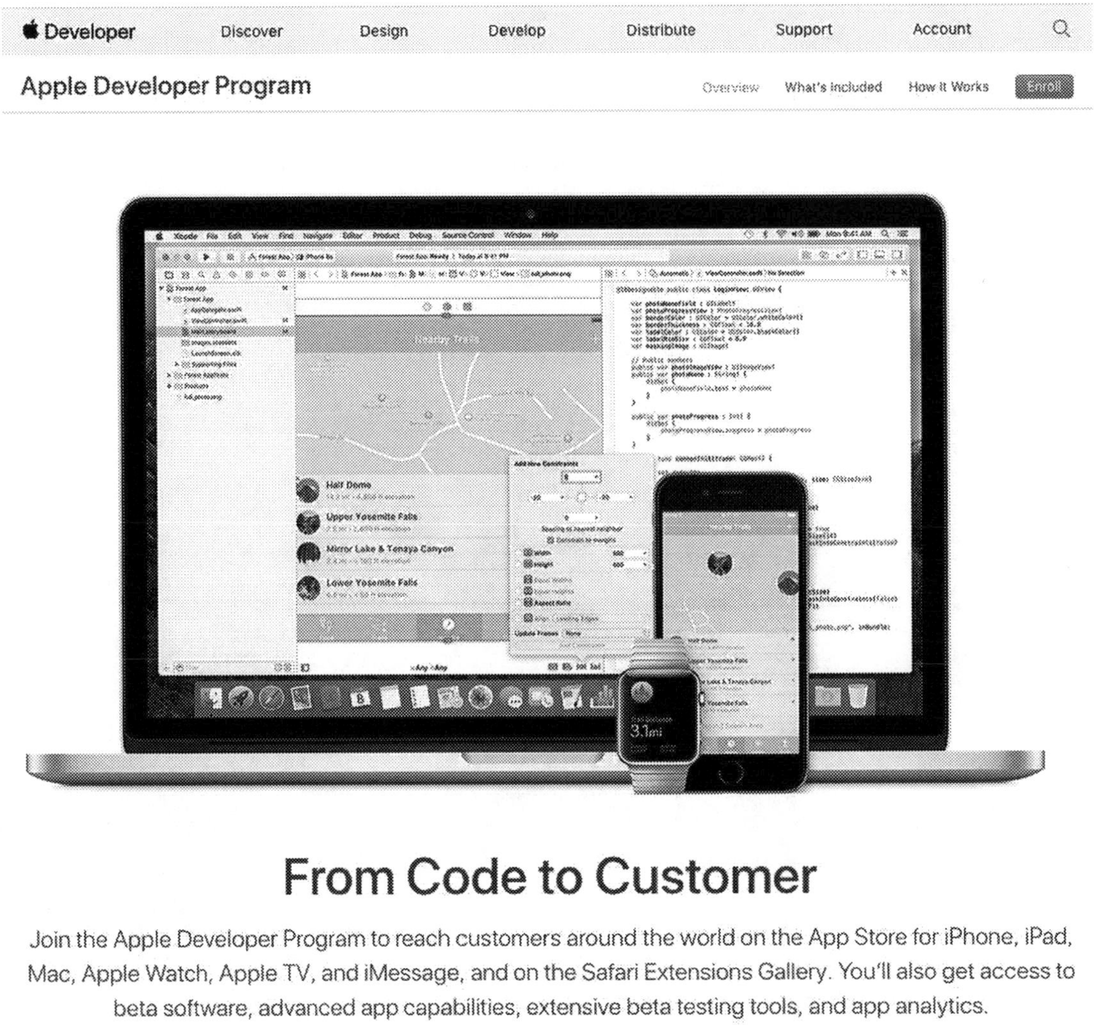
Developer
Discover
Design
Develop
Distribute
Support
Account
Apple Developer Program
Overview
What's Included
How It Works
Enroll
From Code to Customer
Join the Apple Developer Program to reach customers around the world on the App Store for iPhone, iPad, Mac, Apple Watch, Apple TV, and iMessage, and on the Safari Extensions Gallery. You'll also get access to beta software, advanced app capabilities, extensive beta testing tools, and app analytics.

***Figure 2-17.** If you pay $99 to join the Apple Developer Program, beta versions of Xcode and the OS SDKs are available to download. You will also have the ability to submit apps to the App Store.*

Now that you have downloaded and installed Xcode, you can begin writing Objective-C applications, so let's get started. After launching Xcode, follow these steps:

1. Click **Create a new Xcode Project**. See Figure 2-18.

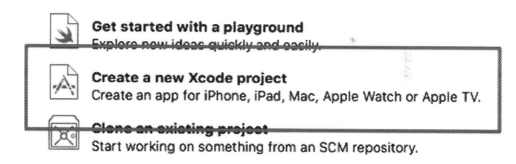

Figure 2-18. *Creating your first Objective-C project*

2. Select **macOS**, then the **Command Line Tool** project template, and then click the **Next** button. See Figure 2-19.

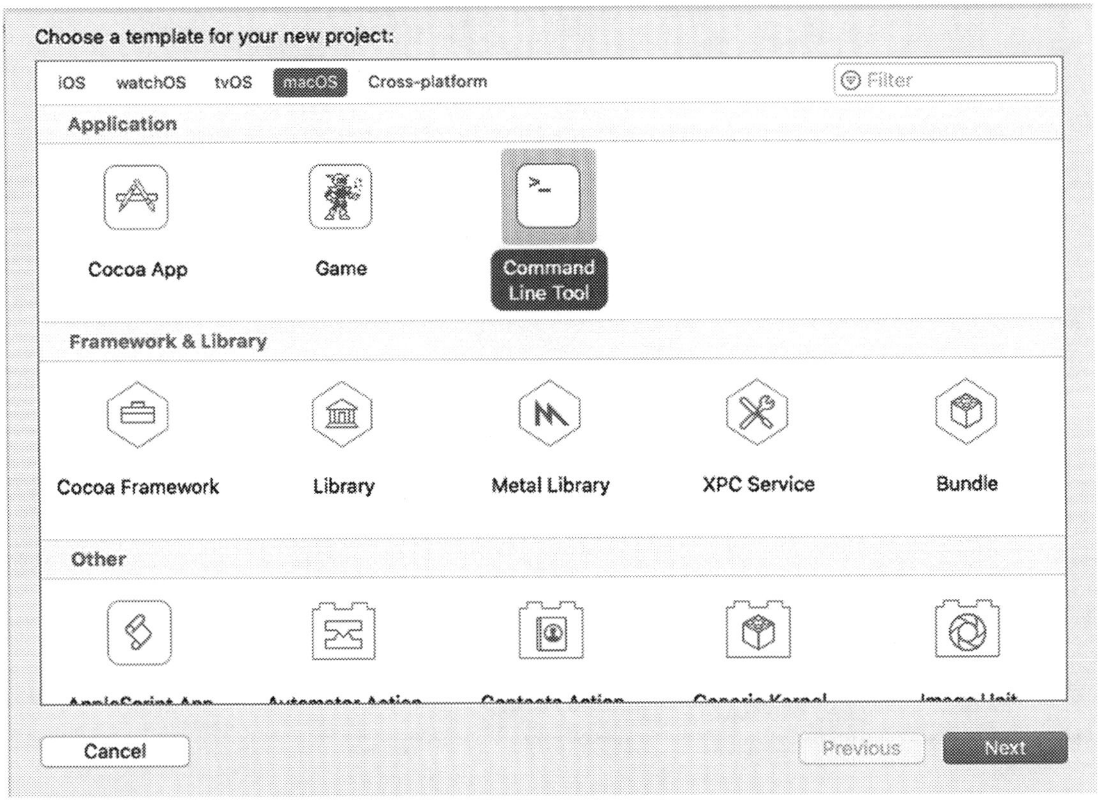

Figure 2-19. *Selecting the Command Line Tool project template*

3. Let's name the app **HelloWorld** and select **Objective-C** as the
    language, as shown in Figure 2-20. Then click the Next button and
    save your app to a folder of your choice.

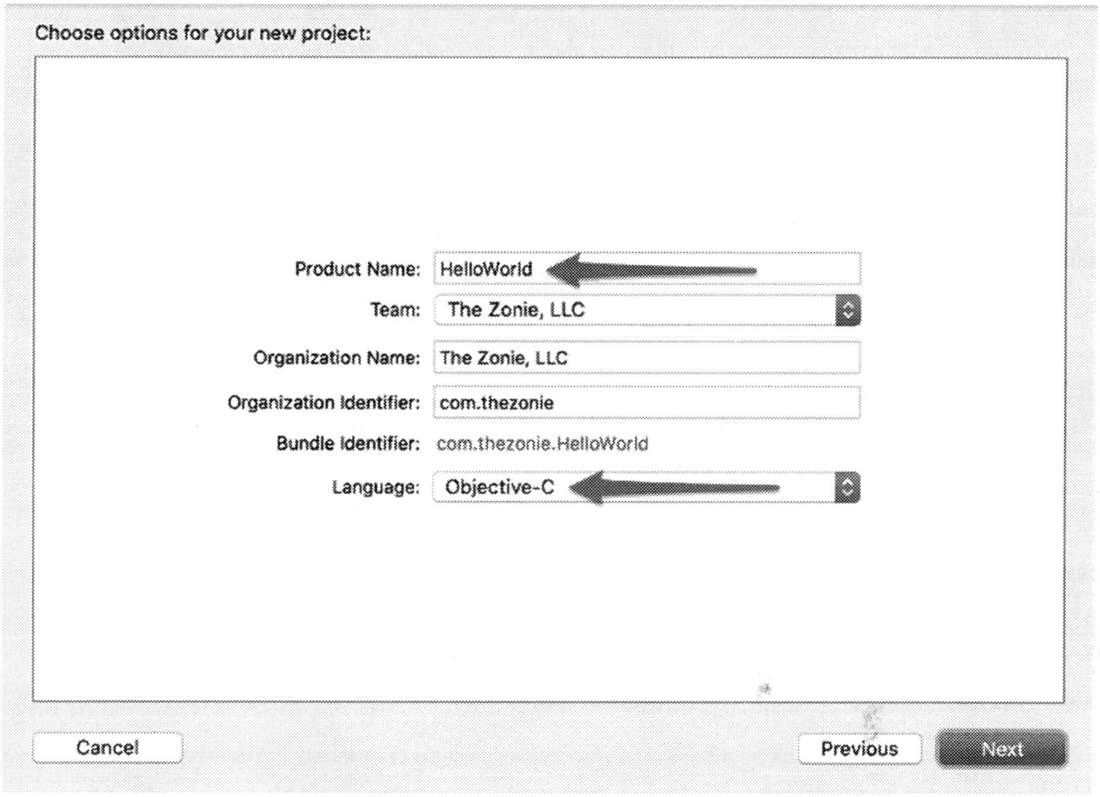

Choose options for your new project:

Product Name:	HelloWorld
Team:	The Zonie, LLC
Organization Name:	The Zonie, LLC
Organization Identifier:	com.thezonie
Bundle Identifier:	com.thezonie.HelloWorld
Language:	Objective-C

Cancel   Previous   Next

Figure 2-20. *Name your app HelloWorld, and select Objective-C as the language*

4. In the Project Navigator, select the `main.m` file.

Xcode does a lot of work for you and creates a directory with files and code ready for
you to use. That is what Xcode templates do: they save you a lot of time.

You need to become familiar with the Xcode IDE. Let's look at two of the most often
used features (see Figure 2-21):

- The Navigator Area

- The Editor Area

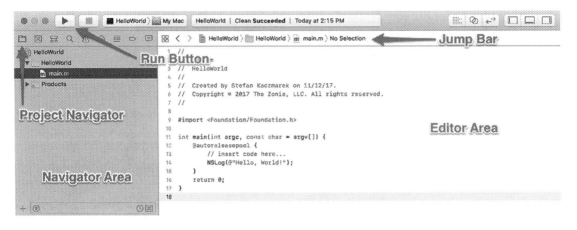

Figure 2-21. *You can run the app right after creating the project by clicking the Run button and seeing "Hello, World!" printed out in the console.*

These sections should look similar to what you used in Alice. The **Navigator Area** contains files needed to build your apps. It will contain your classes, methods, and resources.

The **Editor Area** is the business end of the Xcode IDE, where our dreams are turned into reality. The Editor Area is where you write your code. You will notice that as you write your code it will change color. Sometimes, Xcode will even try to auto-complete words for you. The colors have meanings that will become apparent as you use the IDE. The Editor Area is also where you debug your apps.

Note   Even if we've mentioned it already, it is worth saying again: you will learn Objective-C programming by reading this book, but you will *really* learn Objective-C by debugging your apps. Debugging is where developers learn and become great developers.

The Run button turns your code from plain text to an app that your Macs, iPhones, or iPads know how to execute. With the Alice interface, you used the Run button to run your Alice app.

To run your first program, simply click the Run button. Xcode checks your code syntax, compiles your app, and if no errors are found, makes an app file and runs it.

When the app runs, it prints out **Hello, World!** in the Debug Area Console. Additionally, you can see whether the application terminated and why it terminated. In this case, it terminated normally. You can see this with the message **Program ended with exit code: 0**, which means your app completed without error. See Figure 2-22.

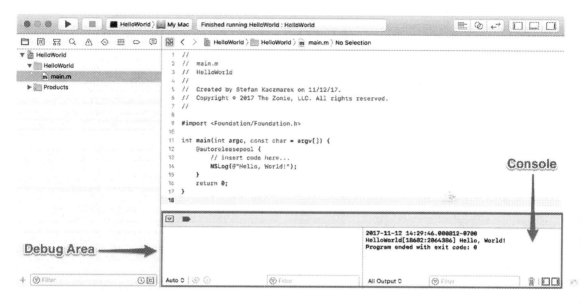

Figure 2-22. *The app executing in the Debug Area Console*

Let's modify the application to do what you did with the Aliens:

1. Select the main.m file from the Project Navigator.

2. Change lines 14 and 15 to look like Figure 2-23.

3. You are going to intentionally forget to add a semicolon at the end of line 15. This will cause a compiler error.

4. Click the Run button.

You can see that something went wrong when you try to compile and run your app. You have a compiler error and a red error icon indicating where the problem is; see Figure 2-23.

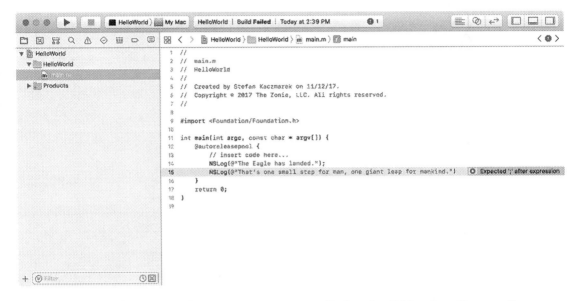

Figure 2-23. *The app with a syntax error caught by the Objective-C compiler*

When you write Objective-C code, everything is important, even semicolons, capitalization, and parentheses. The collection of rules that enable your compiler to compile your code to an executable app is called **syntax**.

NSLog is a function that will print out the contents of its parameters to the console.

Now, let's fix the app by adding the semicolon at the end of line 15. Building and running the app will enable you to see the output in the console. See Figure 2-24.

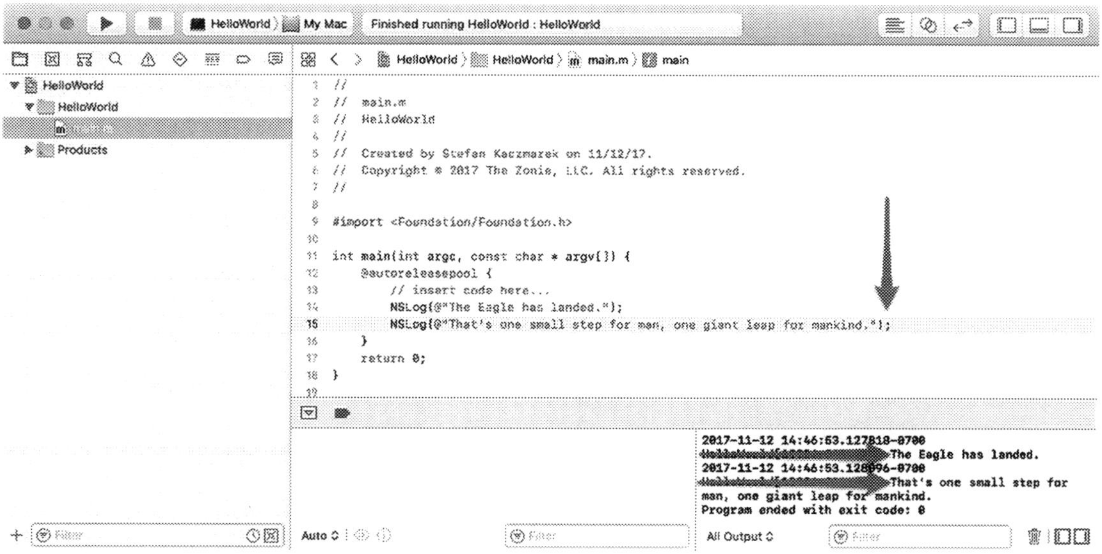

Figure 2-24. *The app compiled with no compiler errors, and completion executed successfully with the output you wanted*

Feel free to play around and change the text that is printed out. Have fun!

Summary

In this chapter, you built your first Alice app. You also installed Xcode and compiled, debugged, and ran your first Objective-C app. You also learned new OOP terms that are key to your understanding of Objective-C.

The terms that you should understand are as follows:

- Classes

- Objects

- Methods

- Parameters

- Instances

- Instantiation

Exercises

Perform the following tasks:

- Extend your `toTheMoon.a3p` Alice app. Place another object of your choosing in the world and have the object say something to the two Aliens when they have finished speaking.

- Extend your Objective-C HelloWorld app by adding a third line of code that prints any text of your choosing to the console.

CHAPTER 3

It's All About the Data

As you probably know, data is stored as zeros and ones in your computer's memory. However, zeros and ones are not very useful to developers or app users, so you need to know how your program uses data and how data is stored on your computer.

In this chapter, you will look at how data is stored on computers and how you can manipulate that data. Then you'll write a fun Alice app illustrating data storage and afterward write the same Alice app in Objective-C. So let's get started!

Numbering Systems Used in Programming

Computers work with information differently than do humans. This section covers the various ways information is stored, tallied, and manipulated by devices such as your Mac, iPhone, and iPad.

Bits

A **bit** is defined as the basic unit of information used by computers to store and manipulate data. A bit has a value of either **0** or **1**. When computers were first introduced, transistors and microprocessors didn't exist. Data was manipulated and stored by vacuum tubes being turned on or off. If the vacuum tube was on, the value of the bit was 1, and if the vacuum tube was off, the value was 0. The amount of data a computer was able to store and manipulate was directly related to how many vacuum tubes the computer had.

The first recognized computer was called the Electronic Numerical Integrator And Computer (ENIAC). It took up more than 136 square meters and had 18,000 vacuum tubes. It was about as powerful as a handheld calculator.

© Stefan Kaczmarek, Brad Lees, Gary Bennett, Mitch Fisher 2018
S. Kaczmarek et al., *Objective-C for Absolute Beginners*, https://doi.org/10.1007/978-1-4842-3429-7_3

Today, computers use transistors to store and manipulate data. The power of
a computer processor depends on how many transistors are placed on its chip or
CPU. Like the vacuum tube, transistors have an off or on state. When the transistor is off,
its value is 0. If the transistor is on, its value is 1. At the time of this writing, Apple's A11
Bionic processor, which powers the iPhone 8, iPhone 8 Plus, and iPhone X, is a 6-core
ARM processor with approximately 4.3 billion transistors, up from 149 million transistors
within the A4 from the first iPad. Figure 3-1 shows Apple's latest iPhone processor, the
A11 Bionic.

Figure 3-1. *Apple's proprietary A11 Bionic processor (source: Wikipedia)*

Moore's Law

The number of transistors within your iPhone's or iPad's processor is directly related
to your device's processing speed, memory capacity, and sensors (accelerometer,
gyroscope, compass) available in the device. The more transistors, the more powerful
your device is.

In 1965, Gordon E. Moore, a cofounder of Intel, described the trend of transistors in
a processor. He observed that the number of transistors in a processor doubled every
18 months from 1958 to 1965 and would likely continue "for at least 18 months." The
observation became famously known as Moore's Law and has proven accurate for more
than 55 years. See Figure 3-2.

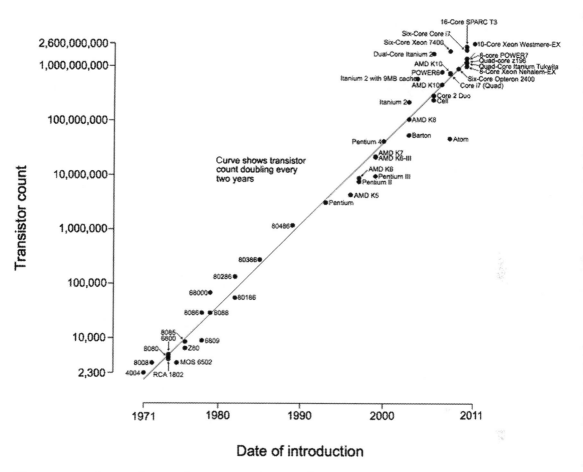

Figure 3-2. *Moore's Law (source: Wikipedia)*

Note   There is a downside to Moore's Law, and you have probably felt it in your pocketbook. The problem with rapidly increasing processing capability is that it renders technology obsolete quickly. So, when your iPhone's two-year cell phone contract is up, the new iPhones on the market will be twice as powerful as the iPhone you just paid for. How convenient for everyone!

Bytes

A byte is another unit used to describe information storage on computers. A **byte** is composed of 8 bits. Whereas a bit can represent up to two different values, a byte can represent up to 2^8, or 256, different values. A byte can contain values from 0–255.

The **binary** number system represents the numerical symbols 0 and 1. To illustrate how the number **71** would be represented in binary, we will use a simple table of 8 bits (1 byte), with each bit represented as a power of 2. To convert the byte value **01000111** to decimal, simply add the "on" bits. See Table 3-1.

Table 3-1. *The Number 71 Represented as a Byte (64 + 4 + 2 + 1)*

Power of 2	2^7	2^6	2^5	2^4	2^3	2^2	2^1	2^0
Value for "on" bit	128	64	32	16	8	4	2	1
Actual bit	0	1	0	0	0	1	1	1

To represent the number **22** in binary, turn on the bits that add up to 22, or **00010110**. See Table 3-2.

Table 3-2. *The Number 22 Represented as a Byte (16 + 4 + 2)*

Power of 2	2^7	2^6	2^5	2^4	2^3	2^2	2^1	2^0
Value for "on" bit	128	64	32	16	8	4	2	1
Actual bit	0	0	0	1	0	1	1	0

To represent the number **255** in binary, turn on the bits that add up to 255, or **11111111**. See Table 3-3.

Table 3-3. *The Number 255 Represented as a Byte (128 + 64 + 32 + 16 + 8 + 4 + 2 + 1)*

Power of 2	2^7	2^6	2^5	2^4	2^3	2^2	2^1	2^0
Value for "on" bit	128	64	32	16	8	4	2	1
Actual bit	1	1	1	1	1	1	1	1

To represent the number **0** in binary, turn on the bits that add up to 0, or **00000000**. See Table 3-4.

Table 3-4. *The Number 0 Represented as a Byte*

Power of 2	2^7	2^6	2^5	2^4	2^3	2^2	2^1	2^0
Value for "on" bit	128	64	32	16	8	4	2	1
Actual bit	0	0	0	0	0	0	0	0

Hexadecimal

Often, it will be necessary to represent characters in another format that is recognized by computers, namely, a hexadecimal format. Hexadecimal is just an easier (more compact) way for humans to parse binary data. You will encounter hexadecimal numbers when you are debugging your apps. The **hexadecimal** system is a base-16 number system. It uses 16 distinct symbols, 0–9, to represent values 0 to 9, and A, B, C, D, E, and F to represent values 10 to 15. For example, the hexadecimal number **2AF3** is equal in decimal to $(2 \times 16^3) + (10 \times 16^2) + (15 \times 16^1) + (3 \times 16^0)$, or 10,995.

Figure 3-3 shows the ASCII table of characters. Because 1 byte can represent 256 characters, this works well for Western characters. For example, hexadecimal **20** represents a space. Hexadecimal **7D** represents a right curly brace (}). You can also see this by playing with the Mac Calculator app in Programmer mode because it can convert numerical values to ASCII.

Dec	Hx	Oct	Char		Dec	Hx	Oct	Html	Chr	Dec	Hx	Oct	Html	Chr	Dec	Hx	Oct	Html	Chr
0	0	000	NUL	(null)	32	20	040	&#32;	Space	64	40	100	&#64;	@	96	60	140	&#96;	`
1	1	001	SOH	(start of heading)	33	21	041	&#33;	!	65	41	101	&#65;	A	97	61	141	&#97;	a
2	2	002	STX	(start of text)	34	22	042	"	"	66	42	102	&#66;	B	98	62	142	&#98;	b
3	3	003	ETX	(end of text)	35	23	043	&#35;	#	67	43	103	&#67;	C	99	63	143	&#99;	c
4	4	004	EOT	(end of transmission)	36	24	044	&#36;	$	68	44	104	&#68;	D	100	64	144	&#100;	d
5	5	005	ENQ	(enquiry)	37	25	045	&#37;	%	69	45	105	&#69;	E	101	65	145	&#101;	e
6	6	006	ACK	(acknowledge)	38	26	046	&	&	70	46	106	&#70;	F	102	66	146	&#102;	f
7	7	007	BEL	(bell)	39	27	047	'	'	71	47	107	&#71;	G	103	67	147	&#103;	g
8	8	010	BS	(backspace)	40	28	050	&#40;	(	72	48	110	&#72;	H	104	68	150	&#104;	h
9	9	011	TAB	(horizontal tab)	41	29	051	&#41;	)	73	49	111	&#73;	I	105	69	151	&#105;	i
10	A	012	LF	(NL line feed, new line)	42	2A	052	&#42;	*	74	4A	112	&#74;	J	106	6A	152	&#106;	j
11	B	013	VT	(vertical tab)	43	2B	053	&#43;	+	75	4B	113	&#75;	K	107	6B	153	&#107;	k
12	C	014	FF	(NP form feed, new page)	44	2C	054	&#44;	,	76	4C	114	&#76;	L	108	6C	154	&#108;	l
13	D	015	CR	(carriage return)	45	2D	055	&#45;	-	77	4D	115	&#77;	M	109	6D	155	&#109;	m
14	E	016	SO	(shift out)	46	2E	056	&#46;	.	78	4E	116	&#78;	N	110	6E	156	&#110;	n
15	F	017	SI	(shift in)	47	2F	057	&#47;	/	79	4F	117	&#79;	O	111	6F	157	&#111;	o
16	10	020	DLE	(data link escape)	48	30	060	&#48;	0	80	50	120	&#80;	P	112	70	160	&#112;	p
17	11	021	DC1	(device control 1)	49	31	061	&#49;	1	81	51	121	&#81;	Q	113	71	161	&#113;	q
18	12	022	DC2	(device control 2)	50	32	062	&#50;	2	82	52	122	&#82;	R	114	72	162	&#114;	r
19	13	023	DC3	(device control 3)	51	33	063	&#51;	3	83	53	123	&#83;	S	115	73	163	&#115;	s
20	14	024	DC4	(device control 4)	52	34	064	&#52;	4	84	54	124	&#84;	T	116	74	164	&#116;	t
21	15	025	NAK	(negative acknowledge)	53	35	065	&#53;	5	85	55	125	&#85;	U	117	75	165	&#117;	u
22	16	026	SYN	(synchronous idle)	54	36	066	&#54;	6	86	56	126	&#86;	V	118	76	166	&#118;	v
23	17	027	ETB	(end of trans. block)	55	37	067	&#55;	7	87	57	127	&#87;	W	119	77	167	&#119;	w
24	18	030	CAN	(cancel)	56	38	070	&#56;	8	88	58	130	&#88;	X	120	78	170	&#120;	x
25	19	031	EM	(end of medium)	57	39	071	&#57;	9	89	59	131	&#89;	Y	121	79	171	&#121;	y
26	1A	032	SUB	(substitute)	58	3A	072	&#58;	:	90	5A	132	&#90;	Z	122	7A	172	&#122;	z
27	1B	033	ESC	(escape)	59	3B	073	&#59;	;	91	5B	133	&#91;	[	123	7B	173	&#123;	{
28	1C	034	FS	(file separator)	60	3C	074	&#60;	<	92	5C	134	&#92;	\	124	7C	174	&#124;		
29	1D	035	GS	(group separator)	61	3D	075	&#61;	=	93	5D	135	&#93;	]	125	7D	175	&#125;	}
30	1E	036	RS	(record separator)	62	3E	076	&#62;	>	94	5E	136	&#94;	^	126	7E	176	&#126;	~
31	1F	037	US	(unit separator)	63	3F	077	&#63;	?	95	5F	137	&#95;	_	127	7F	177	&#127;	DEL

Source: www.LookupTables.com

128	Ç	144	É	161	í	177	▒	193	┴	209	╤	225	ß	241	±
129	ü	145	æ	162	ó	178	▓	194	┬	210	╥	226	Γ	242	≥
130	é	146	Æ	163	ú	179	│	195	├	211	╙	227	π	243	≤
131	â	147	ô	164	ñ	180	┤	196	─	212	╘	228	Σ	244	⌠
132	ä	148	ö	165	Ñ	181	╡	197	┼	213	╒	229	σ	245	⌡
133	à	149	ò	166	ª	182	╢	198	╞	214	╓	230	µ	246	÷
134	å	150	û	167	º	183	╖	199	╟	215	╫	231	τ	247	≈
135	ç	151	ù	168	¿	184	╕	200	╚	216	╪	232	Φ	248	°
136	ê	152	ÿ	169	⌐	185	╣	201	╔	217	┘	233	Θ	249	∙
137	ë	153	Ö	170	¬	186	║	202	╩	218	┌	234	Ω	250	·
138	è	154	Ü	171	½	187	╗	203	╦	219	█	235	δ	251	√
139	ï	156	£	172	¼	188	╝	204	╠	220	▄	236	∞	252	ⁿ
140	î	157	¥	173	¡	189	╜	205	═	221	▌	237	φ	253	²
141	ì	158	₧	174	«	190	╛	206	╬	222	▐	238	ε	254	■
142	Ä	159	ƒ	175	»	191	┐	207	╧	223	▀	239	∩	255	
143	Å	160	á	176	░	192	└	208	╨	224	α	240	≡		

Source: www.LookupTables.com

Figure 3-3. *ASCII characters (source:* www.LookupTables.com*)*

Unicode

Representing characters with a byte worked well for computers until about the 1990s, when the personal computer became widely adopted in non-Western countries where languages have more than 256 characters. Instead of a 1-byte character set, Unicode can have up to a 4-byte character set.

To facilitate faster adoption, the first 256 code points are identical to the ASCII character table. Unicode can have different character encodings. The most common encoding used for Western text is called UTF-8. The "8" is how many bits are used per character, so it's one byte per character, like ASCII.

As an iPhone developer, you will probably use this character encoding the most.

Data Types

Now that we've discussed how computers manipulate data, we need to cover an important concept called **data types**. Humans can generally just look at data and the context in which it is being used to determine what type of data it is and how it will be used. Computers need to be told how to do this. The programmer needs to tell the computer the type of data it is being given. Here's an example: 2 + 2 = 4.

The computer needs to know you want to add these two numbers together. In this example, they are integers. You might first believe that adding these numbers is obvious to even the most casual observer, let alone a sophisticated computer. However, it is common for users of iOS apps to store data as a series of characters, not a calculation. For example, a text message might read "Everyone knows that 2 + 2 = 4."

In this case, we are using our previous example in a series of characters called a **string**. A **data type** is simply the declaration to your program that defines the data you want to store. A **variable** is used to store your data and is declared with an associated data type. All data is stored in a variable, and the variable needs to have a variable type. For example, in Objective-C, the following are variable declarations with their associated data types:

```
int x = 10;
int y = 2;
int z = 0;
char prefix = 'c';
NSString *submarineName  = @"USS Nevada SSBN-733";
```

Data types cannot be mixed with one another. You cannot do the following:

```
z = x + submarineName;
```

Mixing data types will cause either compiler warnings or compiler errors and your app will not run.

Most data you will use in your programs can be classified into three different types: Booleans, numbers, and objects. We will discuss how to work with numbers and object data types in the remainder of this chapter. In Chapter 4, we will talk more about Boolean data types when you learn how to write apps with decision making.

Note   Localizing your app is the process of writing your app so that when users buy and use your app they see strings that are in their native language. This process is too advanced for this book, but it is a relatively simple one to complete when you plan from the beginning. Localizing your app greatly expands the total number of potential customers and revenue for your app without you needing to rewrite it for each language. Be sure to localize your app. It is not hard to do and can easily double or triple the number of people who buy it.

Using Variable and Data Types with Alice

Now that you have learned about data types, let's write an Alice app that adds two numbers and displays the sum using an object and methods.

1. Open Alice to create a new Project.

2. Select the **Grass** template and click **OK**. See Figure 3-4.

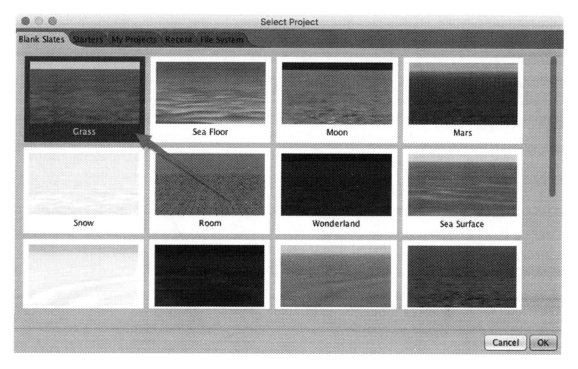

Figure 3-4. *Choosing the Grass template*

Next, you need to create your variables and select their associated data types.

1. **Click and drag the variable tile** from the bottom of your editor to the Editor area, as shown Figure 3-5.

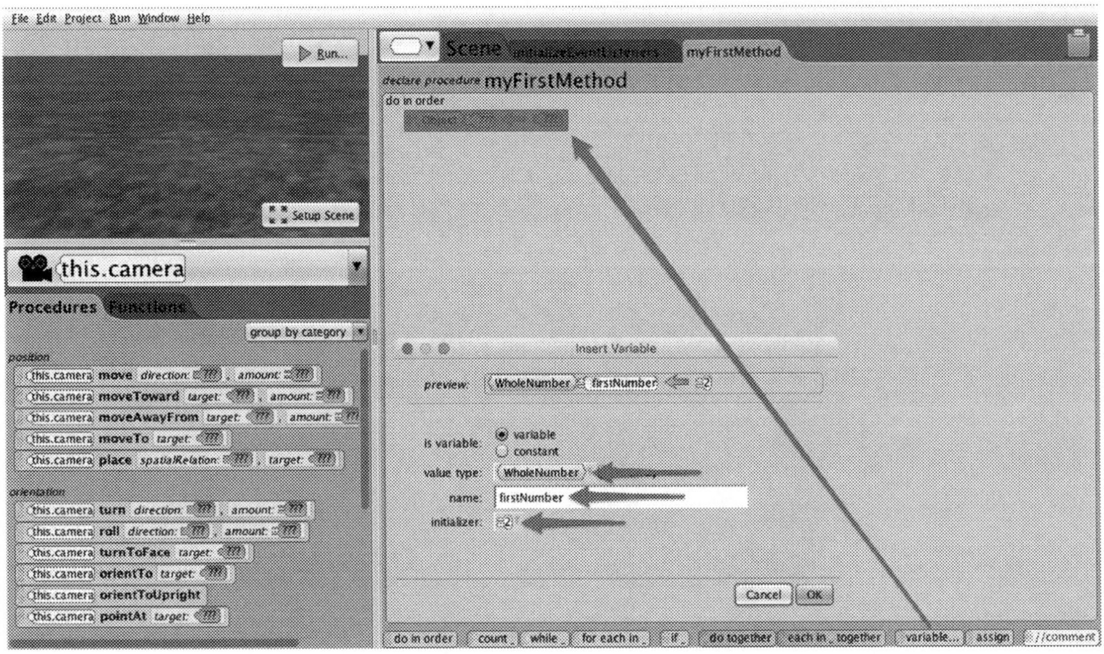

Figure 3-5. *Creating a new variable*

2. Next, name your first variable **firstNumber**.

3. Select **WholeNumber** as the variable's **value type** and set its initial value to **2**.

It is always good programming practice to initialize your variables when they are declared.

4. Create another variable called **secondNumber**, as shown in
   Figure 3-6. Set its **value type** to **WholeNumber** and its initial
   value to **3**.

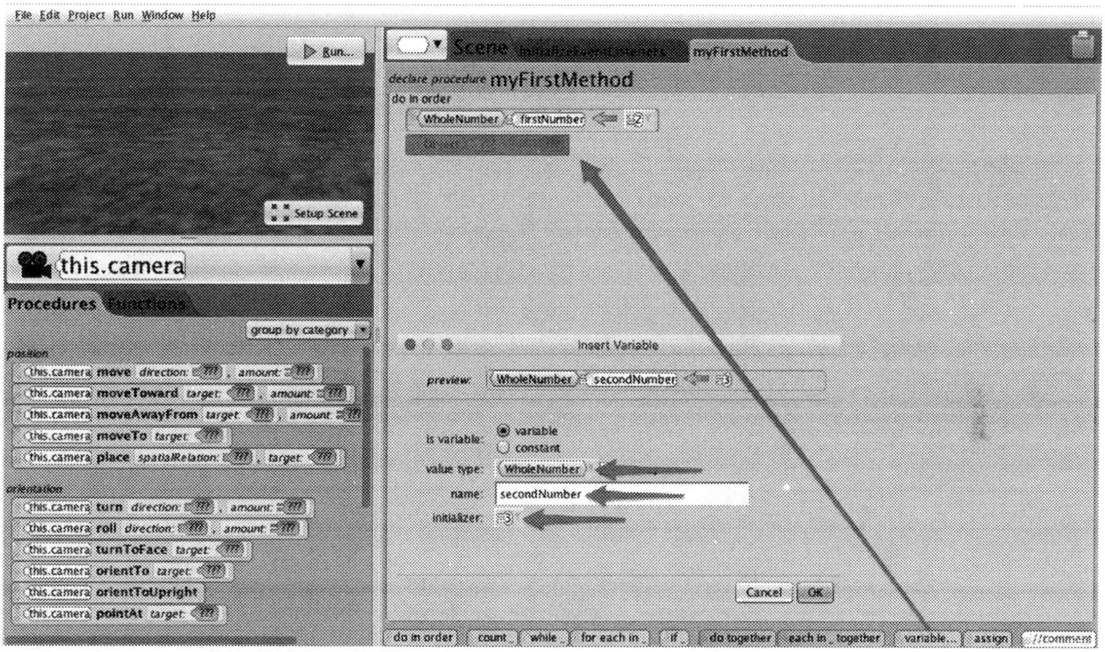

Figure 3-6. *Creating the second variable*

5. Create a third variable called **totalSum**, as shown in Figure 3-7.
    Set the variable's value type to **WholeNumber** and set its initial
    value to **0**. This variable will hold the sum of firstNumber and
    secondNumber.

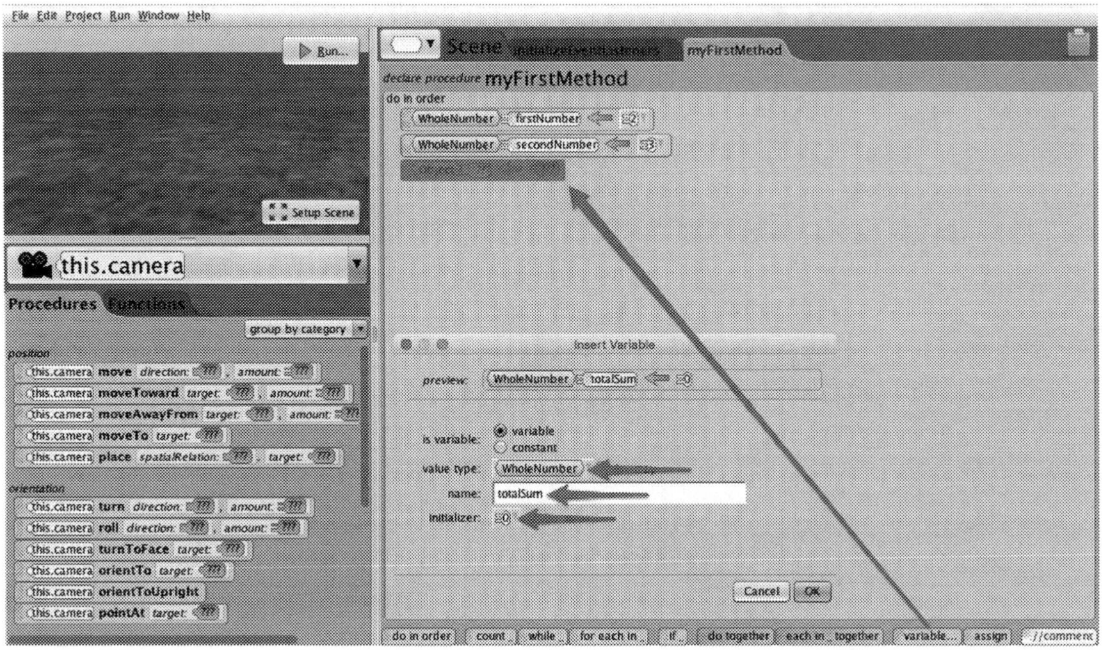

Figure 3-7. *Creating the totalSum variable*

6.   Now to add your two variables together. Drag the **totalSum** tile to the last row of the Editor, as shown in Figure 3-8, and select **0** as its value.

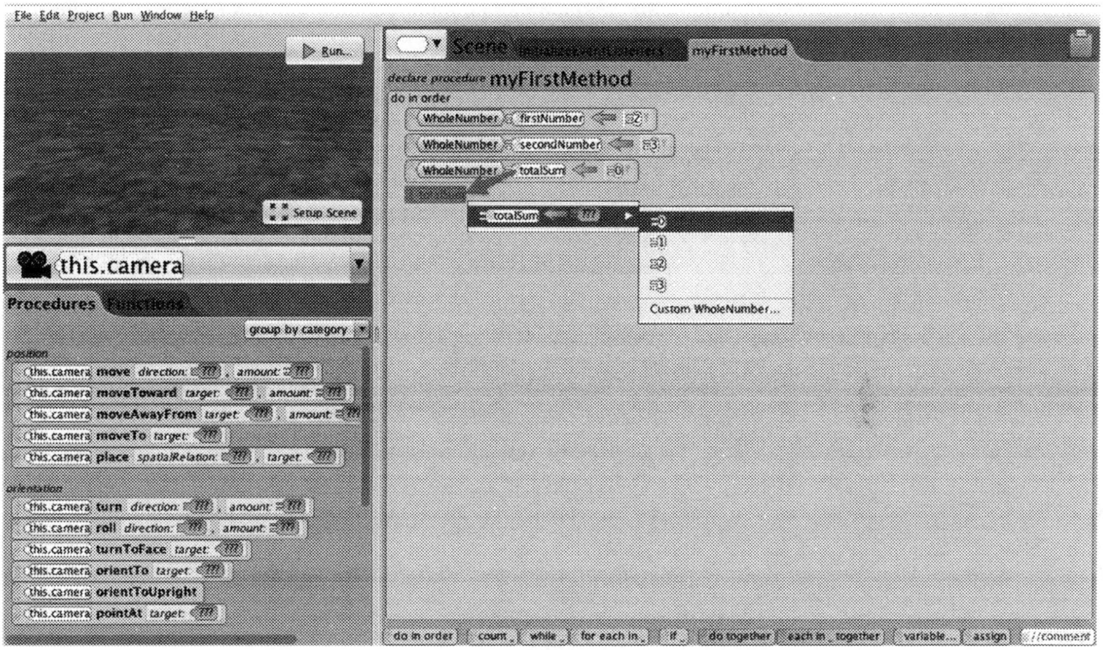

Figure 3-8. *Initializing the variable totalSum*

7. Next, click the **totalSum 0** and change it to **firstNumber**, as shown
    in Figure 3-9.

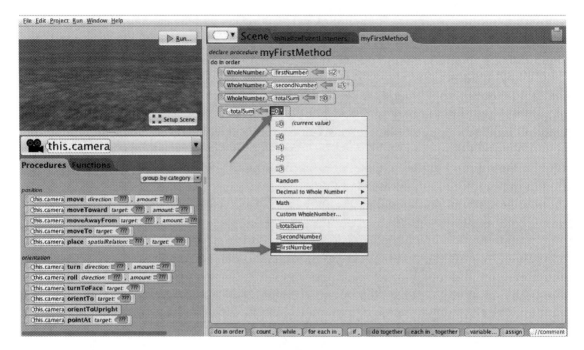

Figure 3-9. *Setting totalSum equal to firstNumber*

8. Now that totalSum is set to firstNumber, click the **firstNumber** tile.

9. Next, select **Math** to add firstNumber to secondNumber as shown in Figure 3-10.

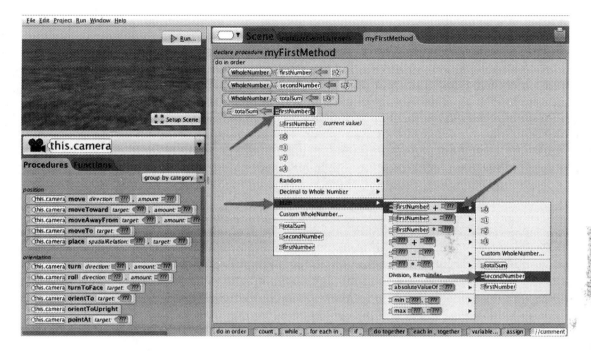

Figure 3-10. *Setting totalSum = firstNumber + secondNumber*

10. totalSum is now set to be the sum of firstNumber and secondNumber. See Figure 3-11.

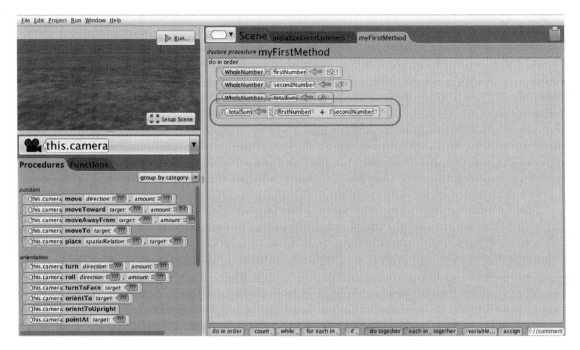

Figure 3-11. *totalSum is now set*

Now you just need to add a character to your world to display your total!

11. Click the Setup Scene button in the Camera View and add any object of your choosing from the Gallery at the bottom of the screen. (We selected an Alien.) See Figure 3-12.

Figure 3-12. *Adding an Alien to your world*

You now need to declare a variable of type **TextString** to hold the text "The sum of 2 + 3 is 5" that the Alien will say.

12. Click the **Edit Code** button in the bottom right corner of the Camera View to go back to the Editor.

13. With your Alien instance selected, drag the **this.alien say text: ???** tile from the **Procedures** tab to the Editor. See Figure 3-13.

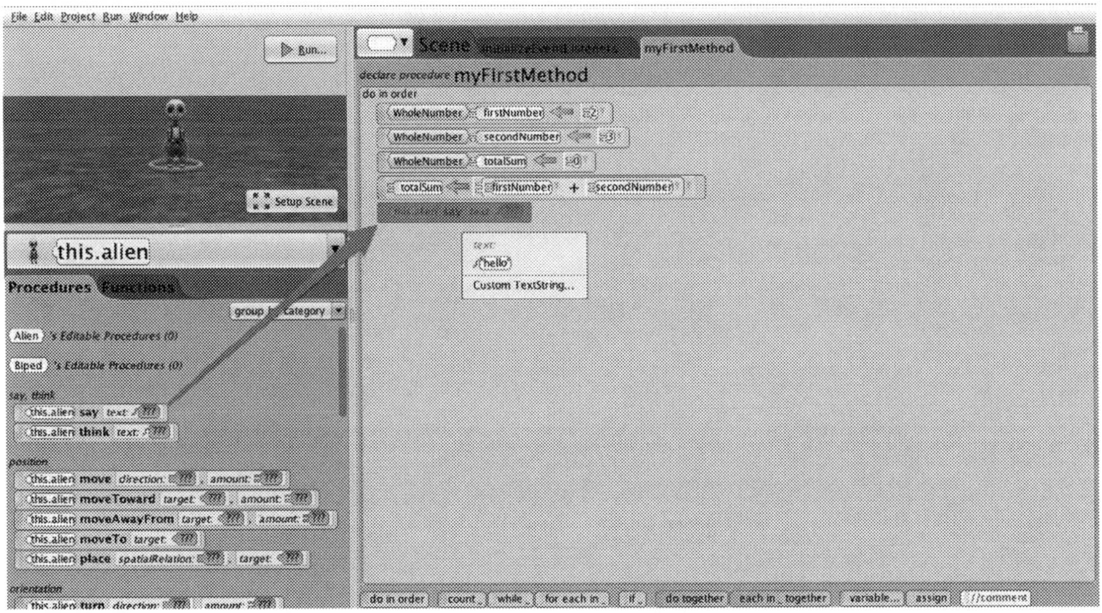

Figure 3-13. *Adding the "say" procedure (method) to the Editor*

14. Click **Custom TextString** and enter the string **The sum of 2 + 3 is**
    (with an extra empty space at the end) as the parameter value.
    See Figure 3-14.

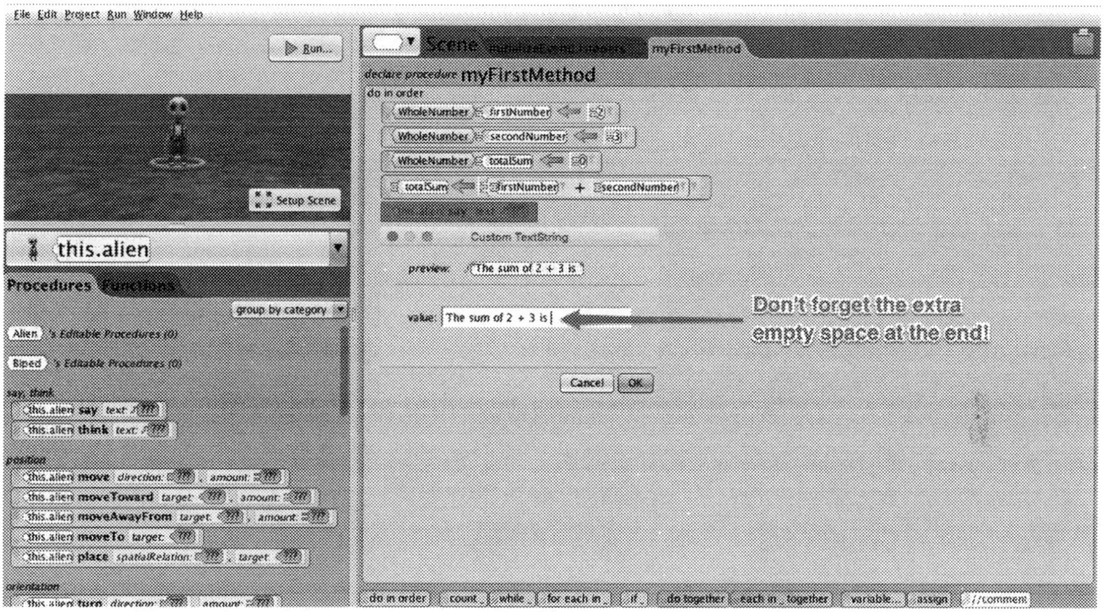

Figure 3-14. *Entering the Custom TextString parameter*

15.   Click **OK,** then click the first parameter of the "say" procedure, and append **totalSum** to the string. See Figure 3-15.

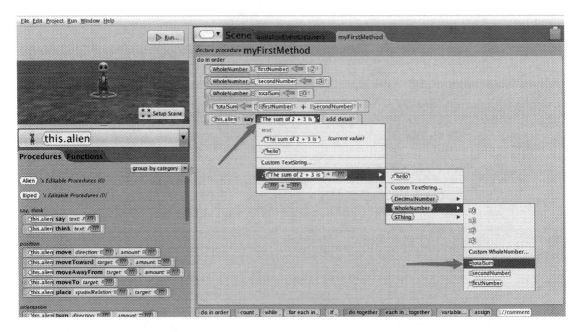

Figure 3-15. *Adding totalSum to your custom string to display to the user*

Alice did something very nice for you in the last step. It automatically converted the data type totalSum from a WholeNumber to a TextString when it appended its value to the "The sum of 2 + 3 is " string. You will also learn how to do this using Objective-C.

You can run the program by clicking the Run button, but you will notice the custom string doesn't display for very long.

To increase the display time of your custom string, click the **add detail** parameter of the "say" procedure and change the **duration** to **2.0** seconds, or any other value you like. See Figure 3-16.

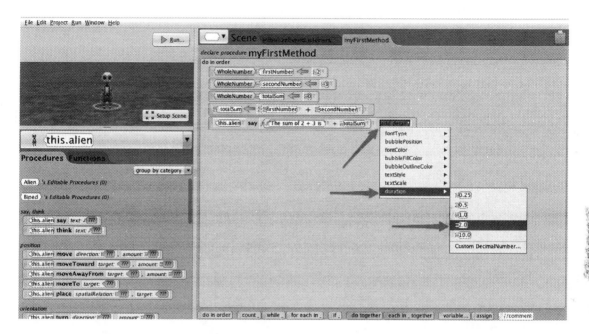

Figure 3-16. *Increasing the "say" duration to 2.0 seconds*

16. Click the Run button, and if you've done everything correctly, your app should look like Figure 3-17 when it runs.

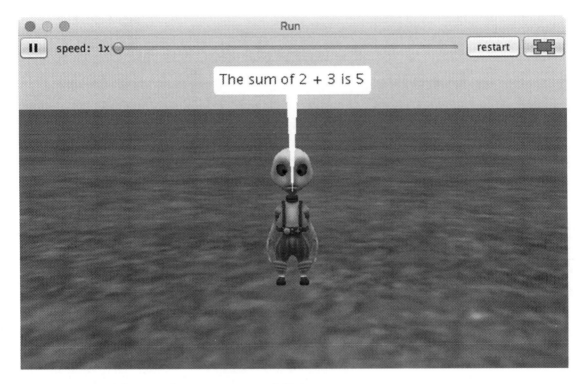

Figure 3-17. *The app has run successfully!*

Data Types and Objective-C

Now that we have covered the principles of data types and have written an Alice app to help show how these principles apply, let's write an Objective-C app that accomplishes what you just did in Alice.

In Objective-C, you have similar data types as you did in Alice. Some of the most frequently used data types for storing numbers are integers, doubles, floats, and longs. Table 3-5 lists several basic data types, many of which will be covered in later chapters.

Table 3-5. *Objective-C Basic Data Types*

Type	Examples	Specifiers
Char	'a', 'O', '\n'	%c
Int	42, -42, 550 0xCCE0	%i, %d
Unsigned int	20u, 101U, 0xFEu	%u, %x, %o
Long int	13, -2010, 0xfefeL	%ld,
Unsigned long int	12UL, 100ul, 0xffeeUL	%lu, %lx, %lo
Long long int	0xe5e5e5LL, 501ll	%lld
Unsigned long long int	11ull, 0xffeeULL	%llu, %llx, %llo
Float	12.30f, 3.2e-5f, 0x2.2p09	%f, %e, %g, %a
Double	3.1415	%f, %e, %g, %a
Long double	3.1e-5l	%Lf, %Le, %Lg, %La
NSObject	Nil	%@

The Objective-C app will add two integers and display their sum in the console. This will be fun and easy, so let's get started!

1. As iOS developers, Xcode is where you make your living, so open up Xcode and create a new project. To do this, select **File ➤ New ➤ Project** and select **macOS** and **Command Line Tool**, as shown in Figure 3-18, before clicking Next.

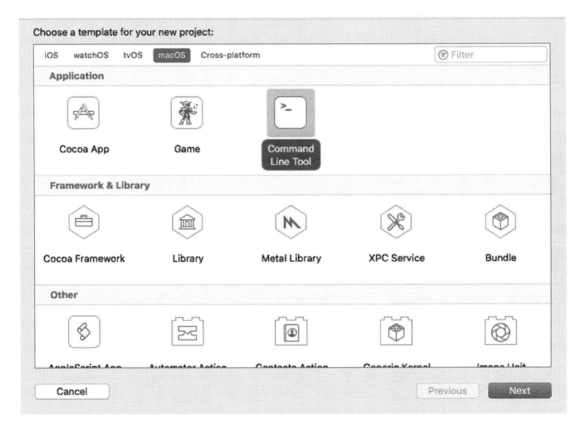

Figure 3-18. *Creating a new project*

2. Enter **Chapter 3** as the Product Name (see Figure 3-19) and choose a folder to save your project after clicking Next.

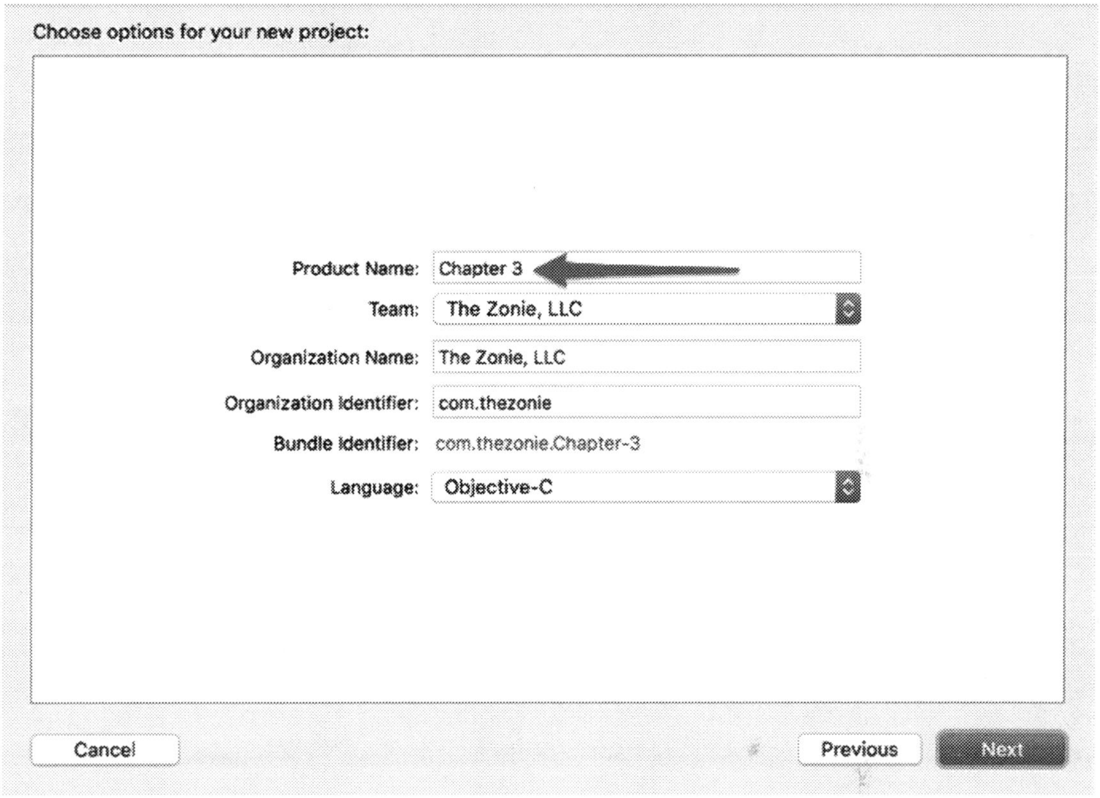

Figure 3-19. *Chapter 3 project settings*

3. After you create the project, you need to open the source code
   file in the Editor. Select the `main.m` source file to open it
   (see Figure 3-20).

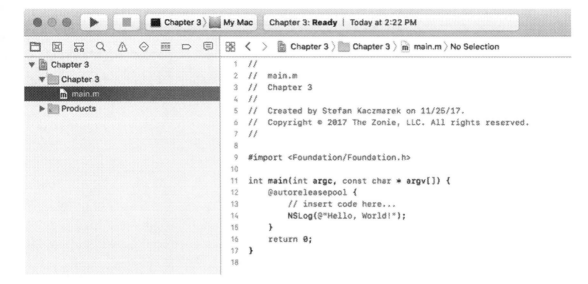

Figure 3-20. *After you create your project and select the main.m file, your Xcode project should look this*

If you haven't seen `//` used in computer programming before, it enables the programmer to comment about the code. Comments are not compiled as part of your application's source code, but are instead used as notes for both you as the original developer and, more importantly, for any other developers who will ultimately review your code. Comments help both the original developer and any follow-up developers understand how the app was developed.

Sometimes it is necessary for comments to span several lines or just part of a line. This can be accomplished with `/*` and `*/`. All the text between `/*` and `*/` is treated as a comment and is not compiled.

In this example, you first need to declare and initialize your variables **firstNumber** and **secondNumber**. It is good practice to always initialize variables when they are declared.

Your application will then calculate the `totalSum` of **firstNumber** and **secondNumber** and print the result to the console. See Figure 3-21.

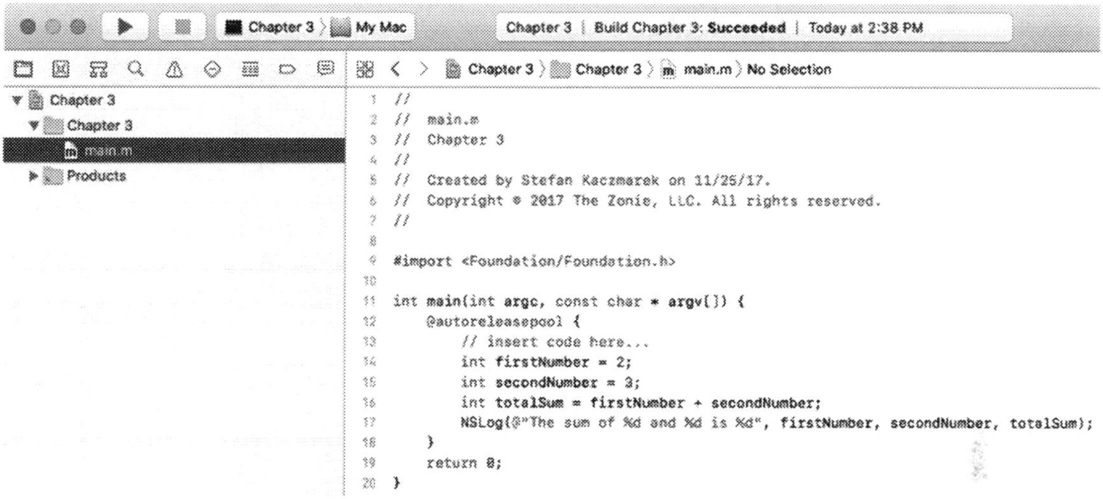

Figure 3-21. *Code for adding two numbers and printing the sum to the console*

NSLog is a function that can take one or more parameters. The first parameter is generally the string that is to be printed to the console. The **@** symbol in front of the string tells the compiler this is an Objective-C type string and not a standard C string. The @ symbol is typically used in front of all your strings for iOS apps. If you don't use the @ symbol, you will probably get a compiler error. NSLog is a helpful function used by developers to test the execution of their code by logging information to the console.

%d tells the compiler an integer will be printed and to substitute the value of the integer for the **%d**. See Table 3-5 for other NSLog format specifiers. Finally, the last three parameters are the integers to be printed.

To compile and run your application, click the **Run** button in the toolbar. If you typed your code in correctly, you should see the resulting NSLog string printed to the console as shown in Figure 3-22.

```
 1  //
 2  //  main.m
 3  //  Chapter 3
 4  //
 5  //  Created by Stefan Kaczmarek on 11/25/17.
 6  //  Copyright © 2017 The Zonie, LLC. All rights reserved.
 7  //
 8
 9  #import <Foundation/Foundation.h>
10
11  int main(int argc, const char * argv[]) {
12      @autoreleasepool {
13          // insert code here...
14          int firstNumber = 2;
15          int secondNumber = 3;
16          int totalSum = firstNumber + secondNumber;
17          NSLog(@"The sum of %d and %d is %d", firstNumber, secondNumber, totalSum);
18      }
19      return 0;
20  }
```

```
2017-11-25 14:53:56.264213-0700 Chapter 3[16200:2043300] The sum of 2 and 3 is 5
Program ended with exit code: 0
```

Figure 3-22. *Console log displaying the results of your Objective-C app*

Note   If your editor doesn't have the same menus or gutter (the left column that contains the line numbers of the program) you saw in the previous screenshots, you can turn these settings on in the Xcode preferences. You can open the Xcode preferences by clicking the Xcode menu in the menu bar and then selecting **Preferences** and then **Text Editing** and checking the **Line numbers** checkbox.

Identifying Problems

Believe it or not, your program may not run the way you thought you told it to. The process of hunting down problems with your app is called **debugging**. To track down bugs in your apps, you can set breakpoints and inspect your variables to see the contents. To do this, simply click in the gutter where you want to set a breakpoint (see Figure 3-23). A breakpoint will stop your application from executing at that line and enable you to inspect your variables.

```
 1  //
 2  //   main.m
 3  //   Chapter 3
 4  //
 5  //   Created by Stefan Kaczmarek on 11/25/17.
 6  //   Copyright © 2017 The Zonie, LLC. All rights reserved.
 7  //
 8
 9  #import <Foundation/Foundation.h>
10
11  int main(int argc, const char * argv[]) {
12      @autoreleasepool {
13          // insert code here...
14          int firstNumber = 2;
15          int secondNumber = 3;
16          int totalSum = firstNumber + secondNumber;
17          NSLog(@"The sum of %d and %d is %d", firstNumber, secondNumber, totalSum);
18      }
19      return 0;
20  }
```

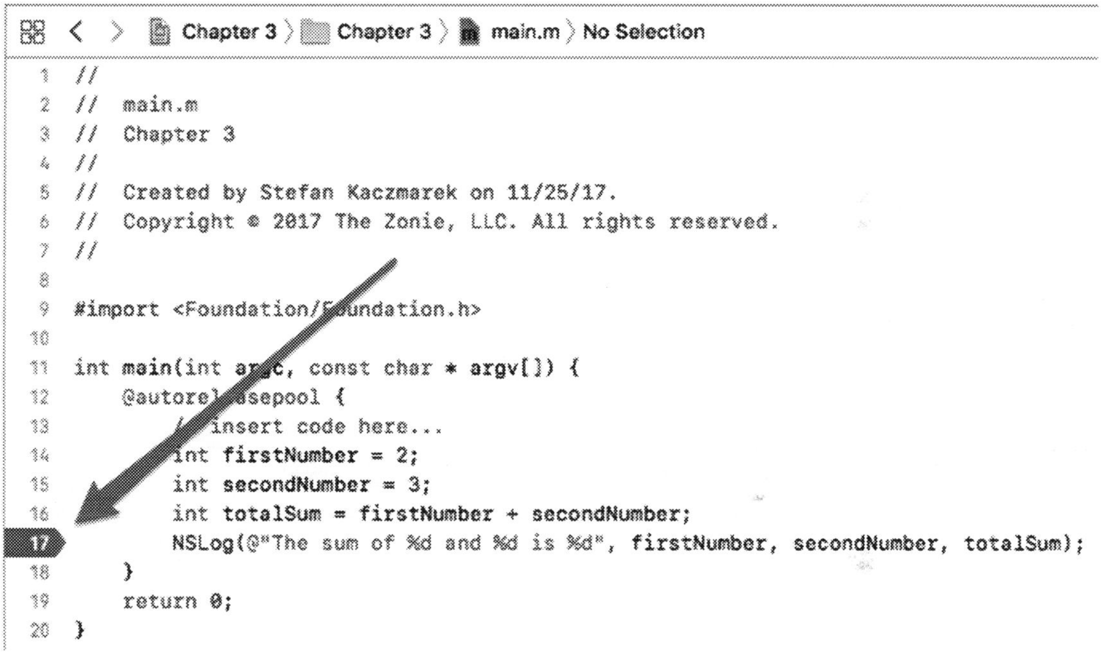

Figure 3-23. *Setting a debugging breakpoint*

A blue pointer in the gutter of your editor denotes a breakpoint. When you run your application and your app is about to execute a line of code that contains a breakpoint, your app will halt and display a green line across that line of code to indicate where it has stopped (see Figure 3-24). Clicking the **Variable view** button (also shown in Figure 3-24) will allow you to inspect the current value of each variable. Additionally, you can inspect each variable by hovering over it in the code with your mouse cursor.

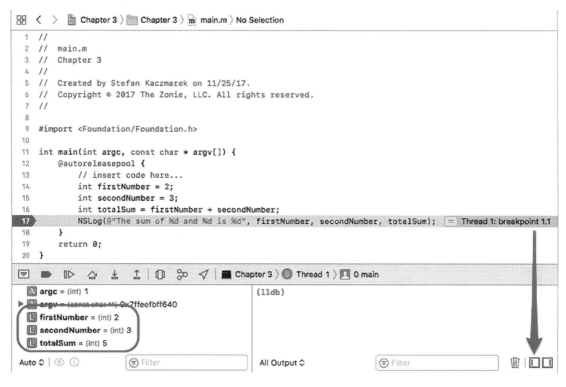

Figure 3-24. *Breakpoint hit*

We will talk more about debugging your apps in Chapter 13.

Summary

In this chapter, you learned about how data is used by your apps. You saw how to initialize variables and how to assign data to them. We explained that when variables are declared, they have a data type associated with them and that only data of the same type can be assigned to variables.

Finally, we showed you how to use variables in your first Alice app and finished by using variables with an Objective-C app.

Exercises

Perform the following tasks:

- Write an Objective-C console app (command-line tool) that multiples two integers together and displays the result in the console.

- Write an Objective-C console app that squares a float. Display the resulting float in the console.

- Write an Objective-C console app that subtracts two floats, with the result stored as an integer. Note that rounding does not occur.

CHAPTER 4

Making Decisions About and Planning Program Flow

One of the cool things about being an Objective-C developer is you get to tell your devices exactly what you want them to do and it will be done—your devices will do tasks over and over again without getting tired. That's because iPhones, iPads, and Macs don't care how hard they worked yesterday, and they don't let feelings get in the way. These devices don't need hugs.

There is a downside to being a developer: You have to think of all possible outcomes when it comes to your apps. Many developers love having this kind of control; they enjoy focusing on the many details of their apps. However, it can be frustrating having to handle so many details. As we mentioned in the introduction to this book, there is a price to pay for developing apps, and that price is time. The more time you spend developing and debugging, the better you will get with all the details, and the better your apps will run. You have to pay this price to become a successful developer.

Computers are black and white; there are no shades of gray. Your devices produce results, many of which are based on true and false conditions.

In this chapter, you will learn about computer logic and controlling the flow of your apps. Processing information and arriving at results is at the heart of all apps. Your apps need to process data based on values and conditions. To do this, you need to understand how computers perform logical operations and execute code based on the information your apps have acquired.

© Stefan Kaczmarek, Brad Lees, Gary Bennett, Mitch Fisher 2018
S. Kaczmarek et al., *Objective-C for Absolute Beginners*, https://doi.org/10.1007/978-1-4842-3429-7_4

Boolean Logic

Boolean logic is a system for logical operations. Boolean logic uses binary operators like AND, OR, and the unary operator NOT to determine whether your conditions have been met. Binary operators take two operands. Unary operators take one operand.

We just introduced a couple of new terms that can sound confusing; however, you probably use Boolean logic every day. Let's look at a couple of examples of Boolean logic with the binary operators AND and OR in a conversation parents sometimes have with their teenage children.

"You can go to the movies tonight if your room is clean AND the dishes are put away."

"You can go to the movies tonight if your room is clean OR the dishes are put away."

Boolean operators' results are either TRUE or FALSE. In Chapter 3, we briefly introduced the Boolean data type. A variable that is defined as Boolean can only contain the values TRUE and FALSE. In Objective-C, the equivalent BOOL primitive type can only contain the more commonly named values YES and NO.

```
BOOL seeMovies = YES;
```

In the preceding example, the AND operator takes two operands: one to the left and one to the right of AND. Each operand can be evaluated independently with a TRUE or FALSE.

For an AND operation to yield a TRUE result, both sides of the AND have to be TRUE. In our first example, the teenager has to clean his or her room AND have the dishes done. If either one of the conditions is FALSE, the result is FALSE—no movies for the teenager.

For an OR operation to yield a TRUE result, only one operand has to be TRUE, or both conditions can be TRUE to yield a TRUE result. In our second example, just a clean bedroom will result in the ability to go to the movies.

Note   Behind the scenes, your iPhone, iPad, or Mac defines a FALSE as a 0 and a TRUE as a 1. To be technically correct, a TRUE is defined as any nonzero value; so, values of 0.1, 1, and 2 will be evaluated as a TRUE when evaluated in a Boolean expression.

A NOT statement is a unary operator. It takes just one operand to yield a Boolean result. Here's an example:

"You can NOT go to the movies."

This example takes one operand. The NOT operator turns a TRUE operand to a FALSE and a FALSE operand to a TRUE. Here, the result is a FALSE.

Note   Performing a NOT operation is commonly referred to as *flipping the bit*, or *negating*. A TRUE is defined as a 1, a FALSE is defined as a 0, and zeros and ones are referred to as *bits*. A NOT operation turns a TRUE to a FALSE and a FALSE to a TRUE, hence *flipping the bit* or *negating* the result.

AND, OR, and NOT are three common Boolean operators. Occasionally, you need to use more complex operators. XOR, NAND, and NOR are other common operations for Objective-C developers.

The Boolean operator XOR means *exclusive-or*. An easy way to remember how the XOR operator works is the XOR operator will return a TRUE result if only one argument is TRUE, not both.

Objective-C does not have the NAND or NOR operators built in, but just know that they simply mean NOT AND and NOT OR, respectively. After evaluating the AND or the OR arguments, simply negate the result.

Truth Tables

Let's use a tool to help you evaluate all the Boolean operators. A **truth table** is a mathematical table used in logic to evaluate Boolean operators. They are helpful when trying to determine all the possibilities of a Boolean operator. Let's look at some common truth tables for AND, OR, NOT, XOR, NAND, and NOR.

In an AND truth table, there are four possible combinations of TRUE and FALSE.

- TRUE AND TRUE = TRUE

- TRUE AND FALSE = FALSE

- FALSE AND TRUE = FALSE

- FALSE AND FALSE = FALSE

Placing these combinations in a truth table results in Table 4-1.

Table 4-1. *An AND Truth Table*

A	B	A AND B
TRUE	TRUE	TRUE
TRUE	FALSE	FALSE
FALSE	TRUE	FALSE
FALSE	FALSE	FALSE

An AND truth table only produces a TRUE result if both of its operands are TRUE. Table 4-2 illustrates an OR truth table and all possible operands.

Table 4-2. *An OR Truth Table*

A	B	A OR B
TRUE	TRUE	TRUE
TRUE	FALSE	TRUE
FALSE	TRUE	TRUE
FALSE	FALSE	FALSE

An OR truth table produces a TRUE result if one or both of its operands are TRUE. Table 4-3 illustrates a NOT truth table and all possible operands.

Table 4-3. *A NOT Truth Table*

NOT	RESULT
TRUE	FALSE
FALSE	TRUE

A NOT *flips the bit* or negates the original operand's Boolean value.

Table 4-4 illustrates an XOR (or exclusive-or) truth table and all possible operands.

Table 4-4. *An XOR Truth Table*

A	B	A XOR B
TRUE	TRUE	FALSE
TRUE	FALSE	TRUE
FALSE	TRUE	TRUE
FALSE	FALSE	FALSE

The operator XOR yields a TRUE result if only one of the operands is TRUE.

Table 4-5 illustrates a NAND truth table and all possible operands.

Table 4-5. *A NAND Truth Table*

A	B	A NAND B
TRUE	TRUE	FALSE
TRUE	FALSE	TRUE
FALSE	TRUE	TRUE
FALSE	FALSE	TRUE

Table 4-6 illustrates a NOR truth table and all possible operands.

Table 4-6. *A NOR Truth Table*

A	B	A NOR B
TRUE	TRUE	FALSE
TRUE	FALSE	FALSE
FALSE	TRUE	FALSE
FALSE	FALSE	TRUE

The easiest way to look at the NAND and NOR operators is to simply negate the results from the AND and OR truth tables, respectively.

Comparison Operators

In software development, the comparison of different data items is accomplished with **comparison operators**. These operators produce a logical TRUE or FALSE result. Table 4-7 shows the list of comparison operators.

Table 4-7. *Comparison Operators*

>	Greater than
<	Less than
>=	Greater than or equal to
<=	Less than or equal to
==	Equal to
!=	Not equal to

Note   If you're constantly forgetting which way the greater-than and less-than signs go, use a crutch I learned in grade school: If the greater-than and less-than signs represent the mouth of an alligator, the alligator always eats the bigger value. It may sound silly, but it works.

Designing Apps

Now that we've introduced Boolean logic and comparison operators, you can start designing your apps. Sometimes it's important to express all or parts of your apps to others without having to write the actual code.

Writing out code helps a developer think out loud and brainstorm with other developers regarding sections of code that are of concern. This helps to analyze problems and possible solutions before coding begins.

Pseudocode

Pseudocode refers to writing out code that is a high-level description of an algorithm you are trying to solve. Pseudocode does not contain the necessary programming syntax for coding; however, it does express the algorithm that is necessary to solve the problem at hand.

Pseudocode can be written by hand on paper (or a whiteboard) or typed on a computer.

Using pseudocode, you can apply what you know about Boolean data types, truth tables, and comparison operators. Refer to Listing 4-1 for pseudocode examples.

Listing 4-1. Pseudocode Examples Using Conditional Operators in If-Then-Else Code

```
x = 5;
y = 6;
isComplete = TRUE;

if (x < y)
{
    // in this example, x is less than y
    do stuff;
}
else
{
    do other stuff;
}

if (isComplete == TRUE)
{
    // in this example, isComplete is equal to TRUE
    do stuff;
}
else
{
    do other stuff;
}
```

```
// another way to check isComplete == TRUE
if (isComplete)
{
    // in this example,  isComplete is TRUE
    do stuff;
}

// one way to check if a value is false
if (isComplete == FALSE)
{
    do stuff;
}
else
{
    // in this example, isComplete is TRUE so the else block will be
executed
    do other stuff;
}

// another way to check isComplete == FALSE
if (!isComplete)
{
    do stuff;
}
else
{
    // in this example,  isComplete is TRUE so the else block will be
executed
    do other stuff;
}
```

Note   Pseudocode is a programming notation resembling a simplified programming language, used in program design. *Pseudocode will not compile and run.* It is for illustrative purposes only.

Note that the **!** switches the value of the Boolean it's applied to; so, using **!** makes a TRUE value a FALSE and a FALSE value a TRUE. This is the logical NOT operator in Objective-C.

Often, it is necessary to combine your comparison tests. A compound relationship test is one or more simple relationship tests joined by either the && or the || (two pipe characters).

&& and || are verbalized as logical AND and logical OR, respectively. The pseudocode in Listing 4-2 illustrates the logical AND and logical OR operators.

Listing 4-2. Using && and || Logical Operators Pseudocode

```
x = 5;
y = 6;
isComplete = TRUE;

// using the logical AND
if (x < y && isComplete == TRUE)
{
    // in this example, x is less than y and isComplete == TRUE
    do stuff;
}

if (x < y || isComplete == FALSE)
{
    // in this example, x is less than y.
    // Only one operand has to be TRUE for an OR to result in a TRUE.
    // See Table 4-2 A OR Truth Table
    do stuff;
}

// another way to test for TRUE
if (x < y && isComplete)
{
    // in this example, x is less than y and isComplete == TRUE
    do stuff;
}
```

```
// another way to test for FALSE
if (x < y && !isComplete)
{
    do stuff;
}
else
{
    // isComplete == TRUE
    do stuff;
}
```

Flowcharting

After the design requirements discussed in Chapter 1 have been finalized, you can pseudocode sections of your app to solve complex development issues. **Flowcharting** is a common method of diagramming an algorithm. An algorithm is represented as different types of boxes connected by lines and arrows. Developers often use flowcharting to express code visually. See Figure 4-1.

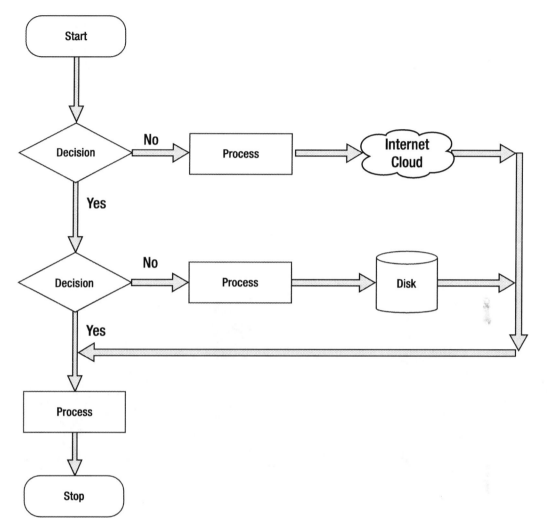

Figure 4-1. *Sample flowchart showing common figures and their associated names*

Flowcharts should always have a start and a stop. Branches should never come to an end without a stop. This helps developers make sure all of the branches in their code are accounted for and that they cleanly stop execution.

Designing and Flowcharting an Example App

You just learned a lot of information about decision making and program flow. It's time to do what programmers do best: write apps!

The app you have been assigned to write generates a random number between 0 and 100 inclusive and asks users to guess the number. Users have to do this until the number is guessed. You can use any object from the Alice gallery to ask users for their guess, and you can also choose any world for your object to be in. The object will provide a visual queue for each high, low, and correct guess. When users guess the correct answer, they will be asked if they want to play again. See Figure 4-2.

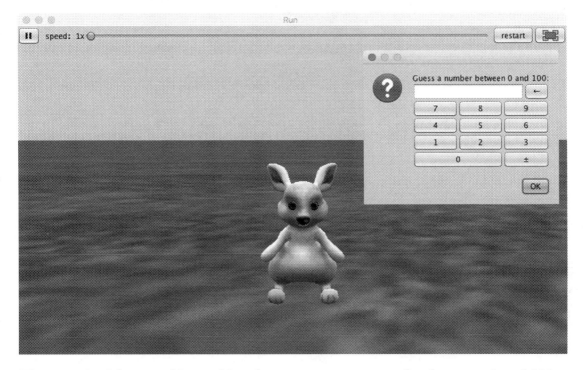

Figure 4-2. *A bunny object asking the user to guess a number between 0 and 100*

The App's Design

Using the design requirements, you can make a flowchart for your app. See Figure 4-3.

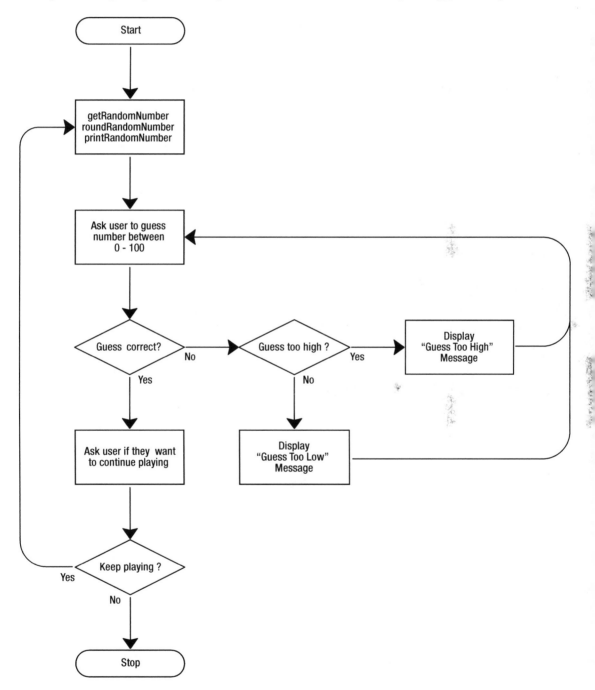

Figure 4-3. *Flowchart for guessing a random number app*

Reviewing Figure 4-3, you'll notice that as you approach the end of a block of logic in your flowchart, there are arrows that go back to a previous section and repeat that section until some condition is met. This is called **looping**. It enables you to repeat sections of programming logic—without having to rewrite those sections of code over—until a condition is met.

Using Loops to Repeat Program Statements

A **loop** is a sequence of program statements that is specified once but can be repeated several times in succession. A loop can repeat a specified number of times (count-controlled) or until some condition (condition-controlled) occurs.

In this section, you'll learn about count-controlled loops and condition-controlled loops. You will also learn how to control your loops with Boolean logic.

Count-Controlled Loops

A count-controlled loop is a loop that repeats a specified number of times. In Objective-C and Alice, this is a **for loop**. A for loop has a counter variable. This variable enables the developer to specify the number of times the loop will be executed. See Listing 4-3.

Listing 4-3. A Count-Controlled Loop

```
int i;
for (i = 0; i < 10; i++)
{
    // repeat all code in braces 10 times
}
....continue
```

The loop in Listing 4-3 will loop ten times. The variable i starts at 0 and increments at the end of the } by 1. The incrementing is done by the i++ in the for statement; i++, which is equivalent to i = i + 1. i is then checked to see whether it is less than 10. This for loop will exit when i = 9 and the } is reached.

> **Note**   It is common for developers to confuse the number of times they think their loops will repeat. If the loop started at 1 in Listing 4-3, the loop would repeat nine times instead of ten.

In Objective-C, for loops can have their counter variables declared in the for loop declaration itself. See Listing 4-4.

Listing 4-4. Counter Variable Is Initialized in the For Loop Declaration

```
for (int i = 0; i < 10; i++)
{
    // repeat all code in braces 10 times
}
....continue
```

Occasionally, you will need to repeat just one line of code in a for loop. This can be accomplished by not using any { }. The first line of code encountered after the for loop declaration is repeated, as specified in the for loop declaration. See Listing 4-5.

Listing 4-5. Counter Variable Is Initialized in the For Loop Declaration

```
for (int i = 0; i < 10; i++)
    do this line of code 10 times;
....continue
```

Condition-Controlled Loops

Objective-C and Alice have the ability to repeat a loop until some condition changes. You may want to repeat a section of your code until a false condition is reached with one of your variables. This type of loop is called a **while loop**. A while loop is a control flow statement that repeats based on a given Boolean condition. A while loop can be thought of as a repeating if statement. See Listing 4-6.

Listing 4-6. An Objective-C While Loop Repeating

```
BOOL isTrue = TRUE;
while (isTrue)
{
    // do something;
     isTrue = FALSE; // a condition occurs that sometimes sets isTrue to FALSE
}
....continue
```

The while loop in Listing 4-6 first checks whether the variable isTrue is TRUE—which it is—so the {loop body} is entered where the code is executed. Eventually, some condition is reached that causes isTrue to become FALSE. After completing all the code in the loop body, the condition (isTrue) is checked once more, and the loop is repeated again. This process is repeated until the variable isTrue is set to FALSE.

Infinite Loops

An infinite loop repeats endlessly, either because of the loop not having a condition that causes termination or because of the loop having a terminating condition that can never be met.

Generally, infinite loops can cause apps to become unresponsive. They are the result of a side effect of a bug in either the code or the logic. See Listing 4-7.

Listing 4-7. An Example of an Infinite Loop

```
x = 0;
while (x  != 5)
{
    do something;
    x = x + 2;
}
....continue
```

Listing 4-7 is an example of an infinite loop caused by a terminating condition that can never be met. The variable x will be checked with each iteration through the while loop but will never be equal to 5. The variable x will always be an even number because it was initialized to zero and incremented by 2 in the loop. This will cause the loop to repeat endlessly. See Listing 4-8.

Listing 4-8. An Example of an Infinite Loop Caused by a Terminating Condition That Can Never Be Met

```
while (TRUE)
{
    do something;
}
....continue
```

Coding the Example App in Alice

Now that you have your design requirements and flowchart completed and you understand looping, you're ready to write your Alice application. See Figure 4-4.

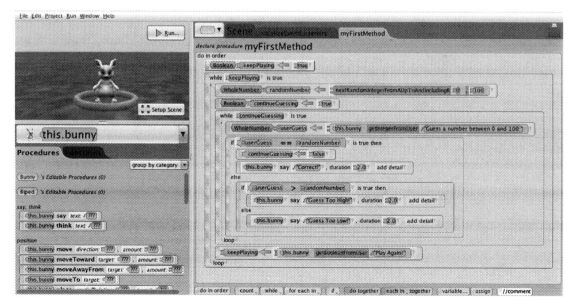

Figure 4-4. *Random number generator app*

Figure 4-5 shows the entire program listing for your random number generator code.

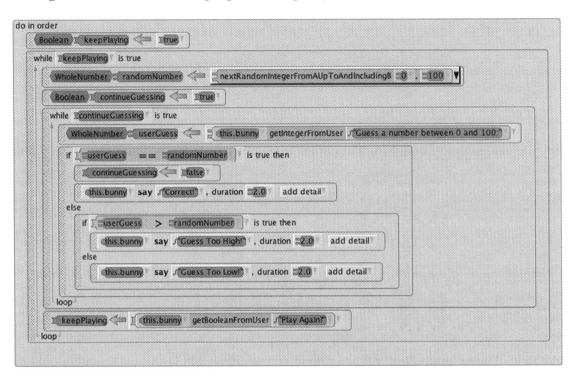

Figure 4-5. *Random number generator; complete program listing*

Note You can download the complete random number generator app at
`http://forum.xcelme.com`. The code will be under the Chapter 4 topic.

Coding the Example App in Objective-C

Using the requirements and what you learned with your Alice app, it's time to write your random number generator in Objective-C.

Your Objective-C app will run from the command line as it asks the user to guess a random number.

1. Open Xcode and start a new project. Choose Command Line Tool.
    See Figure 4-6.

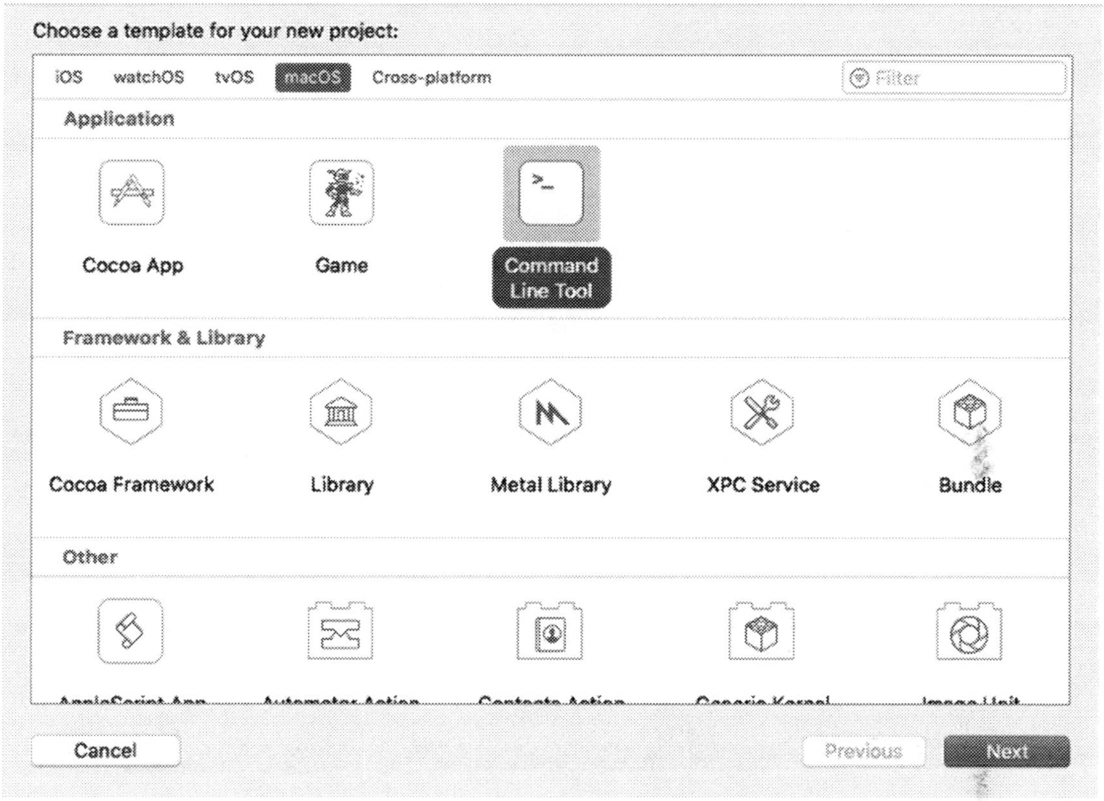

Figure 4-6. *Start a new Command Line Tool project*

2. Call your project RandomNumber (see Figure 4-7). Save the project anywhere you prefer on your hard drive.

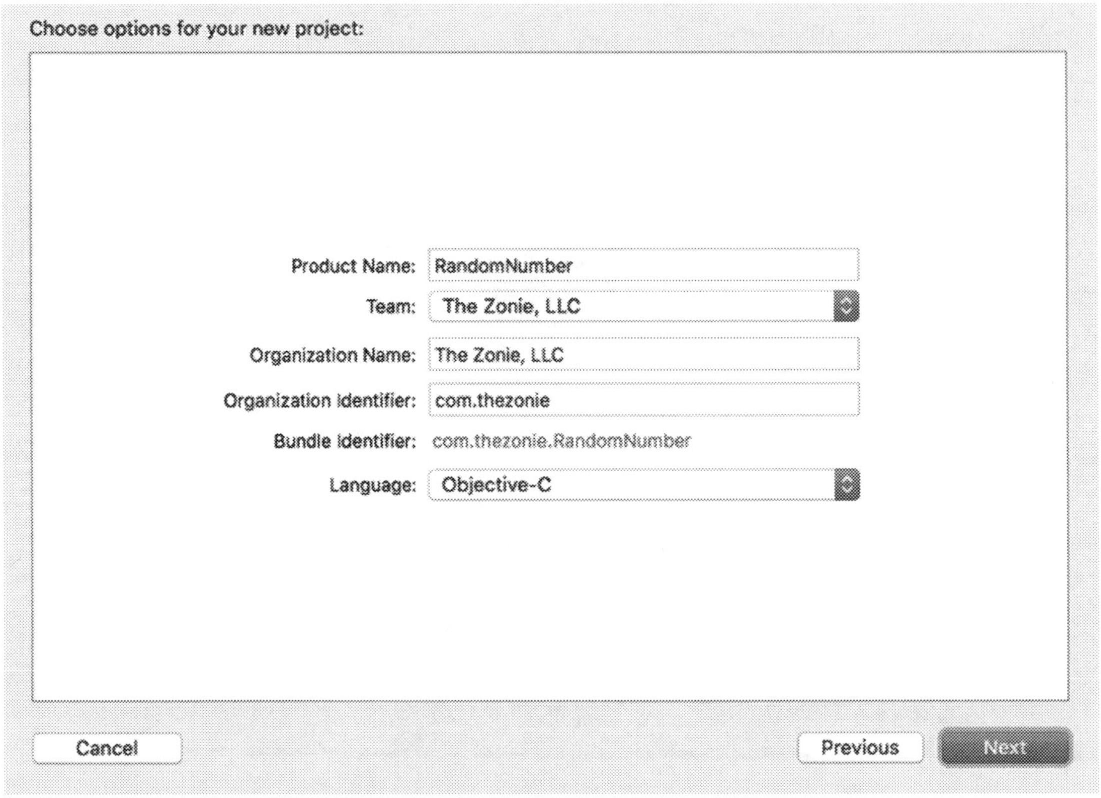

Figure 4-7. *Project options for RandomNumber*

Now, you need to open the implementation file in the Source group. This is where you will write your Objective-C code.

3. Open the main.m file. Delete the following line of code:

```
NSLog(@"Hello, World!");
```

4. You are ready to write your app. Start writing the code under this:

```
// insert code here...
```

See Figure 4-8.

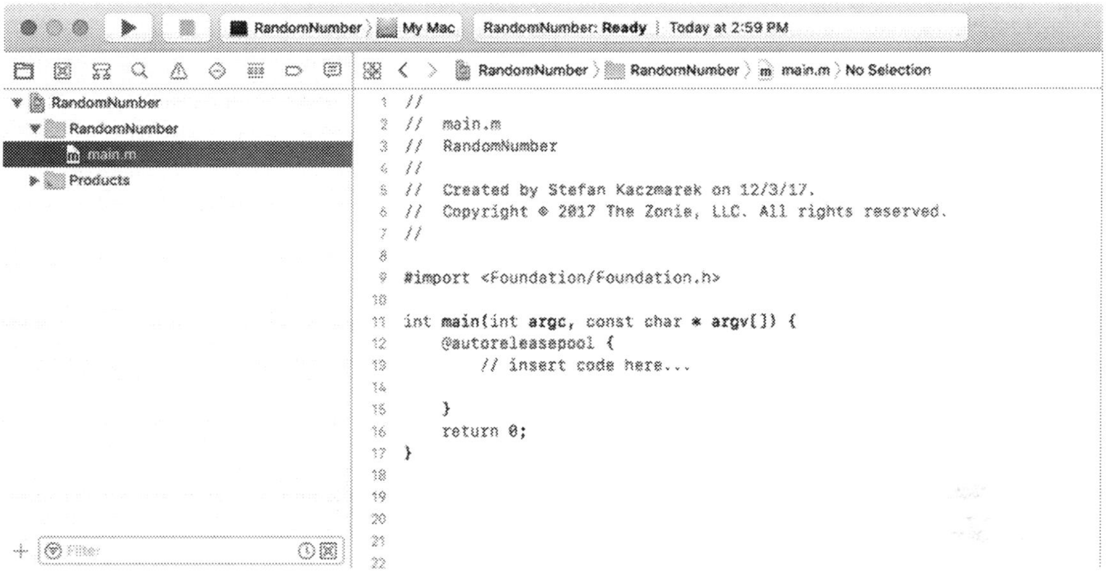

Figure 4-8. *The Editor*

Following your Alice code, you will write your random number generator app. You will notice that most of the code is similar to your Alice app. See Listing 4-9.

Listing 4-9. Source Code for Your Random Number Generator App

```
11 int main(int argc, const char * argv[]) {
12      @autoreleasepool {
13          // insert code here...
14          int randomNumber = 1;
15          int userGuess = 1;
16          BOOL continueGuessing = YES;
17          BOOL keepPlaying = YES;
18          char yesNo = ' ';
19
20          while (keepPlaying) {
21              randomNumber = (arc4random() % 101);
22              NSLog(@"The random number to guess is: %d",randomNumber);
23              while (continueGuessing) {
```

```
24                    NSLog (@"Pick a number between 0 and 100. ");
25                    scanf ("%d", &userGuess);
26                    fgetc(stdin);    // remove CR/LF i.e extra character
27                    if (userGuess == randomNumber) {
28                        continueGuessing = NO;
29                        NSLog(@"Correct number!");
30                    }
31                    // nested if statement
32                    else if (userGuess > randomNumber){
33                        // user guessed too high
34                        NSLog(@"Your guess is too high");
35                    }
36                    else {
37                        // no reason to check if userGuess < randomNumber.
                            It has to be.
38                        NSLog(@"Your guess is too low");
39                    }
40                    // refactored from our Alice app. This way we only have
                        to code once.
41                    NSLog(@"The user guessed %d",userGuess);
42                }
43            NSLog (@"Play Again? Y or N");
44            yesNo = fgetc(stdin);
45            if (yesNo == 'N' || yesNo == 'n') {
46                keepPlaying = FALSE;
47            }
48            continueGuessing = TRUE;
49        }
50    }
51
52    return 0;
53 }
```

In Listing 4-9, there is new code that we haven't discussed before. The first new line of code (line 21) is

```
randomNumber = (arc4random() % 101);
```

This line will produce a random number between 0 and 100; `arc4random()` is a function that returns a random number. Although this will not generate a truly random number, it will work for this example.

The % is called the **modulus operator**. This operator returns the remainder of its two operands; in this case, it's the remainder of `arc4random()` divided by 101. This is what will return a number between 0 and 100.

The next line of new code is

```
scanf ("%d", &userGuess);
```

The function `scanf` reads a value from the keyboard and stores it in `userGuess`.

Note   The source code for this Objective-C project is available for download at `http://forum.xcelme.com`.

Nested If Statements and Else-If Statements

Sometimes, it is necessary to **nest if statements**. This means that you need to have `if` statements nested inside an existing `if` statement. Additionally, it is sometimes necessary to have a comparison as the first step in the `else` section of the `if` statement. This is called an **else-if statement**. Recall line 32 in Listing 4-9:

```
else if (userGuess > randomNumber)
```

Removing Extra Characters

Line 26 is another new line of code:

```
fgetc(stdin);       // remove CR/LF i.e extra character
```

The function `scanf` can be difficult to work with. In this case, `scanf` leaves a remnant in your input buffer that needs to be flushed, so you can read a Y or N from the keyboard to determine whether the user wants to play again.

Improving the Code Through Refactoring

Often, after you get your code to work, you will examine it and find more efficient ways to write it. The process of rewriting your code to make it more efficient, maintainable, and readable is called **code refactoring**.

As you were reviewing your code in Objective-C, you may have noticed that you could eliminate some unnecessary code. Your code had the following line repeated in the if-else statement:

```
// refactored from our Alice app. This way we only have to code once.
NSLog(@"The user guessed %d",userGuess);
```

Note   As developers, we have found that the best line of code you can write is the line that you don't write. Less code means less to debug and maintain.

Running the App

Click the Play button in your Objective-C project and run your app. See Figure 4-9.

```
2017-12-03 15:14:34.329046-0700 RandomNumber[63321:7253782] The random number to guess is: 46
2017-12-03 15:14:34.329334-0700 RandomNumber[63321:7253782] Pick a number between 0 and 100.
50
2017-12-03 15:14:44.300389-0700 RandomNumber[63321:7253782] Your guess is too high
2017-12-03 15:14:44.300448-0700 RandomNumber[63321:7253782] The user guessed 50
2017-12-03 15:14:44.300464-0700 RandomNumber[63321:7253782] Pick a number between 0 and 100.
40
2017-12-03 15:14:48.788895-0700 RandomNumber[63321:7253782] Your guess is too low
2017-12-03 15:14:48.788939-0700 RandomNumber[63321:7253782] The user guessed 40
2017-12-03 15:14:48.788954-0700 RandomNumber[63321:7253782] Pick a number between 0 and 100.
45
2017-12-03 15:14:55.235475-0700 RandomNumber[63321:7253782] Your guess is too low
2017-12-03 15:14:55.235518-0700 RandomNumber[63321:7253782] The user guessed 45
2017-12-03 15:14:55.235533-0700 RandomNumber[63321:7253782] Pick a number between 0 and 100.
47
2017-12-03 15:15:00.298490-0700 RandomNumber[63321:7253782] Your guess is too high
2017-12-03 15:15:00.298555-0700 RandomNumber[63321:7253782] The user guessed 47
2017-12-03 15:15:00.298580-0700 RandomNumber[63321:7253782] Pick a number between 0 and 100.
46
2017-12-03 15:15:04.292061-0700 RandomNumber[63321:7253782] Correct number!
2017-12-03 15:15:04.292103-0700 RandomNumber[63321:7253782] The user guessed 46
2017-12-03 15:15:04.292118-0700 RandomNumber[63321:7253782] Play Again? Y or N
n
Program ended with exit code: 0
```

Figure 4-9. *The console output of the Objective-C random number generator app*

Moving Forward Without Alice

You've used Alice to learn object-oriented programming. It has enabled you to focus on OOP concepts without having to deal with syntax and a compiler; however, it is necessary to become more familiar with the specifics of the Objective-C language. Alice has served you well, and you can now focus on using Objective-C and Xcode for the remainder of the book.

Summary

In this chapter, we covered a lot of important information on how to control your applications. Program flow and decision making are essential to every iPhone/iPad/Mac app. Make sure you have completed the Objective-C example in this chapter. You may review these examples and think you understand everything without having to write this app. This is a fatal mistake, one that will prevent you from becoming a successful Objective-C developer. You must spend time coding this example.

The terms in this chapter are important. You should be able to describe the following:

- AND
- OR
- XOR
- NAND
- NOR
- NOT
- Truth tables
- Negation
- All comparison operators
- Application requirement
- Logical AND (&&)
- Logical OR (||)

- Flowchart

- Loop

- Count-controlled loops

- For loop

- Condition-controlled loops

- Infinite loops

- While loops

- Nested if statements

- Code refactoring

Exercises

Perform the following tasks:

- Extend the random number generator app to print to the console how many times the user guessed before he or she guessed the correct random number. Do this in both Alice and Objective-C.

- Extend the random number generator app to print to the console how many times the user played the app. Print this value when the user quits the app. Do this in both Alice and Objective-C.

CHAPTER 5

Object-Oriented Programming with Objective-C

Over the past 25 years, the programming world has been focusing on the development paradigm of object-oriented programming (OOP). Most modern development environments and languages implement OOP. Put simply, OOP forms the basis of everything you develop today.

You may be asking yourself why we waited until Chapter 5 to present OOP using Objective-C if it is the primary development style of today. The simple answer is that it is not an easy concept for new developers. We will spend this chapter going into detail about the different aspects of OOP and how this will affect your development.

Implementing OOP into your applications correctly will take some up-front planning, but you will save yourself a lot of time throughout the life of your projects. OOP has changed the way development is done. In this chapter, we will look at what OOP is. OOP was initially discussed in the first chapter of this book, but we will go into more detail here. We will revisit what objects are and how they relate to physical objects we find in our world. We will look into what classes are and how they relate to objects. We will also discuss steps you will need to take when planning your classes and some visual tools you can use to accomplish this. When you have read this chapter and have worked through the exercises, you will have a better understanding of what OOP is and why it is necessary for you as a developer.

At first, objects and object-oriented programming may seem difficult to understand, but the hope is that as you progress through this chapter, it will begin to make sense.

© Stefan Kaczmarek, Brad Lees, Gary Bennett, Mitch Fisher 2018
S. Kaczmarek et al., *Objective-C for Absolute Beginners*, https://doi.org/10.1007/978-1-4842-3429-7_5

The Object

As discussed in Chapter 1, OOP is based on objects. Some of our discussion about objects will be a review, but we will also go into more depth. An object is anything that can be acted upon. To better explain what a programming object is, we will first look at some items in the physical world around us. A physical object can be anything around you that you can touch or feel. Take, for example, a television. Some characteristics of a television include type (plasma, LCD, or CRT), size (40 inches), brand (Sony, Vizio), weight, and cost. Televisions also have functions. They can be turned on or off. You can change the channel, adjust the volume, and change the brightness.

Some of these characteristics and functions are unique to televisions and some are not. For example, a couch in your house would probably not have the same characteristics as a television. You would want different information about a couch, such as material type, seating capability, and color. A couch might have only a few functions, such as converting to a bed.

Now let's talk specifically about objects as they relate to programming. An **object** is a specific item. It can describe something physical like a book, or it could be something such as a window for your application. Objects have properties and methods. **Properties** describe certain things about an object such as location, color, or name. Conversely, methods describe actions the object can perform such as close or recalculate. In our example, a TV object would have `type`, `size`, and `brand` properties, while a `Couch` object would have properties such as `color`, `material`, and `comfort level`. In programming terms, a property is a variable that is part of an object. For example, a TV would use a string variable to store the brand and an integer to store the height.

Objects also have commands the programmer can use to control them. The commands are called **methods**. Methods are the way that other objects interact with a certain object. For example, with the television, a method would be any of the buttons on the remote control. Each of those buttons represents a way you can interact with your television. Methods can and often are used to change the values of properties, but methods do not store any values themselves.

As we described in Chapter 1, objects have a **state**, which is basically a snapshot of an object at any given point in time. A state would be the values of all the properties at a specific time.

In upcoming chapters, we will use the example of a bookstore. A bookstore contains many different objects. It contains book objects that have properties such as title, author, page count, and publisher. It also contains magazines with properties such as title, issue, genre, and publisher. A bookstore also has some nontangible objects such as a sale. A sale object would contain information about the books purchased, the customer, the amount paid, and the payment type. A sale object might also have some methods that calculate tax, print the receipt, or void the sale. A sale object does not represent a tangible object, but it is still an object and is necessary for creating an effective bookstore.

Because the object is the basis of OOP, it is important to understand objects and how to interact with them. We will spend the rest of the chapter describing objects and some of their characteristics.

What Is a Class?

We cannot discuss OOP without discussing what a class is. A **class** defines which properties and methods an object will have. A class is basically a cookie cutter that can be used to create objects that have similar characteristics. All objects of a certain class will have the same properties and the same methods. The values of those properties will change from object to object.

A class is similar to a species in the animal world. A species is not an individual animal, but it does describe many similar characteristics of the animal. To understand classes more, let's look at an example of classes in nature. The Dog class has many properties that all dogs have in common. For example, a dog may have a name, an age, an owner, and a favorite activity. An object that is of a certain class is called an **instance** of that class. If you look at Figure 5-1, you can see the difference between the class and the actual objects that are instances of the class. For example, Lassie is an instance of the Dog class. In Figure 5-1, you can see we have a Dog class that has four properties (Breed, Age, Owner, Favorite Activity). In real life, a dog will have many more properties, but we decided to use four for this demonstration.

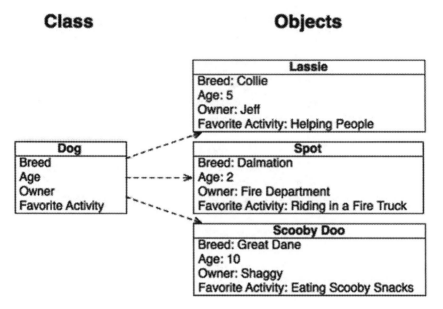

Figure 5-1. *An example of a class and individual objects*

Planning Classes

Planning your classes is one of the most important steps in your development process. While it is possible to go back and add properties and methods after the fact (and you will definitely need to do this), it is important that you know which classes are going to be used in your application and which basic properties and methods they will have. Spending time planning your different classes is important at the beginning of the process.

Planning Properties

Let's look at the bookstore example and some of the classes you need to create. First, it is important to create a Bookstore class. A Bookstore class contains the blueprint of the information each Bookstore object stores, such as the bookstore Name, Address, Phone Number, and Logo (see Figure 5-2). Placing this information in a class rather than hard-coding it in your application will allow you to easily make changes to this information in the future. We will discuss the reasons for using OOP methodologies later in this chapter. Also, if your bookstore becomes a huge success and you decide to open another one, you will be prepared because you can create another object of class Bookstore.

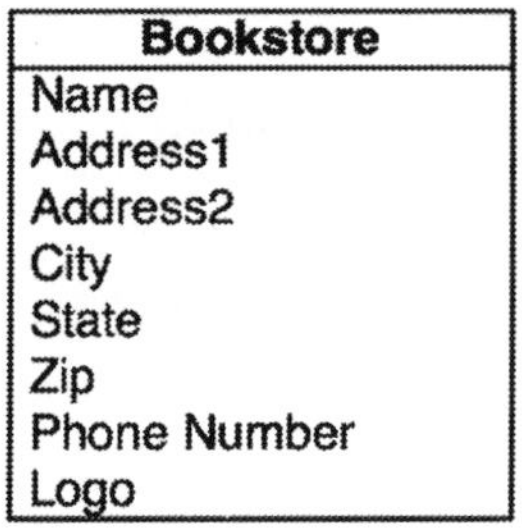

Bookstore
Name
Address1
Address2
City
State
Zip
Phone Number
Logo

Figure 5-2. *The Bookstore class*

Let's also plan a Customer class (see Figure 5-3). Notice how the name has been broken into First Name and Last Name. This is important to do. There will be times in your project when you may want to use only the first name of a customer, and it would be hard to separate the first name from the last if you didn't plan ahead. Let's say you want to send a letter to a customer letting them know about an upcoming sale. You do not want your greeting to say "Dear John Doe." It would look much more personal to say "Dear John."

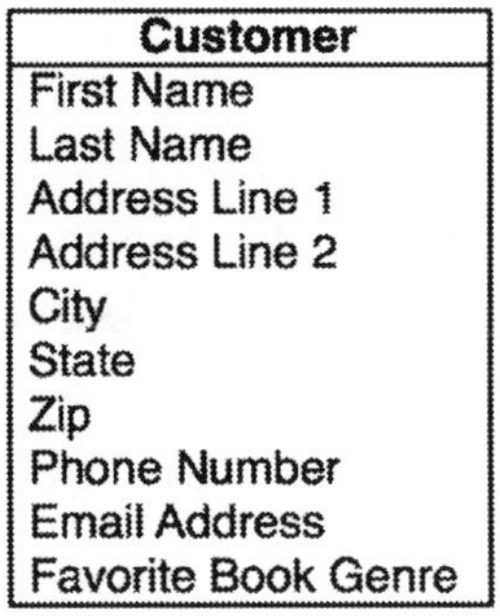

Customer
First Name
Last Name
Address Line 1
Address Line 2
City
State
Zip
Phone Number
Email Address
Favorite Book Genre

Figure 5-3. *The Customer class*

You will also notice how we have broken out the address into its different parts instead of grouping it all together. We separated the Address Line 1, Address Line 2, City, State, and Zip properties. This is important and will be used in your application. Let's go back to the letter you want to send informing your customers of a sale in your store. You might not want to send it to customers who live in different states. By separating the address, you can easily filter out those customers you do not want to include in certain mailings.

We have also added the attribute of Favorite Book Genre to the Customer class. We added this to show you how you can keep many different types of information in each class. This field may come in handy if you have a new mystery title coming out and you want to send an e-mail alerting customers who are especially interested in mysteries. By storing this type of information, you will be able to specifically target different portions of your customer base.

A Book class is also necessary to create your bookstore (see Figure 5-4). You will store information about the book such as Author, Publisher, Genre, Number of Pages, and Edition (in case there are multiple editions). The Book class will also have the Price for the book.

```
          Book
  Author
  Publisher
  Genre
  Year Published
  Number of Pages
  Edition
  Price
```

Figure 5-4. *The Book class*

We also added another class called the Sale class (see Figure 5-5). This class is more abstract than the other classes we have discussed because it does not describe a tangible object. You will notice how we have added a reference to a customer and a book to the Sale class. Because the Sale class will track sales of books, you will need to know which book was sold and to which customer.

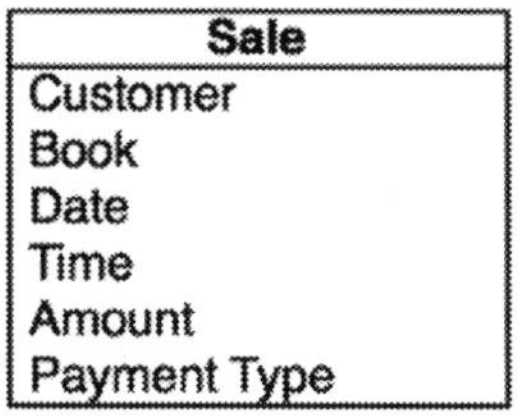

```
          Sale
  Customer
  Book
  Date
  Time
  Amount
  Payment Type
```

Figure 5-5. *The Sale class*

Now that you have planned out the properties of the classes, you will need to look at some methods that each of the classes will have.

Planning Methods

You will not add all of the methods now, but the more planning you can do at the beginning, the easier it will be for you down the line. Not all of your classes will have many methods. Some may not have any methods at all.

Note   When planning your methods, remember to have them focus on a specific task. The more specific the method, the more likely it is that it can be reused.

For the time being, you will not add any methods to the Book class or the Bookstore class. You will focus on the other two classes.

For the Customer class, you will add methods to list the purchase history of that client. There may be other methods that you will need to add in the future, but you will add just that one for now. Your completed Customer class diagram should look like Figure 5-6. Note the line near the bottom that separates the properties from the methods.

Customer
First Name
Last Name
Address Line 1
Address Line 2
City
State
Zip
Phone Number
Email Address
Favorite Book Genre
List Purchase History

Figure 5-6. *The completed Customer class*

For the Sales class, let's add three methods: Charge Credit Card, Print Invoice, and Checkout (see Figure 5-7). For now, you don't need to know how to implement these methods, but you need to know that you are planning on adding them to your class.

Sale
Customer
Book
Date
Time
Amount
Payment Type
Charge Credit Card
Print Invoice
Checkout

Figure 5-7. *The completed Sale class*

Now that you have finished mapping out the classes and the methods you are going to add to them, you have the beginnings of a Unified Modeling Language (UML) diagram. Basically, this is a diagram used by developers to plan out their classes, properties, and methods. Starting your development process by creating such a diagram will help you significantly in the long run. An in-depth discussion of UML diagrams is beyond the scope of this book. If you would like more information about this subject, smartdraw.com has a great in-depth overview of them at `https://www.smartdraw.com/resources/tutorials/uml-diagrams/`.

Figure 5-8 shows the complete diagram.

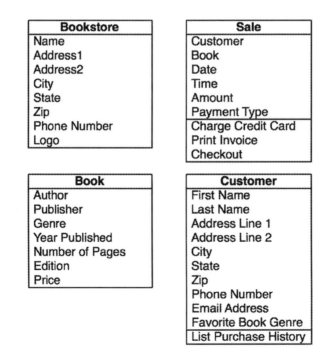

Figure 5-8. *The completed UML diagram for the bookstore*

Implementing the Classes

Now that you understand the objects you are going to be creating, you need to create your first object. To do so, you will start with a new project.

1. Please launch Xcode. Click **File ➤ New ➤ Project**.

2. Select **iOS**, and then select **Master-Detail App**. For what you are doing in this chapter, you could have selected any of the application types (see Figure 5-9). Click **Next**.

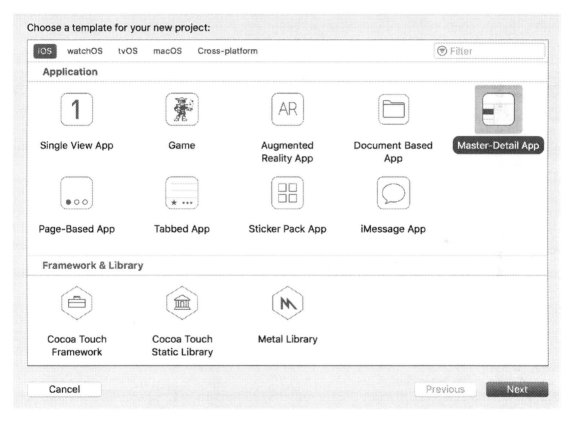

Figure 5-9. *Creating a new project*

3. Enter a product name. For this example, let's use **BookStore**. By default, Xcode will fill in the Organization Name and Organization Identifier fields. Make sure the Language field is set to Objective-C. Leave the check boxes on this screen as they appear by default. You don't need to worry about these items right now. Add a Company Identifier if you have not already set one. The format for the identifier is com.yourcompanyname. Please do not include spaces in your Company Identifier. Click **Next** and select a location to save your project and then save your project.

4. Select the **BookStore** folder on the left side of the screen (see Figure 5-10). This is where the majority of your code will reside.

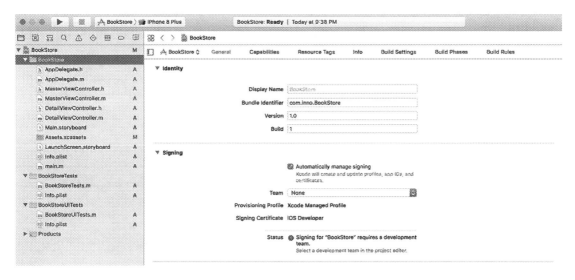

Figure 5-10. *Selecting the BookStore folder*

5. Select **File ➤ New ➤ File**.

6. From the pop-up window, select **iOS** and then **Cocoa Touch Class** (see Figure 5-11). Then click **Next**.

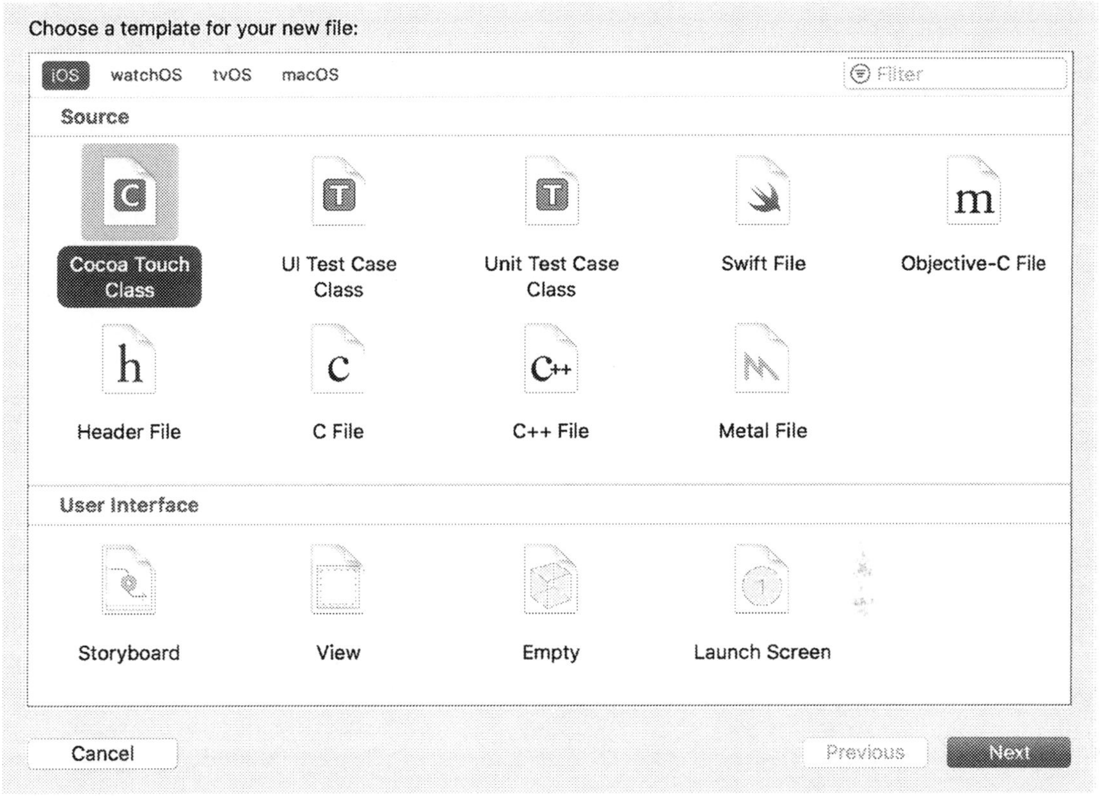

Figure 5-11. *Creating a new Objective-C class*

7.   On the next screen, you need to select the superclass for your
     object. This is what determines what properties and methods your
     object will have by default. You will select NSObject for now
     (see Figure 5-12).

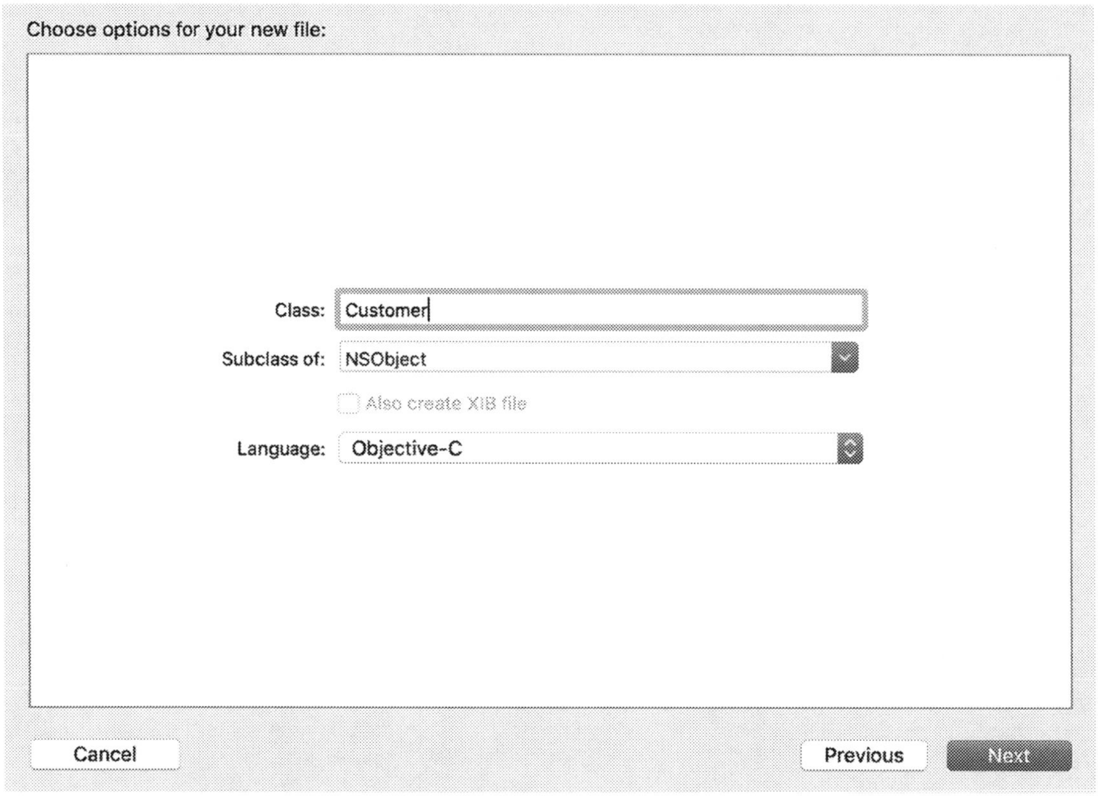

Figure 5-12. *Selecting the superclass*

Note   NSObject is the base class in Objective-C. It contains properties and methods required for most objects used.

---

8. You will now be given the opportunity to name your class. For this exercise, you will create the Customer class. For now, name the class Customer. Now click **Next** and then **Create**.

Note   For ease of use and for understanding your code, remember that class names should always be capitalized in Objective-C. Object names should always start with a lowercase letter. For example, Book would be an appropriate name for a class, and book would be a great name for an object based on the Book class. For a two-word object, such as the book author, an appropriate name would be bookAuthor. This type of capitalization is called **lower camelcase**.

9. Now look in your main project folder; you should have two new files. One is called Customer.h and the other is called Customer.m. The .h file is the header or interface file that will contain information about your class. The header file will list all of the public properties and methods in your class, but it will not actually contain the code related to them. The .m file is the implementation file, which is where you write the code for your methods.

10. Click the Customer.h file and you will see the window shown in Figure 5-13. You will notice that it does not contain a lot of information currently. The first part, with the double slashes (//), is all comments and is not considered part of the code. Comments allow you to tell those who might read your code what each portion of code is meant to accomplish. We will not go into more detail now about the other portions of the header file, except to say that all of the instance variables of a class need to be inside the braces ({}) of the @interface portion.

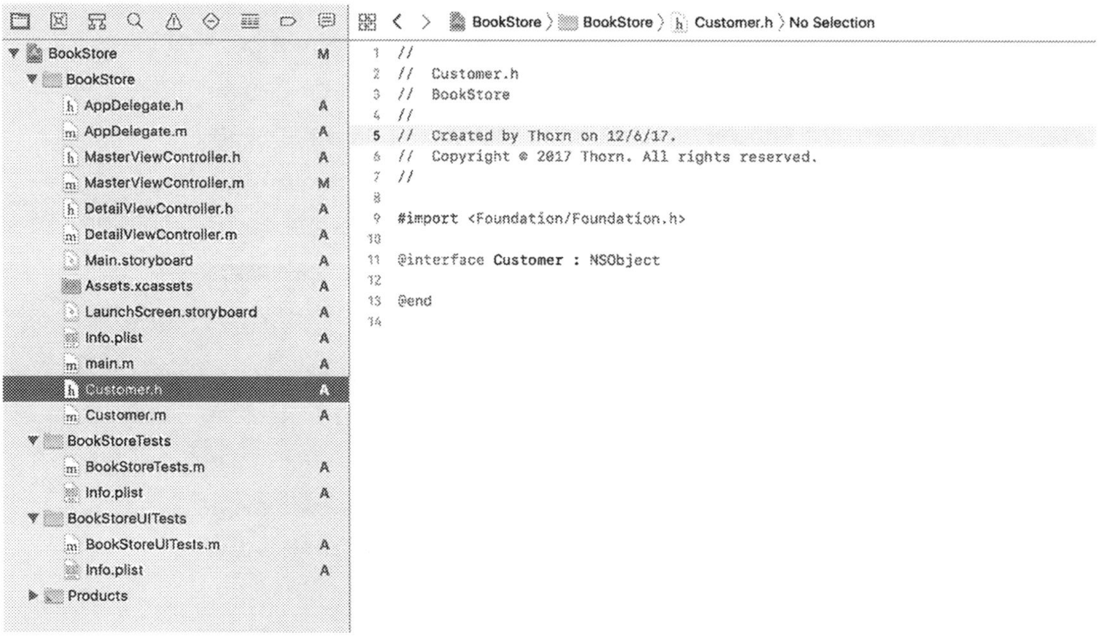

Figure 5-13. *Your empty customer class*

Now let's transfer the properties from your UML diagram to your actual class.

Tip   Properties should always start with a lowercase letter. There can be no spaces in a property name.

For the first property, firstName, you will add this line to your file:

```
NSString* firstName;
```

Note   NSString is a class that holds and performs actions on a string. A string is a set of characters. NSString can hold letters, numbers, and punctuation.

This creates a string object in your class called firstName. Because all of the properties for the Customer class are strings also, you will just need to repeat the same procedure for the other ones. When that is complete, your @interface portion should look like Figure 5-14.

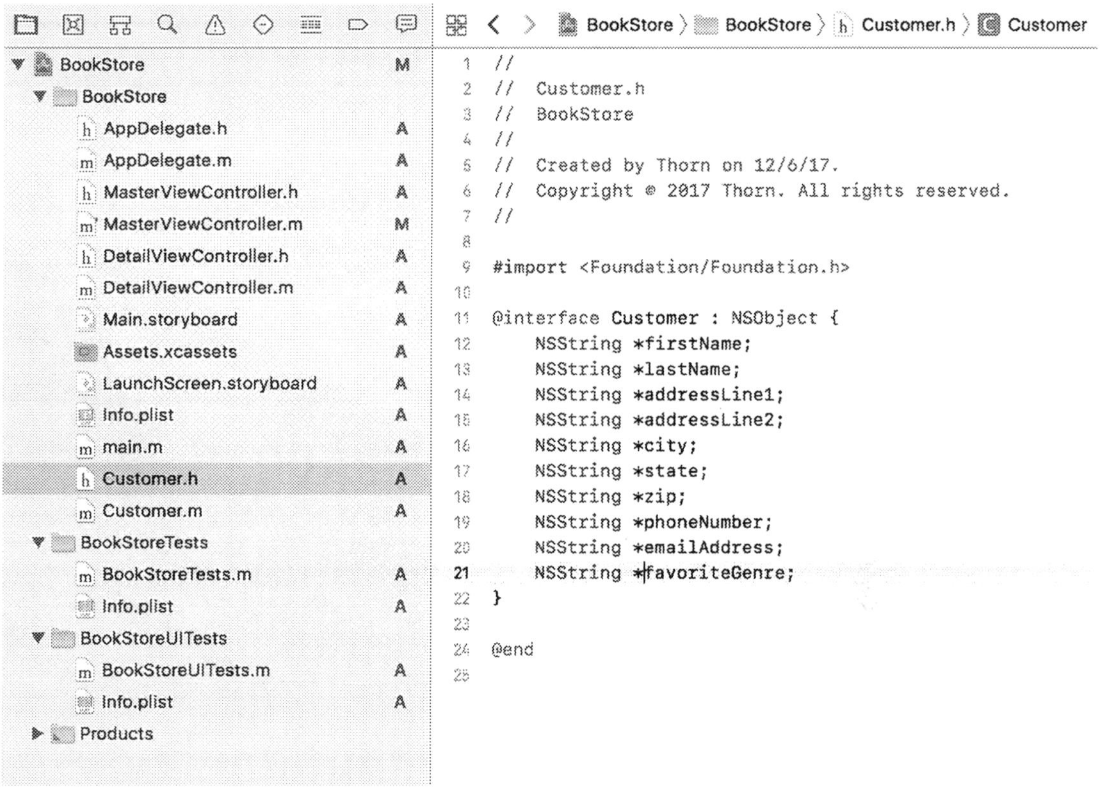

```
 1  //
 2  //  Customer.h
 3  //  BookStore
 4  //
 5  //  Created by Thorn on 12/6/17.
 6  //  Copyright © 2017 Thorn. All rights reserved.
 7  //
 8
 9  #import <Foundation/Foundation.h>
10
11  @interface Customer : NSObject {
12      NSString *firstName;
13      NSString *lastName;
14      NSString *addressLine1;
15      NSString *addressLine2;
16      NSString *city;
17      NSString *state;
18      NSString *zip;
19      NSString *phoneNumber;
20      NSString *emailAddress;
21      NSString *favoriteGenre;
22  }
23
24  @end
25
```

Figure 5-14. *The Customer class interface with instance variables*

Now that the @interface portion is complete, you will need to add your method. Methods need to go outside the curly brace portion but still inside the @interface portion of the header file. You will add a new method that returns an NSArray. This code will look as follows:

- (NSArray *)listPurchaseHistory;

That is all that needs to be done in the header file to create your class. Figure 5-15 shows the final header file. In the next chapter, we will go into more detail about the implementation file.

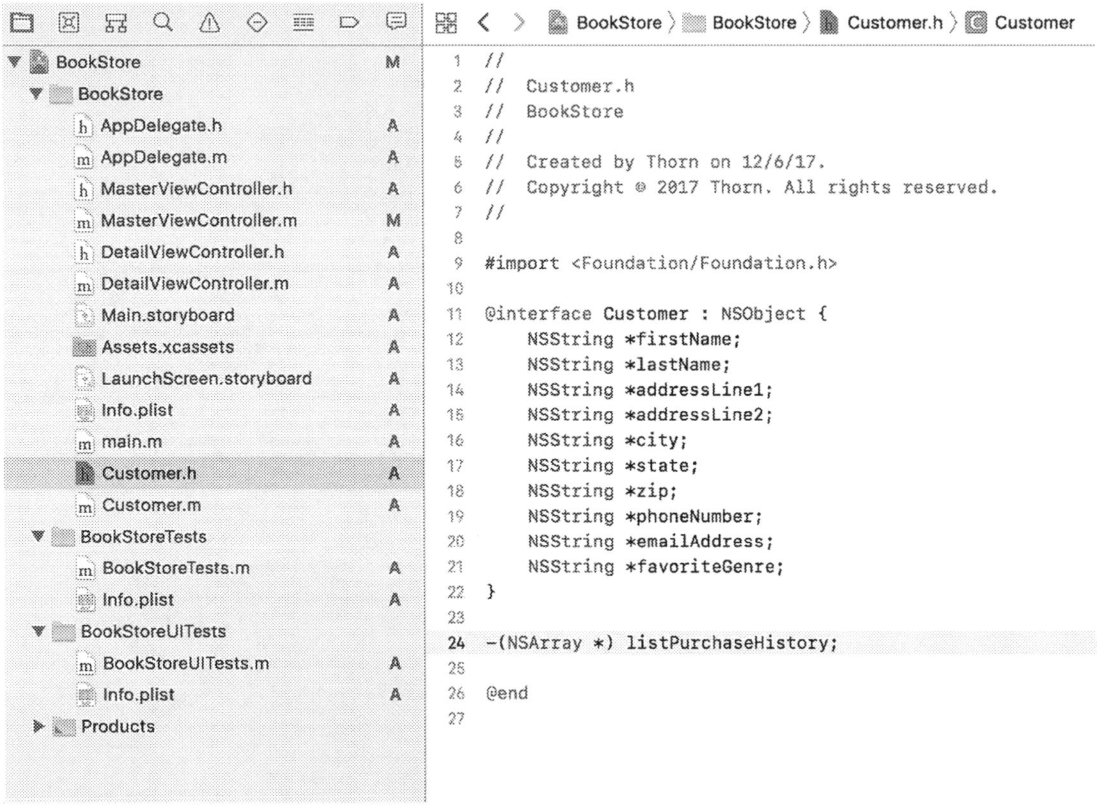

Figure 5-15. *The finished customer class header file*

Inheritance

Another major quality of OOP is **inheritance**. Inheritance in programming is similar to genetic inheritance. You might have inherited your eye color from your mother or hair color from your father, or vice versa. Classes can, in a similar way, inherit properties and methods from their parent classes. In OOP, a parent class is called a **superclass** and a child class is called a **subclass**.

In Objective-C, all classes created by a programmer have a superclass that is similar in properties and methods to itself. The class will inherit characteristics from that parent class. So, just as in all other OOP languages, the class is called a subclass of the parent class. In this chapter, all of your classes are subclasses of the NSObject. In Objective-C, many classes will be subclasses of NSObject. In the previous example, the Customer class was a subclass of NSObject.

You could, for example, create a class of printed materials and use subclasses for books, magazines, and newspapers. Printed materials can have many things in common, so you could assign properties to the superclass of printed materials and not have to redundantly assign them to each individual class. By doing this, you further reduce the amount of redundant code that is necessary for you to write and debug.

Figure 5-16 shows a layout for the properties of a `Printed Material` superclass and how that will affect the subclasses of `Book`, `Magazine`, and `Newspaper`. The properties of the `Printed Material` class will be inherited by the subclasses, so there is no need to define them explicitly in the class. Note that the `Book` class now has significantly fewer properties. By using a superclass, you significantly reduce the amount of redundant code in your programs.

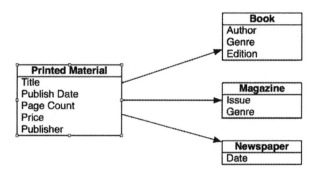

Figure 5-16. *Properties of the superclass and its subclasses*

Why Use OOP?

Throughout this chapter, we have discussed what OOP is and we have even discussed how to create classes and objects. However, we think it is important to discuss why you want to use OOP principles in your development.

If you take a look at the popular programming languages of the day, all of them use the OOP principles to a certain extent. Objective-C, Swift, C++, Visual Basic, C#, and Java all require the programmer to understand classes and objects to successfully develop in those languages. To become a developer in today's world, you need to understand OOP. But why use it?

It Is Everywhere

Just about any development you choose to do today will require you to understand object-oriented principles. In macOS and iOS, almost everything you interact with will be an object. For example, simple windows, buttons, and text boxes are all objects and have properties and methods. If you want to be successful as a programmer, you need to understand OOP.

Eliminate Redundant Code

By using objects, you can reduce the amount of code you have to retype. If you write code to print a receipt when a customer checks out, you will want that same code available when you need to reprint a receipt. If you placed your code to print the receipt in the Sales class, you will not have to rewrite this code. This not only saves you time but often helps you eliminate mistakes. If you do not use OOP and there is a change to the invoice (even something as simple as a graphic change), you have to make sure you make the change in your desktop application and the mobile application. If you miss one of them, you run the risk of having the two interfaces behave differently.

Ease of Debugging

By having all the code relating to a book in one class, you know where to look when there is a problem with the book. This may not sound like such a big deal for a little application, but when your application gets to hundreds of thousands or even millions of lines of code, it will save you a lot of time.

Ease of Replacement

If you place all of your code in a class, then as things change in your application, you can change out classes and give your new class completely different functionality. However, it can interact with the rest of the application in the same way as your current class. This is similar to car parts. If you want to replace a muffler on a car, you do not need to get a new car. If you have code related to your invoice scattered all over the place, it makes it much more difficult to change items about a class.

Advanced Topics

We have discussed the basics of OOP throughout this chapter, but there are other topics that are important to your understanding.

Interface

As we have discussed in this chapter, the way the other objects interact through each other is with methods. We discussed the header files created when you create a class. This is often called the **interface** because it tells other objects how they can interact with your objects. Implementing a standard interface throughout your application will allow your code to interact with different objects in similar ways. This will significantly reduce the amount of object-specific code you need to write.

Polymorphism

Polymorphism is the ability of an object of one class to appear and be used as an object of another class. This is usually done by creating methods and properties that are similar to those of another class. A great example of polymorphism that we have been using is the bookstore. In the bookstore, you have three similar classes: `Book`, `Magazine`, and `Newspaper`. If you wanted to have a big sale for your entire inventory, you could go through all of the books and mark them down. Then you could go through all of the magazines and mark them down, and then go through all of the newspapers and mark them down. That would be a lot of work. It would be better to make sure all of the classes have a `Markdown` method. Then you could call it on all of the objects without needing to know which class they were as long as they were subclasses of a class that contained the methods needed. This would save a bunch of time and coding.

As you are planning your classes, look for similarities and methods that might apply to more than one type of class. This will save you time and speed up your application in the long run.

Summary

You've finally reached the end of the chapter! Here is a summary of the things that were covered:

- *Object-oriented programming (OOP)*: We discussed the importance of OOP and the reasons why all modern code should use this methodology.

- *Object*: You learned about objects and how they correspond to real-world objects. You learned that many programming objects relate directly to real-world objects. You also learned about abstract objects that do not correspond to real-world objects.

- *Class*: You learned that a class determines the types of data (properties) and the methods that each object will have. Every object needs to have a class. It is the blueprint for the object.

- *Creating a class*: You learned how to map out the properties and methods of your classes.

  - You used Xcode to create a class file.

  - You edited the class header file to add your properties and methods.

Exercises

Perform the following tasks:

- Create the class files for the rest of the classes you mapped out.

- Map out an `Author` class. Choose the kind of information you need to store about an author.

For the daring and advanced:

- Create a superclass called `PrintedMaterials`. Map out the properties that a class might have.

- Create classes for the other types of printed materials a store might carry.

CHAPTER 6

Learning Objective-C and Xcode

For the most part, all computer languages perform the typical tasks any computer needs to do: store information, compare information, make decisions about that information, and perform some action based on those decisions. Objective-C is a language that makes these tasks easier to understand and accomplish. The real trick with Objective-C (actually, the trick with any C language) is to understand the symbols and keywords used to accomplish these tasks. This chapter continues our examination of Objective-C and Xcode so you can become even more familiar with them.

A Brief History of Objective-C

Objective-C is really a combination of two languages: the C language and a lesser-kwnown language called Smalltalk. In the 1970s, several bright engineers from Bell Labs created a language named **C** that made it easy to port their pet project, the Unix operating system, from one machine to another. Prior to C, people had to write programs in assembly languages. The problem with assembly languages is that each is specific to its machine, so moving software from one machine to another was nearly impossible. The C language, created by Brian Kernighan and Dennis Ritchie, solved this problem by providing a language that wrote out the assembly language for whatever machine it supported, a kind of Rosetta Stone for early computer languages. Because of its portability, C quickly became the *de facto* language for many types of computers, especially early PCs.

121

© Stefan Kaczmarek, Brad Lees, Gary Bennett, Mitch Fisher 2018
S. Kaczmarek et al., *Objective-C for Absolute Beginners*, https://doi.org/10.1007/978-1-4842-3429-7_6

Fast-forward to the early 1980s and the C language was on its way to becoming one of the most popular languages of the decade. Around this time, an engineer from a company called Stepstone was mixing the C language with another up-and-coming language called Smalltalk. The C language is typically referred to as a *procedural language*, that is, a language that uses procedures to divide up processing steps. Smalltalk, on the other hand, was something entirely different. It was an *object-oriented programming language*. Instead of processing things procedurally, it used programming objects to get its work done. This new superset of the C language became known as "C with Objects" or, more commonly, **Objective-C**.

In 1985, Brad Cox sold the Objective-C language and trademark to NeXT Computer, Inc. NeXT was the brainchild of Steve Jobs, who had been fired from his own company, Apple Computer, that same year. NeXT used the Objective-C language to build the NeXTSTEP operating system and its suite of development tools. In fact, the Objective-C language gave NeXT a competitive advantage with all of its software. Programmers using NeXTSTEP and Objective-C could write programs faster than those writing in the traditional C language. While the hardware part of NeXT computers never really took off, the operating system and tools did. Quite interestingly, NeXT was purchased by Apple Computer in late 1996 with the intention of replacing its aging operating system, which had been in existence since the first Macintosh was developed in 1984. Four years after the acquisition, what had been NeXTSTEP reemerged as Mac OS X, with Objective-C still at the heart of the system. In 2014, Apple introduced Swift as its new language for iOS/Mac development. However, Objective-C is still the most common language used in the majority of iOS and Macintosh apps and will continue to be so in the near future.

Understanding the Language Symbols and Basic Syntax

Even though Objective-C integrates a great deal of object-oriented language, at the heart of Objective-C is C. Here are some of the symbols and language constructs used in Objective-C, some of which are part of the C language and most of which you've already encountered in previous chapters. It's not important to know which are pure C and which are not; just know that the old and new*er* symbols/constructs together make the Objective-C language.

Pretty much every language shares at least the following concepts:

- Create a variable and assign it a value.
- Begin and end a section of code.
- Signify the end of a line of code.
- Write a comment.

Objective-C has these syntactical differences from other object-oriented languages:

- Define a class.
- Define a method.
- Define an Objective-C variable.
- Call a method.

Create a Variable

A **variable** is something that stores a value that can change (i.e., vary). Creating a variable requires at least two parts.

```
1   int count;
```

In this code, a variable is declared. The first word, int, indicates that the variable is an integer. An integer is a whole number that can range from negative to positive values (there are other variable types that will be described when Objective-C properties are descried in Chapter 7).

The second word is the actual variable name, count. It's always proper form to name the variable with what it is intended to store. From the looks of the name, it's going to store the count of something.

Note   As a standard, an integer in most operating systems, including iOS, can range from -2,147,483,648 to 2,147,483,647.

Begin and End a Section of Code

Every language needs some way to indicate where the code begins and ends. Objective-C has a few different ways to designate this. The following is the most common in Objective-C (and standard C as well): { and }, the begin and end braces, which specify the beginning and ending of a section of code.

A good example is the conditional, or if statement, shown here:

```
1   if (a == b) {
2       *** do something cool if a is equal to b ***
3   }
```

First, there is a conditional: if (a == b). This simply tests to see whether the value of a is equal to the value of b. The block of code for the conditional is surrounded by the braces ({ and }) and is executed if the conditional is true (conditionals are described in more detail in Chapter 9).

Signify the End of a Line of Code

C and therefore Objective-C are free-form languages. This means that the code can be formatted however the programmer likes. This gives the programmer a lot of flexibility as far as how the code looks. Because of this, Xcode needs to know when there is an end of a line of code. So ; is used to represent the end of a line of code:

```
1   cost = 100.0;  // Assign a value to something
2   NSLog(@"Hello!"); // Call a function/method (described later)
```

Note   Because Objective-C is a free-form language, it is possible to write Objective-C as one really loooooooong single line. Yes, it will work and, yes, your co-workers and everyone on the planet will hate your code.

There is an exception to this general rule, and that is code that requires a block to define it. Using the example from earlier again, look at this code:

```
1   if (a == b) {
2       *** do something cool if a is equal to b ***
3   }
```

In this code, there is no semicolon after if (a == b) or after any of the braces. You will see other statements in upcoming chapters that are similar to this one. The takeaway is that if the code you're writing requires braces, don't add a semicolon at the end of the line.

Write a Comment

Comments in any language are useful to document or explain a piece of code. Actually, you've already seen a comment in some sample code:

```
1   cost = 100.0;  // Assign a value to something
2   NSLog(@"Hello!"); // Call a function/method (described later)
```

The // characters indicate that the text that follows is a comment and should not be treated as code. The thing with the // comment is that it is only good until the end of that line. What if you have a lot to write and want the comment to span multiple lines? In this case, there are more special characters: /* is used to begin the comment and */ is used to end the comment. This is referred to as a **block comment**.

```
1   /* This is a block comment
2   and can span multiple lines.
3   This is useful if I have a lot to say!
4   */
```

Notice that /* or */ can appear on lines all by themselves or be combined with text. It doesn't really matter how it's formatted, even like this: /* This is a block comment too */. A block comment doesn't mean that the comment *has* to span multiple lines.

Note   It is a good habit to write and maintain comments within your code. Comments are not so much about writing *what* the code does but why it's doing it. This code may seem obvious: cost = 100.0. It's a variable assignment. What's important here is not that there is a variable assignment but *why* the variable is being assigned 100.0.

Define a Class

In all object-oriented languages there is the concept of a **class**. The definition of that class is also generally different from language to language, and Objective-C is no exception.

Objective-C divides the definition of a class within two distinct sections. The first section is what is called the **interface**. The interface simply defines the methods and properties that make up the class. It also indicates the superclass to your object. (You'll learn more about this in Chapter 7.)

```
1   @interface MyObject : NSObject
2   *** Stuff explained in Chapter 7 here
3   @end
```

The interface to an object is defined by @interface...@end. This object has the unique and creative name of MyObject. The : NSObject part denotes the superclass, meaning MyObject acts just like NSObject but builds upon it with the methods and properties defined in MyObject. NSObject is a **superclass**; conversely, MyObject is a **subclass** of NSObject.

```
1   @implementation MyObject
2   *** Stuff explained in Chapter 7 here
3   @end
```

The implementation as denoted by @implementation...@end is the part of the class that actually has the code that does all the stuff MyObject is supposed to do. This is where all the coding of a class really takes place.

It's common to see the @interface...@end part in a separate file from the @implementation...@end part, but they don't have to be separate. Also important to note is that since the @interface and @implementation sections are just like code blocks, they don't require a ; at the end of the line (see the "Signify the End of a Line of Code" section earlier). That said, it is a best practice to put the @interface in an .h file and the @implementation in an .m file.

Define a Method

A **method** is defined in two ways. The first is the definition of the method in the @interface part of the class.

```
1   @interface MyObject : NSObject
2   - (int)howMany;
3   @end
```

Here is the interface to the MyObject class, and what you see on line 2 is the method **definition**. It's called a definition because all it does is *define* the method's name (howMany) and what value it returns, which in this case is an int (as in integer, like used when defining a variable). And, of course, you need to end the definition of the method with a semicolon. A **return** value is like asking an object a question. So, if you ask the object the question howMany, it responds with a number (int). Methods that don't need to return anything would have a (void) in place of the (int).

Chapter 7 will detail the actual code of the howMany method that is found in the @implementation part of the code.

Define an Objective-C Variable

Objective-C variables aren't too different from other variables (like you saw earlier in the "Create a Variable" section) with the exception of a special character.

```
1   MyObject *myObjectInstance;
```

While this may look a little odd, it's not too different than this:

```
1   int count;
```

In line 1, you see the Objective-C class name of MyObject being used, but it has an asterisk (*) character after it. We won't go into technical details on what * actually does; just know that when a variable is defined and that variable is an Objective-C object, you *always* put an asterisk after it (sometimes * is referred to as a **splat** or **star**). If you don't do this, Xcode will point it out as an error and you will have to fix it.

Call a Method

Once a class has a method defined, there needs to be a way to actually call it. So, when you have an instance (or object) of the `MyObject` class, the `count` object can be called and used as such:

```
1   int value;
2   value = [myObjectInstance howMany];
```

Line 1 defines a variable that is an integer called `value`.

Line 2 calls the `howMany` method from the object named `myObjectInstance`. Now, how you define `myObjectInstance` is shown in the next chapter, but what's more important here is the odd-looking [and] characters. These characters are used to surround Objective-C code that deals with objects calling methods.

Note   Technically in Objective-C you don't call a method but instead send a **message** to an object. In the previous example, the howMany message is being sent to the `myObjectInstance` object. There are technical details in how Objective-C has been built as to why there is this difference in semantics. However, for simplicity's sake, the term **method** is used in order to maintain similar terms as other object-oriented languages.

Putting the "Objective" into Objective-C

The majority of what makes Objective-C, well, objective, is its basis in Smalltalk. Smalltalk is a 100% object-oriented language, and Objective-C borrows heavily from Smalltalk concepts and syntax. Here are a few of the high-level concepts borrowed from Smalltalk. Don't worry if some of these terms seem unfamiliar; they will be discussed in later chapters (Chapters 7 and 8 cover the basics).

- A class defines an object. That definition is made up of methods and properties.

- Objects can contain instance variables.

- Instance variables (and variables in general) have a defined scope.

- Classes hide details of an implementation.

Note   As you saw in Chapter 5, the term **class** is used to represent, generically, the definition or type of something. An object is what is created from the class. For example, a recipe is like a class because it defines how to create a certain dish. The result of following a recipe is the completed meal. You can't eat a recipe, but you can eat what that recipe creates, just like you can't use a class, but you can use what it creates, and that is an object.[1]

Let's look at a simple example of the complete definition of an Objective-C class called HelloWorld. The following is the interface file (HelloWorld.h):

```
1    @import Foundation;
2
3    @interface HelloWorld : NSObject
4
5    - (void)printGreeting;
6
7    @end
```

And this is the implementation file (HelloWorld.m):

```
8    #import "HelloWorld.h"
9
10   @implementation HelloWorld
11
12   - (void)printGreeting
13   {
14       NSLog(@"Hello World!");
15   }
16
17   @end
```

---

[1]There are some general exceptions to this. We mean exceptions to the class/object example. No, you still can't eat a recipe.

In this example, a class, HelloWorld, is being defined. This class has only one method defined: printGreeting. What do all these strange symbols mean? Using the line numbers as a reference, you can review this code line by line.

Line 1 contains the compiler directive @import Foundation;. For the program to know about certain other objects (for example, the NSObject on line 3), importing Foundation defines the objects and interfaces to the **Foundation framework**. This framework contains the definition of most non-user-interface base classes of the iOS and macOS systems. The actual start of the object is on line 3, as follows:

```
@interface HelloWorld : NSObject
```

HelloWorld is the object, but what does : NSObject mean? Well, the colon (:) after the class's name indicates you plan to derive additional functionality from another class. In this case, NSObject is that class. HelloWorld is now a *subclass* of NSObject.

Fun Fact   Why the name NSObject and not just Object? Well, as you recall, Mac OS X actually started out as a port from the NeXTSTEP system. NS is an abbreviation for NeXTSTEP and is used in many of the base objects in Mac OS X and iOS: NSObject, NSString, NSDictionary, and so on.

Line 5 contains a message definition for this class, as follows:

```
- (void)printGreeting;
```

When you're defining a method, the definition line must start with either a - or + character. In the case of the HelloWorld object, you are using - to indicate this message can be used *after* the object is created. The + character is used for messages that can be used *before* the object is created (more on this in Chapter 7).

On line 7, @end indicates that the definition of the object's interface is complete.

That's the complete description of the interface of the HelloWorld object; there's not a whole lot here. More complicated objects simply just have more methods and properties.

For the implementation, the source code is stored in a different file, HelloWord.m. For starters, line 8 starts with the statement #import "HelloWorld.h". This simply allows the object to know its own interface. While the separation of the interface and implementation files might seem a little odd at first, this convention is consistent in Objective-C programming. Whenever an object is to be used, simply include its interface.

Line 10 is the start of the implementation of the object, as follows:

```
@implementation HelloWorld
```

Line 12 is the definition of the object's method, `printGreeting`. It looks identical to the method definition in the interface file. The only difference here is that code is being defined that implements the `printGreeting` method.

Lines 13–15 form the block of code that implements the method `printGreeting`. For this simple method, the function `NSLog` is called. This base-level function simply takes in a formatted `NSString` object and outputs the result to the console. The `NSString` class is an Objective-C class that implements the behavior of a string of characters. Why have a class for this? For one thing, it gives the framework a consistent class for representing a string. Plus, there is a lot of functionality in `NSString` that can be used to manipulate, compare, and convert the actual string.

The `NSString` object is specified here in a shorthand method. The `@"Hello World!"` part is a way of quickly declaring an `NSString` object. The at sign (@) is the symbol used to indicate that the text in quotes is an `NSString` object.

Line 17 indicates to the compiler that the definition of the implementation section is finished.

But wait, there's more. Now that you have a new Objective-C class defined, how is it used? The following is another piece of code that uses the newly created class, the main program (`main.m`):

```
1    #import "HelloWorld.h"
2
3    void main(void)
4    {
5       HelloWorld *myObject = [HelloWorld new];
6       [myObject printGreeting];
7    }
```

In this new file, the program first starts by including the `HelloWorld.h` file, which allows this piece of the application access to the `HelloWorld` object.

In line 3 is the `main` function. Remember, every Objective-C program must have a `main` function.

Line 5 is a complicated one. It defines and creates, or **instantiates**, a new object of the HelloWorld class. You first see the text HelloWorld* myObject. This defines a variable named myObject of the type HelloWorld, which is the new class.

The next part of the line is [HelloWorld new]. This creates a new HelloWorld object. Wait a second; you never defined the message new, so how is this going to work? Well, when the HelloWorld class was defined, it was defined as a subclass of NSObject. When you call the new method of the HelloWorld object, the system knows that HelloWorld doesn't know that particular message, so it automatically checks the superclass; in this case, this is the NSObject class.

Now that you've created a new object, you can use it. Line 6, [myObject printGreeting], puts the object to use. In this piece of code, you use the newly instantiated object by calling the printGreeting method. The program will output the text Hello World!.

Line 7 ends the code block that defines main and the end of the program.

Note   Methods can also accept multiple arguments. Consider, for example, [myCarObject switchRadioBandTo:FM andTuneToFrequncy:104.7];. The message here would be switchRadioBandTo:andTuneToFrequency:. After each colon, the argument values are placed when a message is actually sent. You might also notice that these messages are named in such a way as to make interpreting what they actually do easy to understand. Using helpful message names is an ideal convention to follow when developing classes because it makes using the classes much more intuitive. Being consistent in naming messages is also critical.

Writing Another Program in Xcode

When you first open Xcode, you'll see the screen shown in Figure 6-1.

Version 9.2 (9C40b)

No Recent Projects

Get started with a playground
Explore new ideas quickly and easily.

Create a new Xcode project
Create an app for iPhone, iPad, Mac, Apple Watch or Apple TV.

Clone an existing project
Start working on something from an SCM repository.

☑ Show this window when Xcode launches   Open another project...

Figure 6-1. *Xcode opening screen*

Figure 6-1 shows a great screen to always keep visible at the launch of Xcode. Until you are more comfortable with Xcode, keep the **Show this window when Xcode launches** check box selected. This window allows you to select the most recently created projects or start a new project.

Creating the Project

You are going to start a new project, so click the **Create a new Xcode project** icon. Whenever you want to start a new iOS or macOS application, library, or anything else, use this icon. Once a project has been started and saved, the project will appear in the Recents list on the right side of the display.

For this Xcode project, you're going to choose something simple. Make sure **iOS** is chosen. Then select **Single View App**, as shown in Figure 6-2. Then simply click the **Next** button.

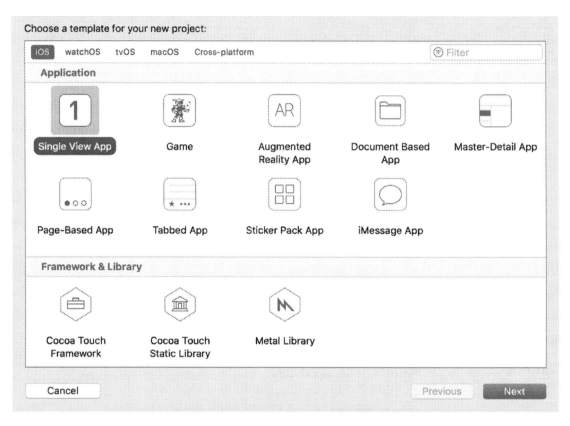

Figure 6-2. *Choosing a new project from a list of templates*

There are several different types of templates. These templates make it easier to start a project from scratch in that they provide a starting point by automatically creating simple source files.

Once the template has been chosen and the Next button clicked, Xcode presents you with a dialog box asking for the project's name and some other information, as shown in Figure 6-3. Type a product name of **MyFirstApp**. The Company Identifier field needs to have some value, so just enter **MyCompany**. Also make sure the Language field is set to **Objective-C**.

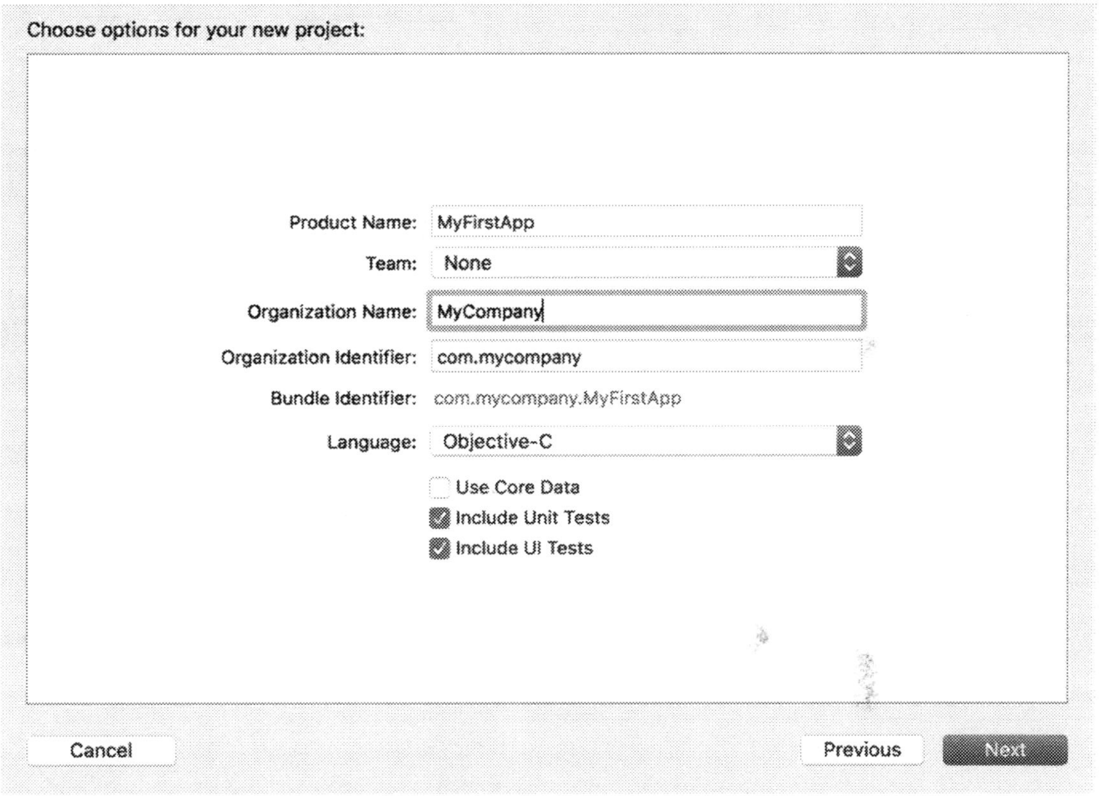

Choose options for your new project:

Product Name:	MyFirstApp
Team:	None
Organization Name:	MyCompany
Organization Identifier:	com.mycompany
Bundle Identifier:	com.mycompany.MyFirstApp
Language:	Objective-C

☐ Use Core Data
☑ Include Unit Tests
☑ Include UI Tests

Cancel   Previous   Next

Figure 6-3. *Setting up the product name, company, and type*

The Use Core Data, Include Unit Tests, and Include UI Tests check boxes can be left as the default. In your example, it doesn't matter if they are checked or not. Once all the information has been supplied, click the **Next** button. Xcode will ask you where to save the project. You can save it any place, but the desktop is a good choice because it's always easy to find.

When the project is initially created, Xcode will display details about your project (Figure 6-4). Everything can be left as is except for the devices within the Deployment Info section. Change the Devices field from Universal to **iPhone**. Universal apps are optimized to run on both iPhones and iPads, but for simplicity's sake, you're just going to stick to the iPhone.

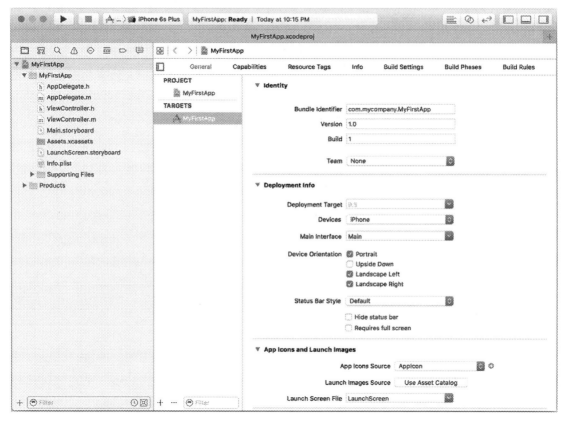

Figure 6-4. *The Xcode 9.2 main screen*

In the leftmost pane is the list of source files. The main area of the screen is dedicated to the context-sensitive editor. Click a source file, like an .h or .m, and the editor will show the source code. Clicking a .storyboard file will show the user interface editor.

Your first app is going to be simple. This iPhone app will simply contain a pushbutton and a label. When the button is pushed, your name will appear on the screen. So, let's start by first looking more closely at some of the stub source code that Xcode built for you. The nice thing with Xcode is that it will create a stub application that will execute without any modification. Before you start adding some code, let's look at the main toolbar of Xcode, shown in Figure 6-5.

Figure 6-5. *The Xcode 9.2 toolbar*

At first glance, there are three distinct areas of the toolbar. The left area is used to run/debug the application. The middle window displays the status as a summary of compiler errors and/or warnings. The far-right area contains a series of buttons that customize the editing view.

As shown in Figure 6-6, the left portion of the toolbar contains a Run button (similar to the iTunes Play button) that will compile and run the application. If the application is running, the Stop button will not be grayed out. Since it's grayed out, you know the application is not running. The last part of the toolbar is the build status. This is where you can see what application (or target) is being built, in this case MyFirstApp.

Figure 6-6. *Close-up of the left portion of the Xcode toolbar*

The right side of the Xcode toolbar contains buttons that change the editor. The three buttons represent the Standard Editor (selected), the Assistant Editor, and the Version Editor. For now, just choose the **Standard Editor**, as shown in Figure 6-7.

Figure 6-7. *Close-up of the right portion of the Xcode toolbar*

Next to the editor choices are a set of View buttons. These buttons represent which panes of the Xcode workplace are visible: left, bottom, and right. Blue indicates that a pane is active, and gray indicates that it is inactive. These buttons can be toggled on and off. Figure 6-8 shows all three panes. Figure 6-9 shows Xcode when no panes are used.

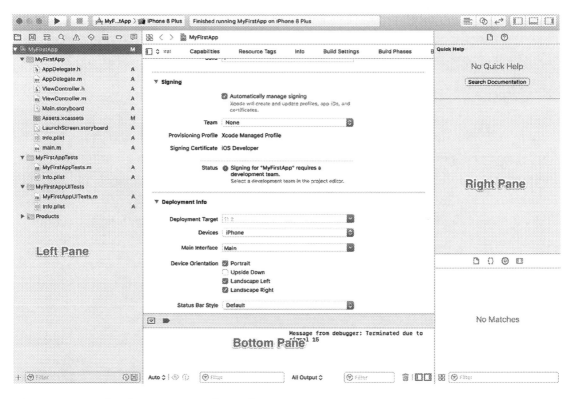

Figure 6-8. *The three panes of Xcode*

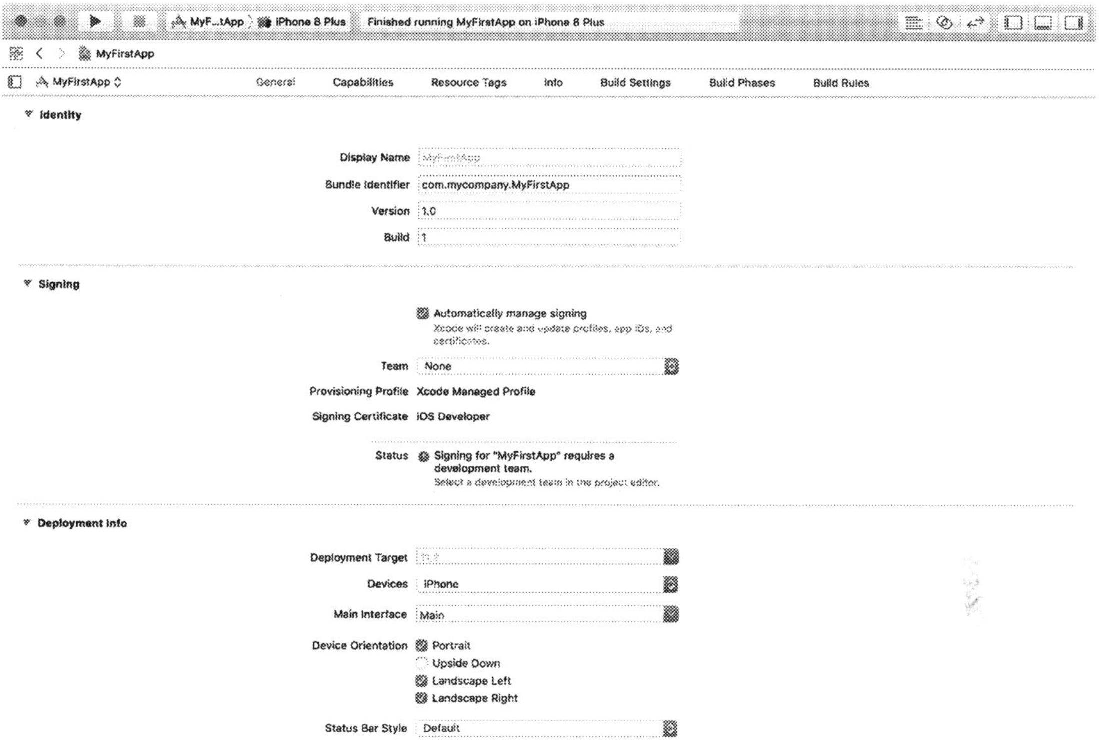

Figure 6-9. *No panes selected. Just one big editor!*

Generally, when Xcode starts up with a new project, the left and right panes are selected.

So what are these different panes?

- The left pane is called the **Navigator**. This is because the pane contains different "tabs" that allow you to navigate the source (among other things).

- The right pane is the **Utilities** pane. It has all the tools that are used to configure the app and build the interface, which is what the user sees.

- The bottom pane is the **Debug area**. It appears when Xcode is debugging the app.

Let's now get into your iOS app.

Click the ViewController.h file once, as shown in Figure 6-10.

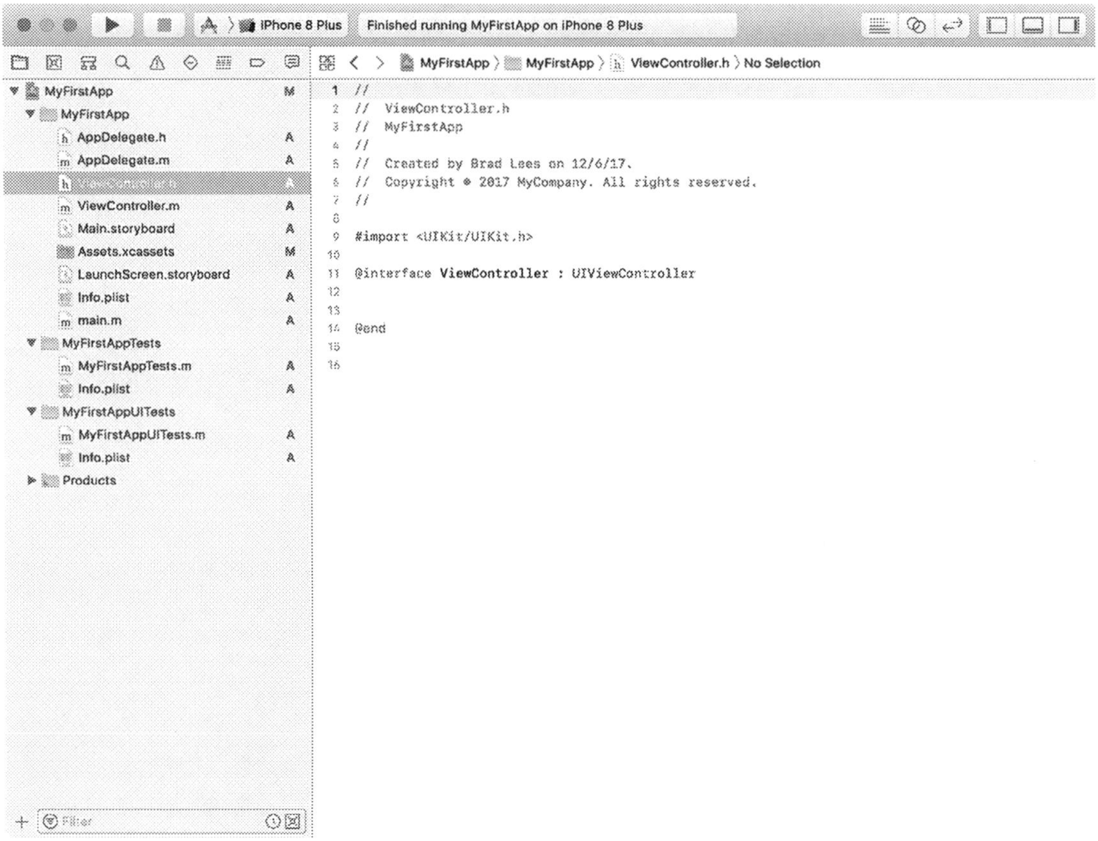

Figure 6-10. *Looking at the source code in the Xcode editor*

Note   For now, you're simply going to add a few lines of code and see what they do. It's not expected that you understand what this code means right now. What's important is simply going through the motions to become more familiar with Xcode. Chapter 7 goes into more depth about what makes up an Objective-C program, and Chapter 10 goes into more depth about building an iPhone interface.

Next, you're going to add two lines of code into this file, as shown in Figure 6-11. Line 12 defines an iPhone label on the screen where you can put some text. Line 15 tells the compiler this ViewController object can be sent a message called showName:. You'll be calling this method to populate the iPhone label. A label is nothing more than an area on the screen where you can put some text information.

```
1   //
2   //  ViewController.h
3   //  MyFirstApp
4   //
5   //  Created by Thorn on 12/6/17.
6   //  Copyright © 2017 MyCompany. All rights reserved.
7   //
8
9   #import <UIKit/UIKit.h>
10
11  @interface ViewController : UIViewController
12
○   @property (nonatomic, strong) IBOutlet UILabel *nameLabel;
14
○   - (IBAction)showName:(id)sender;
16
17
18  @end
19
20
```

Figure 6-11. *Code added to the ViewController.h interface file*

Caution   Type the code *exactly* as shown in the example. For instance, UILabel can't be uilabel or UILABEL. Objective-C is a case-sensitive language, so UILabel is completely different from uilabel.

Next, you're going to add the code to make the message showName: do something. First, click the ViewController.m file on the left once. This file is an **implementation** file. You can tell it's an implementation file because of the @implementation Objective-C directive on line 11, shown in Figure 6-12.

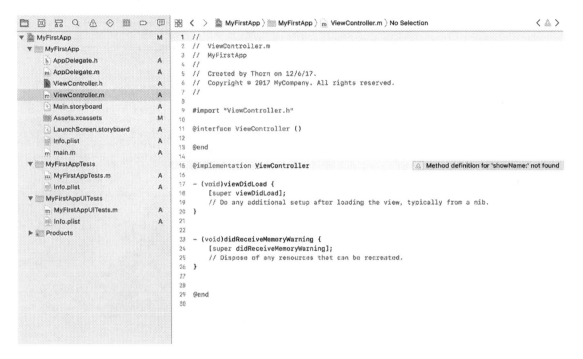

Figure 6-12. *The ViewController.m implementation file*

Note the warning symbol on line 15. Clicking the warning will show the warning "Method definition for 'showName:' not found." This basically means you've added a new method in the interface file, but it's not been added to the implementation file.

What may appear wrong are lines 11–13. This is what is called a **class extension** and is meant to be only in the .m file. This is meant to contain properties that are strictly kept private to the ViewController class.

Figure 6-13 is the updated implementation file. The warning disappears since the showName: method is now in the implementation file. Xcode is nice that way. If a method is defined in the interface file, it will generate a warning if it's not in the implementation file. Xcode does make things easier, but it's still up to the programmer (you) to make any necessary corrections.

```
1   //
2   //  ViewController.m
3   //  MyFirstApp
4   //
5   //  Created by Thorn on 12/6/17.
6   //  Copyright © 2017 MyCompany. All rights reserved.
7   //
8
9   #import "ViewController.h"
10
11  @interface ViewController ()
12
13  @end
14
15  @implementation ViewController
16
17  - (void)viewDidLoad {
18      [super viewDidLoad];
19      // Do any additional setup after loading the view, typically from a nib.
20  }
21
22
23  - (void)didReceiveMemoryWarning {
24      [super didReceiveMemoryWarning];
25      // Dispose of any resources that can be recreated.
26  }
    - (IBAction)showName:(id)sender {
28
29  }
30
31
32  @end
33
```

Figure 6-13. *Code added to the ViewController.m implementation file*

Once lines 27–29, shown in Figure 6-13, have been added, the warning message will disappear. The nice thing with Xcode is that it will report any warnings or errors with the code typed in without first having to try to compile and run the program. This immediate feedback can sometimes be a pain, but it does save time. You now have the necessary code in place, but you don't yet have a user interface on the iPhone. Next, you're going to create the user interface to your app.

To edit the iPhone's interface, you need to click the `Main.storyboard` file once. You will use Xcode's interface editor to **connect** a user interface object, such as a label, to the code you just created. Connecting is as easy as click, drag, and drop.

Note that the right pane is visible, as shown in Figure 6-14. This opens up the Utilities pane for the interface. Among other things, this Utilities pane shows you the various interface objects you can use in your app. You're going to be concerned with only two: Button and Label.

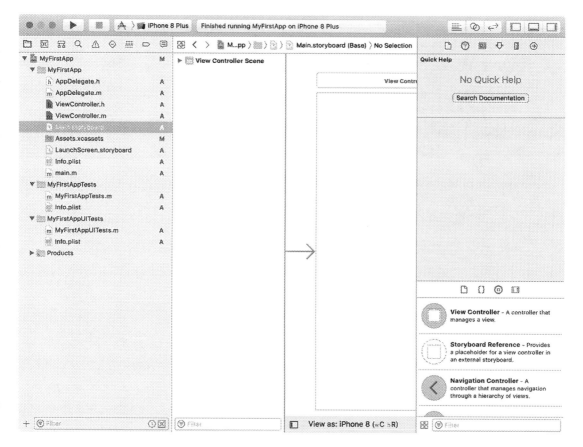

Figure 6-14. *The iPhone interface that you're going to modify*

The first step is to click the **Button** control once from the Utilities pane; you may have to scroll the list of controls to find the Button control. Next, drag the object to the iPhone view, as shown in Figure 6-15. Don't worry; dragging the object doesn't remove it from the list of objects in the Utilities pane. Dragging it out will create a new copy of that object on your iPhone interface.

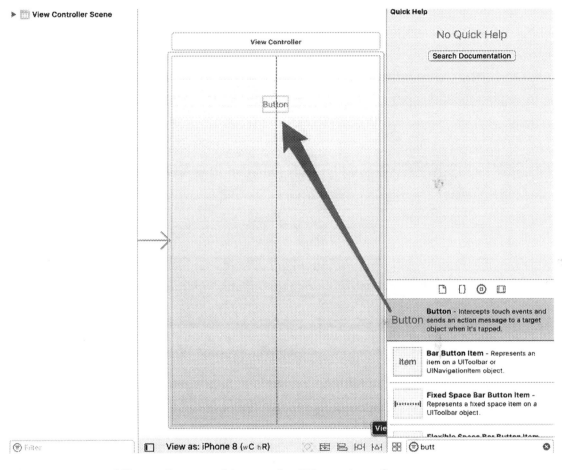

Figure 6-15. *Adding a Button object to the iPhone interface*

Next, double-click the **Button** that was just added to the iPhone interface. This allows the title of the button to be changed. So, change the title from Button to **Name**, as shown in Figure 6-16. Many different interface objects work just like this. Simply double-click and the title or text of the object can be changed. Changing the text of a button can also be done in the actual code, but it's much simpler doing as much as possible in the interface editor.

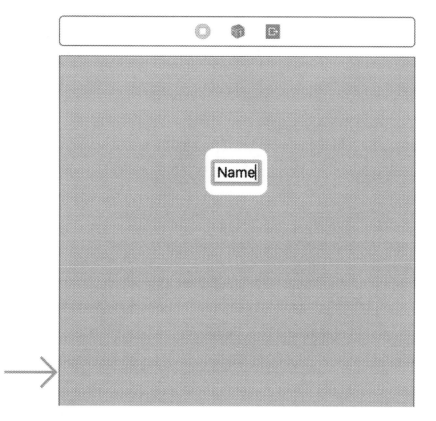

Figure 6-16. *Modifying the button's title*

Once the title has been changed, drag and drop a **Label** object and place it right below the button, as shown in Figure 6-17.

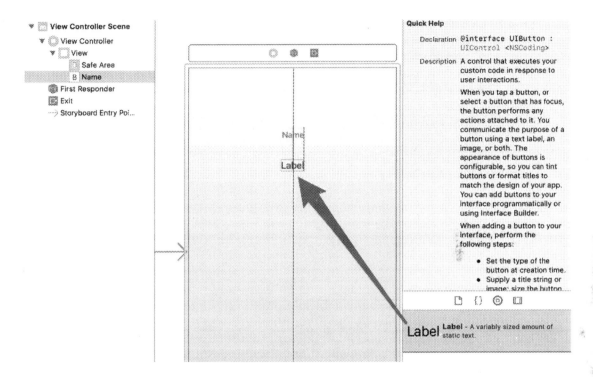

Figure 6-17. *Adding a Label object to the iPhone interface*

For now, you can leave the label's title as Label because you're going to make it change within the program. You also want to leave something in the title so you can actually see it on the screen. If you clear the label's text, the object will still be there, but there is nothing visible to click in order to select. Expand the size of the label by dragging the center handle ball to the right, as shown in Figure 6-18. You'll also need to drag the sizing handle to the left to make "My Name is Awesome" fit and match the final centering of the label.

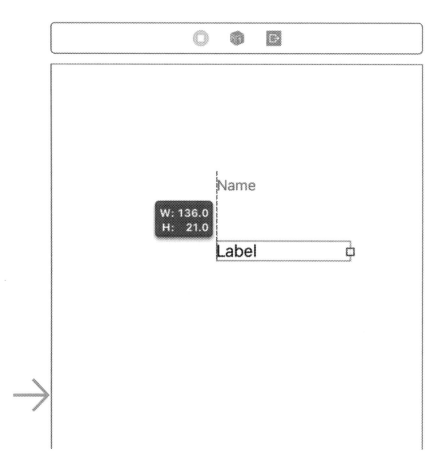

Figure 6-18. *Expanding the label's size*

Now that you have both the button and the label, you can connect these visual objects to your program. You start by Control-clicking (or right-clicking) the button control and **dragging** the blue line to the yellow view controller icon at the top of the screen, as shown in Figure 6-19.

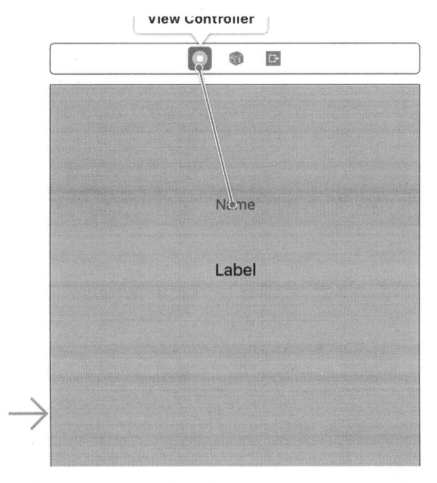

Figure 6-19. *Start the connection from the button to the view controller*

At this point, just stop dragging and release the mouse button. You will see a list of things related to the button. In this case, you care only about selecting the showName: event, as shown in Figure 6-20. It's called an **event** because something happens when, in this case, the button is tapped.

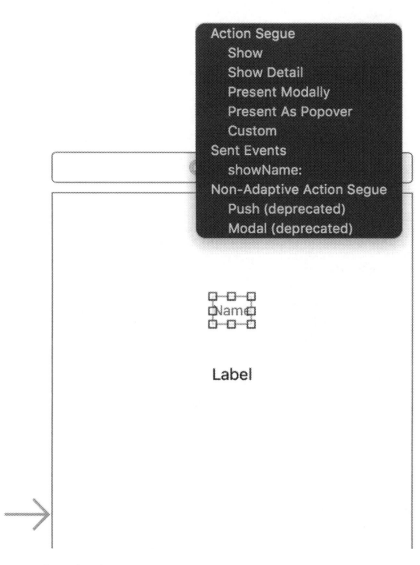

Figure 6-20. *Select the showName: event*

What happens once the showName: is selected is that it **connects** the touch-up inside button event to the showName: method inside the implementation. The event is called **touch-up inside** since the event is sent only when the button is released (touch up) and only when the touch-up occurs **inside** the button (versus if you drag your finger **outside** the button and then release).

Next, you need to create a connection for the Label object. In this case, you don't care about the label events; instead, you want to connect the ViewController's nameLabel outlet to the object on the iPhone interface. This **connects** the label shown on the iPhone interface to the property in the program.

Start by Control-clicking or right-clicking the Label object on the iPhone interface. This brings up the connection menu for the label, as shown in Figure 6-21. There are not as many options for a Label object as there were for the Button object.

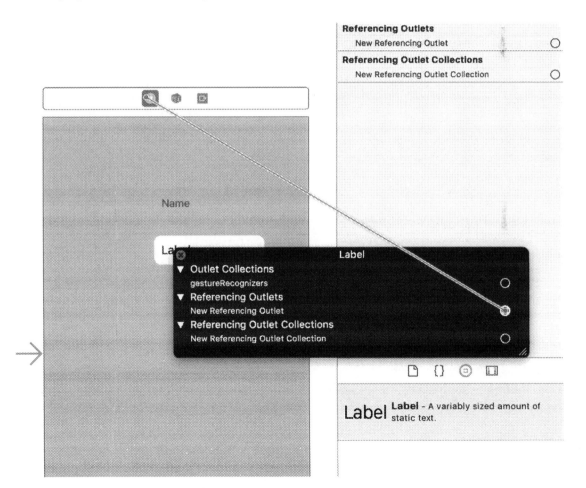

Figure 6-21. *Connection menu for the Label object*

Note   You can control-click and drag from the ViewController icon to the label and then choose nameLabel.

As mentioned, you are not here to connect an event. Instead, you connect what's referred to as a **Referencing Outlet**. The Outlet is the property in your program. Just like the Button, drag and drop the connection to the ViewController icon, as shown in Figure 6-22.

Figure 6-22.   *Connecting the Referencing Outlet to the object*

Once the connection is dropped on the ViewController icon, a list of possible outlets in your ViewController object will be displayed, as shown in Figure 6-22. Of the two choices, you want to choose nameLabel. This is the name of the variable in the ViewController object you are using.

Lastly, you need to add the code that will put something into your new label. In Figure 6-23, line 28 sets the text to the nameLabel property. Notice that you're adding code to the showName: method. If you recall, this is the method that is called during the touch-up inside event. Don't worry too much about understanding everything, but some things should look familiar based upon what you've learned in this chapter.

```
1   //
2   //  ViewController.m
3   //  MyFirstApp
4   //
5   //  Created by Thorn on 12/6/17.
6   //  Copyright © 2017 MyCompany. All rights reserved.
7   //
8
9   #import "ViewController.h"
10
11  @interface ViewController ()
12
13  @end
14
15  @implementation ViewController
16
17  - (void)viewDidLoad {
18      [super viewDidLoad];
19      // Do any additional setup after loading the view, typically from a nib.
20  }
21
22
23  - (void)didReceiveMemoryWarning {
24      [super didReceiveMemoryWarning];
25      // Dispose of any resources that can be recreated.
26  }
27  - (IBAction)showName:(id)sender {
28      [self.nameLabel setText:@"My Name is Awesome"];
29  }
30
31
32  @end
33
```

Figure 6-23. *Setting the text to the new label*

Now you're ready to run the program. Click the **Run** button (it looks like a Play button) at the top-left corner of the Xcode window (see Figure 6-6). This will automatically save your changes and run the application in the iPhone emulator, as shown in Figure 6-24.

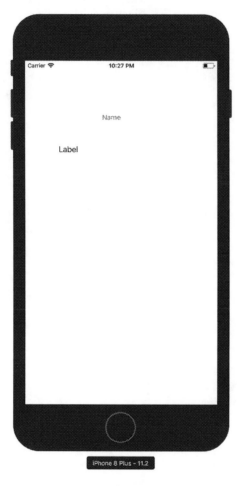

Figure 6-24. *Your app running, before and after the button is pressed*

Click the Name button and the label's text will change from its default value of "Label" to "My Name is Awesome" or whatever text you put in. If you want to, go back into the interface and clear the default label text. Changing the default of "Label" to something more appropriate will give the user interface a more polished look.

Summary

The examples in this chapter were simple, but we hope they've whetted your appetite for more complex applications using Objective-C and Xcode. In later chapters, you can expect to learn more about object-oriented programming and more about what Objective-C can do. Pat yourself on the back because you've learned a lot already. Here is a summary of the topics discussed in this chapter:

- The origins and brief history of the Objective-C language

- Some common language symbols used in Objective-C

- An Objective-C class example

- The `@interface` and `@implementation` sections of a program

- Using Xcode a bit more, including compiling the MyFirstApp project

- Connecting visual interface objects with methods and properties in the `ViewController` object

Exercises

Perform the following tasks:

- Change the size of the Label object on the interface to be smaller in width. How does that affect the text message?

- Delete the Referencing Outlet connection of the label and rerun the project. What happens?

- If you feel you have the hang of this, add a new button and label both to the `ViewController` object and to the interface. Change it from displaying your name to displaying something else.

Objective-C Classes, Objects, and Methods

If you haven't already read Chapter 6, please do so before reading this chapter because it provides a great introduction to some of the basics of Objective-C. This chapter builds on that foundation. By the end of this chapter, you can expect to have a greater understanding of the Objective-C language and how to use the basics to write simple programs. The best way to learn is to take small programs and write (or rewrite) them in Objective-C just to see how the language works.

This chapter will cover what composes an Objective-C class and how to interact with Objective-C objects via methods. We will use a `SimpleLabelData` class as an example of how an Objective-C class is written. This will impart an understanding of how an Objective-C class can be used. This chapter will teach you how to formulate a design for objects that are needed to solve a problem. We'll also touch on how to create custom objects and how to use existing objects provided in the Foundation classes.

If you're coming from a C-like language, you'll find that Objective-C shares several similarities. As described in Chapter 6, Objective-C's roots are firmly planted in the C language. This chapter will expand on Chapter 6's topics and incorporate some of the concepts described in Chapter 8.

Creating an Objective-C Class

Chapter 6 introduced some of the common elements of the Objective-C language, so let's quickly review them.

- An Objective-C class is divided into two parts: a class interface and a class implementation.

157

© Stefan Kaczmarek, Brad Lees, Gary Bennett, Mitch Fisher 2018
S. Kaczmarek et al., *Objective-C for Absolute Beginners*, https://doi.org/10.1007/978-1-4842-3429-7_7

- The @interface keyword is used to define an interface to a new Objective-C class. This is written in an .h, or header, file.

- Methods are the blocks of code defined in the @interface section of a class and implemented in the @implementation section in an .m file.

- The @implementation keyword is used to define the actual code that implements the methods defined in the interface. This is written in an .m, or Objective-C class, file.

As explained in Chapter 6, an Objective-C class consists of an interface and a corresponding implementation. For now, let's concentrate on the interface. At the most basic level, the interface of a class tells you the name of the class, what class it's derived from, and what **methods** the class understands.

Note   It was mentioned in Chapter 6 that technically an Objective-C object sends and receives messages. However, for simplicity sake, we're going to stick to the more common term **method** instead.

Here is a sample of the first line from a class's interface:

```
@interface SimpleLabelData : NSObject
```

Here, the class name is SimpleLabelData. The colon (:) after the class name indicates that the class is derived from another class; that is, the SimpleLabelData object **inherits** functionality from the NSObject class. Put another way, in the example shown in Figure 7-1, the SimpleLabelData class is derived from the NSObject class, which is the base class for all classes.

Tip   If your object is not inheriting from any other Foundation or UIKit class (like UILabel), *always* inherit from NSObject. NSObject provides the base functions that make new objects behave correctly. NSObject is the base class for all Foundation classes. So, inheriting from any Foundation or UIKit class is also fine.

Once the class name is defined, the rest of the interface file contains the main components of the class (see Figure 7-1).

```
1  //
2  //  SimpleLabelData.h
3  //  MyFirstApp
4  //
5  //  Created by Thorn on 12/7/17.
6  //  Copyright © 2017 MyCompany. All rights reserved.
7  //
8
9  #import <Foundation/Foundation.h>
10
11 @interface SimpleLabelData : NSObject
12
13 @property (nonatomic) NSString *title;
14 @property (nonatomic) NSString *value;
15
16 + (instancetype)simpleLabelDataWithTitle: (NSString *)title
17                              andValue: (NSString *)value;
18
19 - (NSString *)combinedString;|
20
21 @end
22
```

Figure 7-1. *An interface file: SimpleLabelData.h*

Declaring Interfaces and Properties

An Objective-C class is defined by its **interface**. Since objects, for the most part, are communicated with using methods, the interface of an object defines what methods the object will respond to. Line 9 imports the Foundation class definitions (more on that in a bit). Line 11 is the start of the definition of the class's interface by defining its name (SimpleLabelData) (sometimes called the type) and the superclass (NSObject). Next are two @property lines. These are properties of the class that both define the class' instance variables and make them publicly accessible from other objects.

Whenever the SimpleLabelData class is instantiated, the resulting SimpleLabelData object has access to these properties. If there are ten SimpleLabelData objects, each object has its own properties independent of the other objects. This is also referred to as **scope**, in that the object's properties are specific to that object only. Other objects manage their own properties and so on.

Calling Methods

Every object has methods. In Objective-C, the common concept to interact with an object is to call methods, like so:

```
[aSimpleLabelData combinedString];
```

The preceding line will call a method of an instance of the `SimpleLabelData` class from a variable named `aSimpleLabelData`. The method (`combinedString`) is the name of the method to call.

If a class does not have that method defined, the parent object checks for it, and its parent object checks for it, and so on, until the method is either found or not. This behavior is called **dynamic binding**, which means the method is found at runtime instead of compile time. Dynamic binding allows an Objective-C program to react to changes while the program is running; this is one of the huge advantages Objective-C has over other languages.

Methods can also have parameters passed along with them. Parameters are used to control behavior or are simply passed to the object to store for later use. So, the following method accepts some parameters:

```
someLabelData = [SimpleLabelData simpleLabelDataWithTitle:@"Name"
            andValue:@"What's in a name?"];
```

It's important to understand the method and how it's structured, especially once you actually implement the code. In your code, you'll need to make sure you implement the `simpleLabelDataWithTitle:andValue:` method; otherwise, the program won't work. (Please note that this is the name that this example uses. A method name can be pretty much any combination of words.)

In the preceding example, the method consists of two parameters: the title and a title value. What's interesting about Objective-C relative to other languages is that the methods are essentially named parameters. It's easy to understand `simpleLabelDataWithTitle:andValue:` in that it's obvious what the method is looking for as input. Here are a few other examples:

```
[NSDictionary dictionaryWithContentsOfFile:filename];
[myString characterAtIndex:1];
[myViewController addChildViewController:otherViewController];
```

Using Class Methods

A class doesn't always have to be instantiated to be used. In some cases, classes have methods that can actually perform some simple operations and return values. These methods are called **class methods**. In Figure 7-1, the method names that start with a plus sign (+) are class methods (all class methods must start with a + sign).

Class methods have limitations. One of their biggest limitations is that none of the properties can be used. Being unable to use properties makes sense since we haven't instantiated anything. A class method can have its own local variables within the method itself but can't use any of the variables defined as properties.

A call to a class method would look like this:

```
[SimpleLabelData new];
```

Notice that the call is similar to how a method is passed to an instantiated object. The big difference is that instead of a class instance, the class name itself is used. Class methods are used quite extensively in the macOS and iOS frameworks. They are used mostly for returning some fixed or well-known types or values or for returning a new instance of an object. These types of class methods are sometimes referred to as **factory methods** since, like factories, they create something new (in this case, a new instance of a class). Here are some factory method examples:

```
1.  [NSDate timeIntervalSinceReferenceDate]; // Returns a number
2.  [NSString stringWithFormat:@"%d", 1000]; // Returns a new NSString
                                                        object
3.  [NSDictionary new];                      // Returns a new NSDictionary
                                                        object.
```

All of the preceding methods are class methods being called.

Line 1 simply returns a value that represents the number of seconds since January 1, 2001, which is the reference date.

Line 2 returns a new NSString object that has been formatted and has a value of 1000.

Line 3 is a form that is commonly used because it actually allocates a new object. Typically, the line is not used by itself but in a line, like this:

```
NSDictionary  *myDict = [NSDictionary new];
```

So when would you use a class method? As a general rule, a class method is used in two ways:

- To create a new instance of the class

- When the method being called does not require an instance of the class

In our sample class, the second way doesn't apply but an example would be as follows:

```
NSDate *now = [NDate date];
```

This class method returns the current date/time and doesn't require an instance of NSDate.

There are also a few things that are important to note:

- Every class needs a class method to create itself.

- In *most* cases you don't have to create one since it's handled by NSObject for you.

It would be entirely possible to write the SimpleLabelData class without a class method, but we're adding one for instructive purposes.

Using Instance Methods

Instance methods (line 19 in Figure 7-1) are methods that are available only once a class has been instantiated. Here's an example:

```
1.  SimpleLabelData *myLabel;
2.  myLabel = [SimpleLabelData simpleLabelDataWithTitle:@"My Title"
                                   andValue:@"A Value"];
3.  NSString *combined = [myLabel combinedString];
4.  NSString *title = myLabel.title;
```

Line 1 declares the variable to hold the instance of the class.

Line 2 calls the class method to create the object, set its properties, and return it as an instance to be stored in the myLabel variable.

Line 3 calls an instance method to combine the title/value into a combined string.

Line 4 gets the `title` property from the instance and stores it into a new variable called `title`.

Another thing of note is that the code in the `Class` method cannot access the properties, which are the instance variables, until *after* the class is instantiated. You will see this when we go over the implementation file.

All instance methods must start with a hyphen (`-`); this easily distinguishes them from class methods, which use a plus (+) sign.

Working with the Implementation File

Now that you've seen what an interface file looks like, let's take a look at the **implementation file**. First, the interface file has an `.h` extension, as in `SimpleLabelData.h`. The implementation file has an `.m` extension, as in `SimpleLabelData.m`, as shown in Figure 7-2.

Another important thing to note is that the interface and implementation files have the same name (excluding the extension). This convention is used universally. While there is nothing preventing an interface and an implementation file from having different file names, having different names can cause much confusion. Moreover, tools like Xcode won't work as well. For example, the Xcode key sequence Control+Command+up-arrow key moves between implementation and interface files, and it will not work if the two file names are not the same.

When Xcode creates a class, it creates a rudimentary stub of an implementation file. Figure 7-2 starts with the `#import` statement to your interface file. The `#import` statement reads in your interface file for the class. As the compiler goes through your implementation (`.m`) file, it needs to know what class it's implementing, and the interface file provides all the information that it needs.

Note   Class method parameter names `initialTitle` and `initialValue` do not need to match the ones in the interface, `title` and `value`. Many times, the internal variable names used are different than the external ones.

```
1   //
2   //  SimpleLabelData.m
3   //  MyFirstApp
4   //
5   //  Created by Thorn on 12/7/17.
6   //  Copyright © 2017 MyCompany. All rights reserved.
7   //
8
9   #import "SimpleLabelData.h"
10
11  @implementation SimpleLabelData
12
13  + (instancetype)simpleLabelDataWithTitle:(NSString *)initialTitle
14                                  andValue:(NSString *)initialValue
15  {
16      SimpleLabelData *newLabel = [self new];
17      newLabel.title = initialTitle;
18      newLabel.value = initialValue;
19
20      return newLabel;
21  }
22
23
24  - (NSString *)combinedString
25  {
26      NSMutableString *newString = [NSMutableString new];
27      [newString appendString:self.title];
28      [newString appendString:@": "];
29      [newString appendString:self.value];
30
31      return [NSString stringWithString:newString];
32  }
33
34  @end
35
```

Figure 7-2. *Your implementation file*

An #import statement tells the compiler to read in the specified file because the compiler needs to know about certain predefined things. For example, in your interface file, the SimpleLabelData class is a subclass of NSObject. The NSObject class needs to be defined for the program to compile successfully. All of these objects are part of the iOS Foundation framework and are included via line 9 in the interface file from Figure 7-1.

```
#import <Foundation/Foundation.h>
```

Note   Look at the #import statements: one uses angle brackets (< >) and the other uses plain double quotation marks (" "). The difference is that a file in the angle brackets indicates a system-level file, which is located using a predefined path that Xcode automatically sets up for your project. Any file that has double quotation marks is searched for in the current project. In this example, the SimpleLabelData.h interface file is part of the project, so it gets double quotation marks, whereas the Foundation.h file is a system file and uses the angle brackets.

Coding Your Methods

Figure 7-2 is a simple example, but it demonstrates what many methods look like in a class. First, if you look at the implementation and interface files for one of the class methods, you can see the similarities. The following line is from the interface file:

```
+ (instancetype)simpleLabelDataWithTitle:(NSString *)initialTitle
                                andValue:(NSString *)initialValue;
```

As you can see, it's a class method because it starts with a +. The next item, (NSString*), is a parameter called initialTitle, and the second item is initialValue, another NSString*. These will be used by the instance to set its own title and value.

Listing 7-1 is from the implementation file.

Listing 7-1. The Implementation of a Class Method

```
1.  + (instancetype)simpleLabelDataWithTitle:(NSString *)initialTitle
                         andValue:(NSString *)initialValue
2.  {
3.      SimpleLabelData *newLabel = [SimpleLabelData new];
4.      newLabel.title = initialTitle;
5.      newLabel.value = initialValue;
6.      return newLabel;
7.  }
```

Listing 7-1 represents an implementation of the method defined in the interface. The word **implementation** indicates that the method is coded here. It looks almost identical to the interface file but now contains a block with some code, rather than simply ending with a semicolon.

Generally, a class has a definition of a method in an interface file and the actual code of the method in an implementation file.

So what does this class method do?

Line 1 is the class method declaration and is the implementation of the class method defined in the interface file.

Line 2 and line 7 begin and end the method.

Line 3 looks a little odd. It creates a new instance of the object by calling [SimpleLabelData new]. The new class method is defined in NSObject and creates a new instance of a class.

Remember, class methods cannot use the instance variables defined in the class but in the case of lines 4 and 5, you're using the newLabel variable, which is now the instance of the new class.

Line 6 returns the instance of the class to the caller.

Now, you will look at the implementation of an **instance method** (see Listing 7-2). There are some significant differences between an instance and a class method; for one, instance methods have the option to use the instance variables defined in the interface file, in this case two properties that represent the title and value. Also, instance methods are available only once the class has been instantiated.

Listing 7-2. The Implementation of an Instance Method

```
1.   - (NSString *)combinedString
2.   {
3.       NSMutableString *newString = [NSMutableString new];
4.       [newString appendString:self.title];
5.       [newString appendString:@": "];
6.       [newString appendString:self.value];

7.       return [NSString stringWithString:newString];

8.   }
```

Listing 7-2 illustrates the implementation of one of the instance methods of your SimpleLabelData class. In this case, the instance method combines the title and value properties with a : between them.

Line 1 is the start of the implementation of the method defined in the interface file.

Line 3 declares a new variable called newString. In this case, it's a variable that is an NSMutableString. This is a string that you can modify, as you will see next.

Line 4 appends the instance's property title to the newString, which is blank up to now. appendString: simply adds the string in the argument to the newString variable.

Lines 5 and 6 do the same as line 4 but use different string values.

Line 7 returns a copy of the new string. A copy is returned since you don't want to return the modifiable temporary string to the caller since the caller could modify it and that would be bad.

What's important to mention is the use of the name self in lines 4 and 6. When working in an instance method, the "instance" of the class is referred to as self.

Using Your New Class

You've created a simple SimpleLabelData class, but by itself, it doesn't accomplish a whole lot. In this section, you will create the Radio class and have it maintain a list of SimpleLabelData classes.

Updating MyFirstApp

Let's start up Xcode and load the project from Chapter 6, MyFirstApp. See Figure 7-3

1. You may have to click **Open another project** if the file isn't listed (Figure 7-3). Once you've loaded the file, you should see the project screen (Figure 7-4).

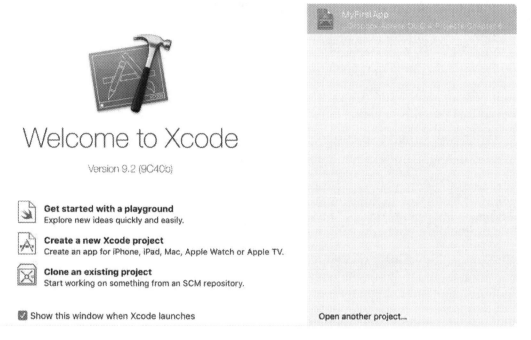

Figure 7-3. *Open Xcode so you can load an existing project*

2. If you don't see the project screen shown in Figure 7-4, just click **MyFirstApp** with the blue icon at the top of the Project Navigator window.

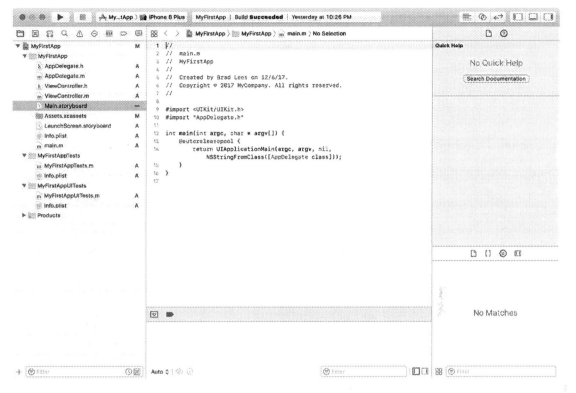

Figure 7-4. *The workspace window in Xcode*

Adding Objects

Now you can add your new objects.

1. First, create your `SimpleLabelData` object. Click the `MyFirstApp` group folder and click the + button at the bottom. Next, choose **File** (as shown in Figure 7-5).

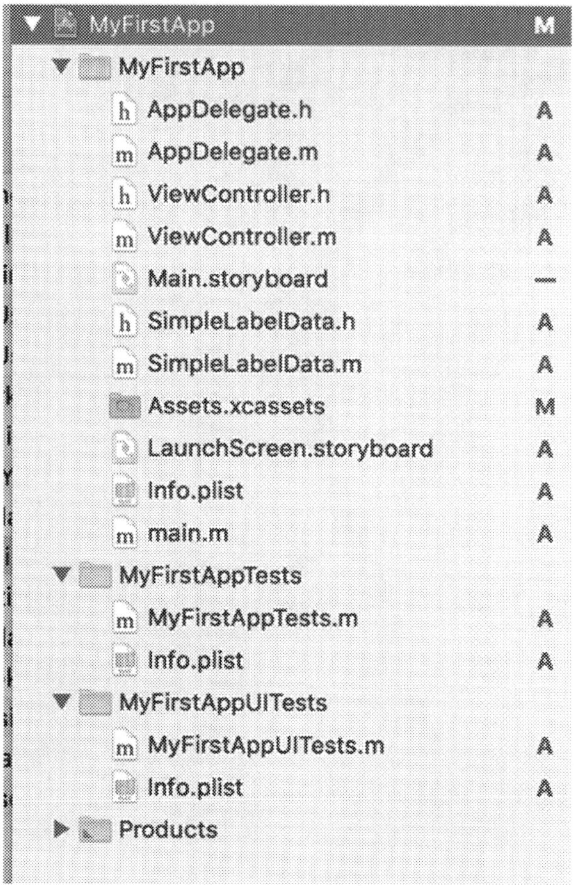

Figure 7-5. *Adding a new file*

Note   There are a few other ways to add a new file instead of just clicking the +
sign. Alternatively, you can right-click in the MyFirstApp folder and the new file
(or files) will be inserted right below the right-click.

The method shown here is an easy and consistent way to add items to the
Xcode project. There are + signs in other areas where right-clicks don't work as
expected.

2. The next screen, shown in Figure 7-6, asks for the new file type. Simply choose **Cocoa Touch Class** from the list of templates and then click **Next**.

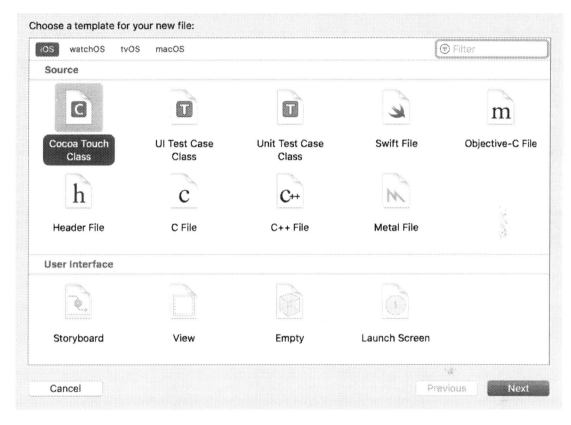

Figure 7-6. *Selecting the new file type*

3. On the next screen, enter **SimpleLabelData** as the class and select **NSObject** (you can just start typing **NSO** and Xcode will find it) for "Subclass of." This means your new class will be a subclass of NSObject, as shown in Figure 7-7.

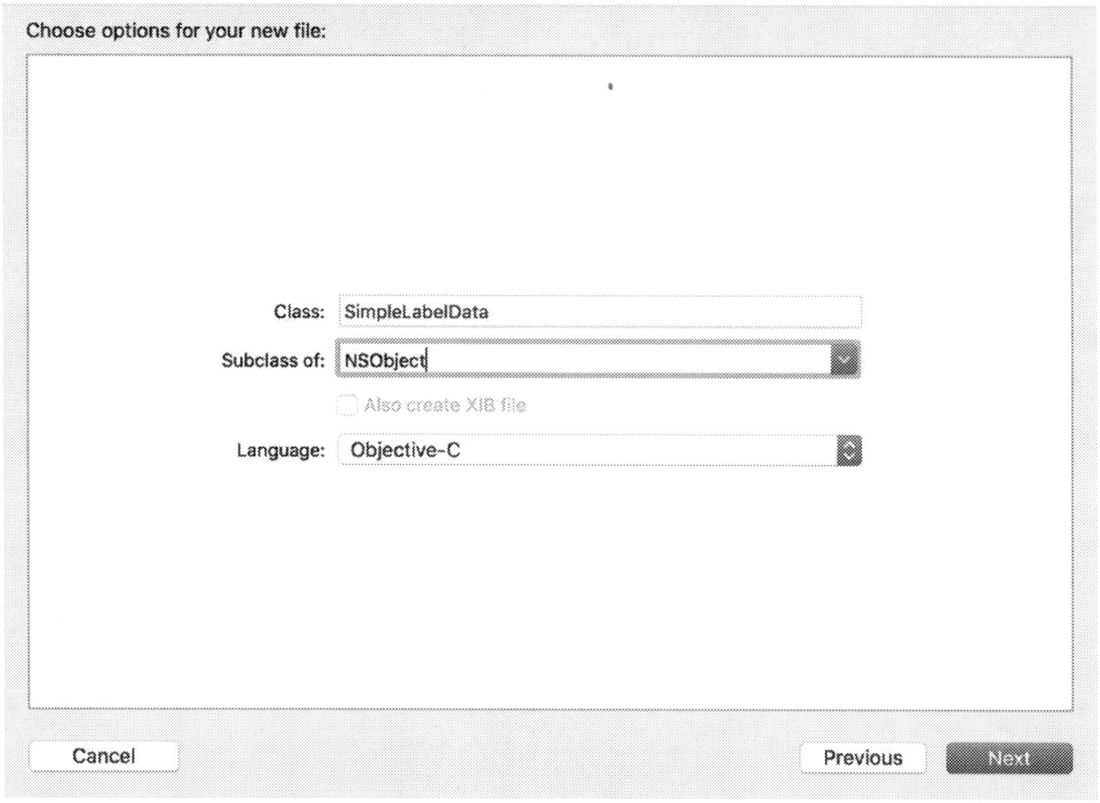

Figure 7-7. *Choosing your new object's subclass*

4. Click Next and the next screen will ask you where to put the files. Simply click the **Create** button since the location in which Xcode chooses to save the files is within the current project.

5. Your project window should now look like Figure 7-8. Click the `SimpleLabelData.h` file. Notice that the stub of your new `SimpleLabelData` class is already present. Now, fill in the empty class so it looks like Figure 7-1, which is the filled-out `SimpleLabelData` interface file.

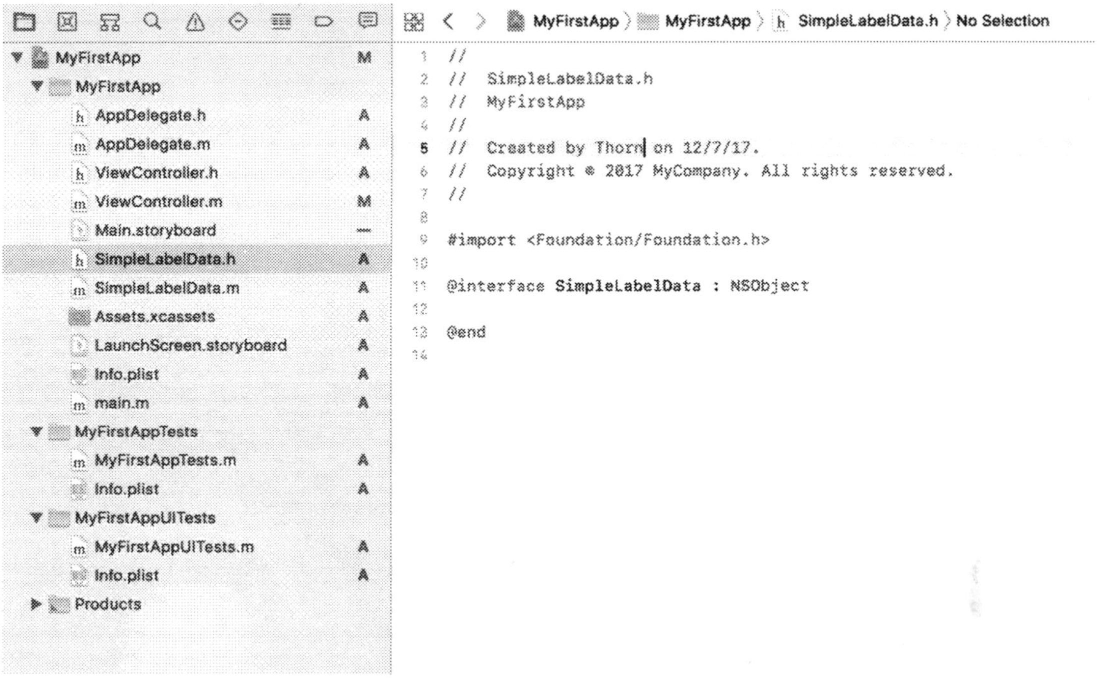

```
 1  //
 2  //  SimpleLabelData.h
 3  //  MyFirstApp
 4  //
 5  //  Created by Thorn on 12/7/17.
 6  //  Copyright © 2017 MyCompany. All rights reserved.
 7  //
 8
 9  #import <Foundation/Foundation.h>
10
11  @interface SimpleLabelData : NSObject
12
13  @end
14
```

Figure 7-8. *Your newly created file in the workspace window*

Writing the Implementation File

The SimpleLabelData.h file now defines the properties, class methods, and instance methods of your new class. Let's move on to the implementation file, SimpleLabelData.m, which looks quite empty, as in Figure 7-9. Fill out the implementation file just like Figure 7-2.

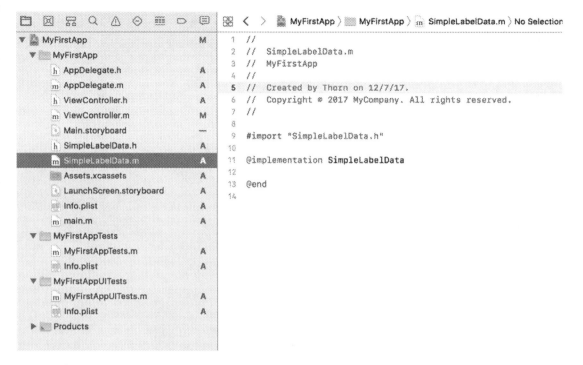

Figure 7-9. *The SimpleLabelData implementation file template*

Note   Xcode is intelligent enough to highlight issues in the interface or implementation file as you type (or soon after you stop typing). Issues can be warnings or errors and are represented by a yellow or red highlight, respectively. After filling out the interface and implementation files, there should not be any errors or warnings. If they are, carefully look at Figures 7-1 and 7-2.

Next, you need to update the storyboard so you can move SimpleLabelData to some new labels. You're going to be adding two new labels and then hook them up to instances of your new class.

Updating the User Interface

To start off, click the Main.storyboard file; the screen should now look like Figure 7-10. This file is the main iPhone screen.

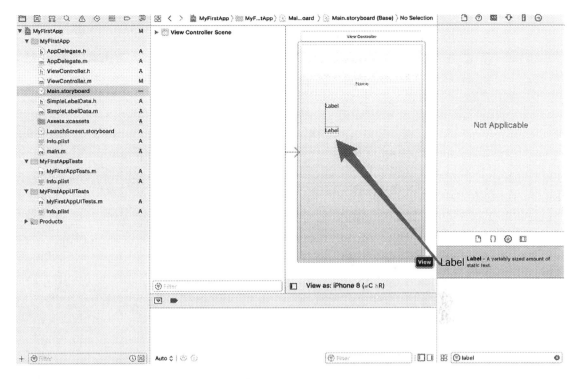

Figure 7-10. *The main storyboard*

1. Drag a new **Label** from the list of objects (called the Object
    Library), as shown in Figure 7-10.

2. Next, you need to resize the label to be the width of the view,
    as shown in Figure 7-11. You want to resize all labels to be long
    enough to hold some of the text you add. Any text added to the
    label will by default truncate with an ellipsis (...) at the end of the
    text. Something also to note is that as you drag and get close to the
    edge of the view, a blue line will be displayed. This is the default
    margin. The label can go further (to the very edge of the display if
    you want), but leaving the margin is more aesthetically pleasing
    than text that ends right at the edge of the phone's display.

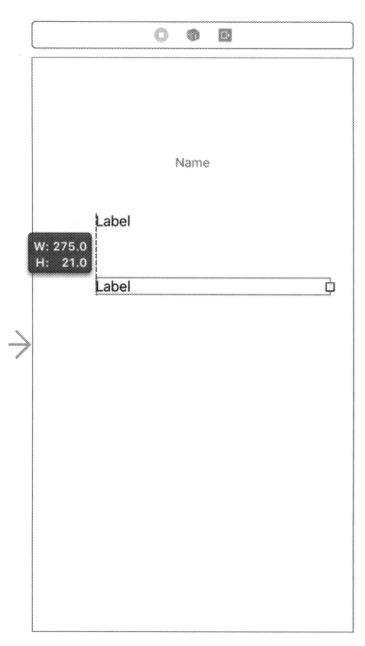

Figure 7-11. *Resizing the second label*

3. Lastly, add the third label to the view, as shown in Figure 7-12, and
    resize it just like the previous labels. All three labels should now be
    the same width (less the side margins). The spacing between the

labels isn't critical, and what is done in the figures is just one way of spacing out the labels. They could even be stacked on top of each other, which would make for one messy view! (Don't do that.)

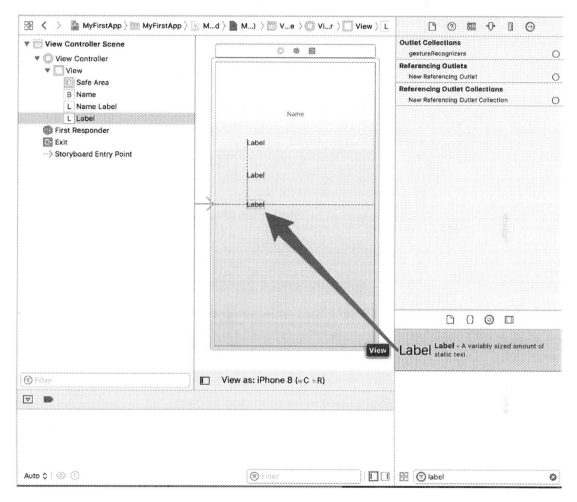

Figure 7-12. *Adding a third and final label*

Hooking Up the Code

Now that all the user interface objects are in place, you can begin to hook up these interface elements to the variables in your program. As you saw in Chapter 6, you do this by **connecting** the user interface objects with the objects in your program.

1. Let's start by adding two more variables that represent the two new labels added. The original MyFirstApp already had a `nameLabel` variable that represented the first label. You're going to change its name to `firstLabel`. But before you do that, you need to disconnect the Name Label item on the storyboard with the `nameLabel` variable in the code. To do this, select the Name Label item on the storyboard and then choose the Connections Inspector tab on the right, as shown in Figure 7-13.

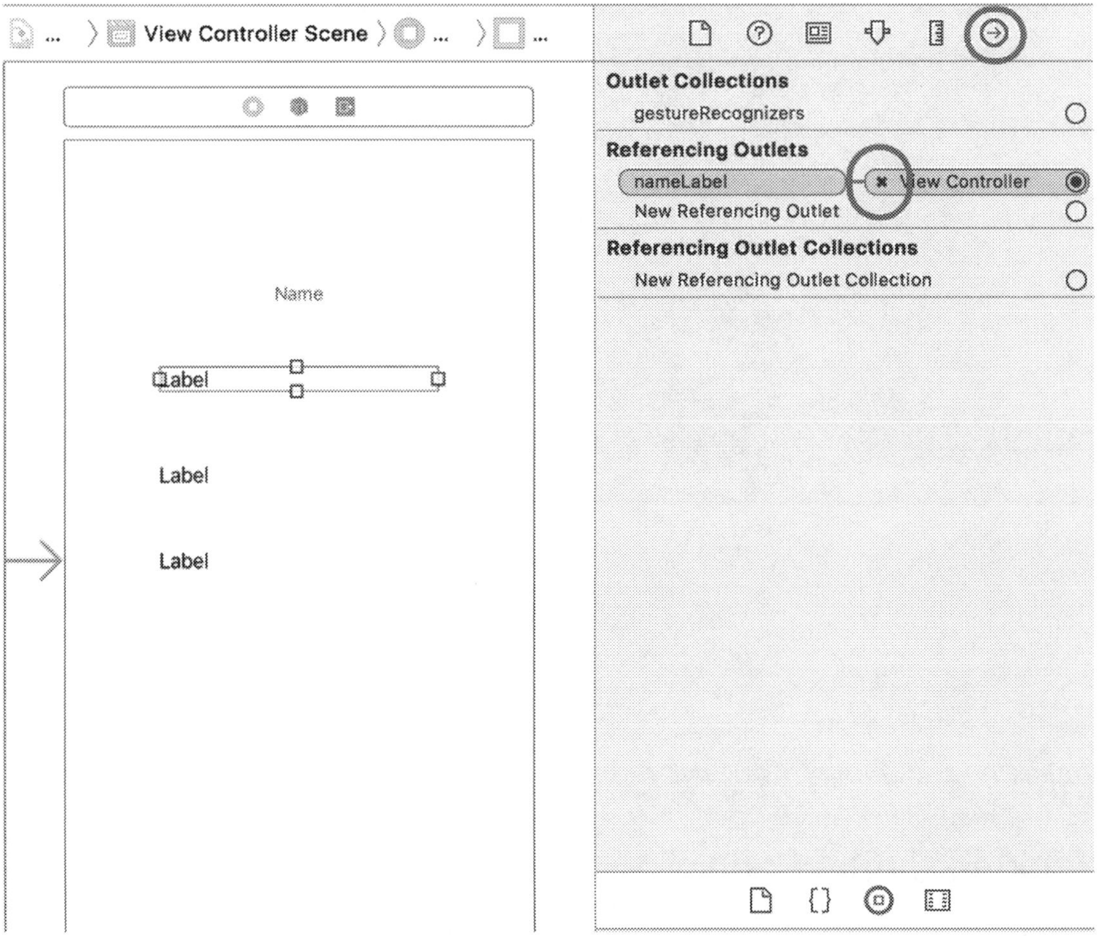

Figure 7-13. *Viewing the connection of the nameLabel variable*

2. Clicking the X in Figure 7-13 will delete the connection between the storyboard and the variable. Even though you are just renaming the variable, the storyboard knows it as `nameLabel` and not the new name you are going to use.

3. Next, go into the `ViewController.h` file and change the variable `nameLabel` to `firstLabel`, as shown in Figure 7-14. Also, add two additional labels, as shown in the figure.

```
1   //
2   //   ViewController.h
3   //   MyFirstApp
4   //
5   //   Created by Thorn on 12/6/17.
6   //   Copyright © 2017 MyCompany. All rights reserved.
7   //
8
9   #import <UIKit/UIKit.h>
10
11  @interface ViewController : UIViewController
12
    @property (nonatomic, strong) IBOutlet UILabel *firstLabel;
    @property (nonatomic, strong) IBOutlet UILabel *secondLabel;
    @property (nonatomic, strong) IBOutlet UILabel *thirdLabel;
16
    - (IBAction)showName:(id)sender;
18
19
20  @end
21
22
```

Figure 7-14. *Adding the additional labels*

4. Now it's time to connect the variables that you've just defined in the `ViewController.h` file to the three labels in the storyboard. Start by going back to the `Main.storyboard` to select the first label, as shown in Figure 7-15. Also make sure that the Connections Inspector is selected.

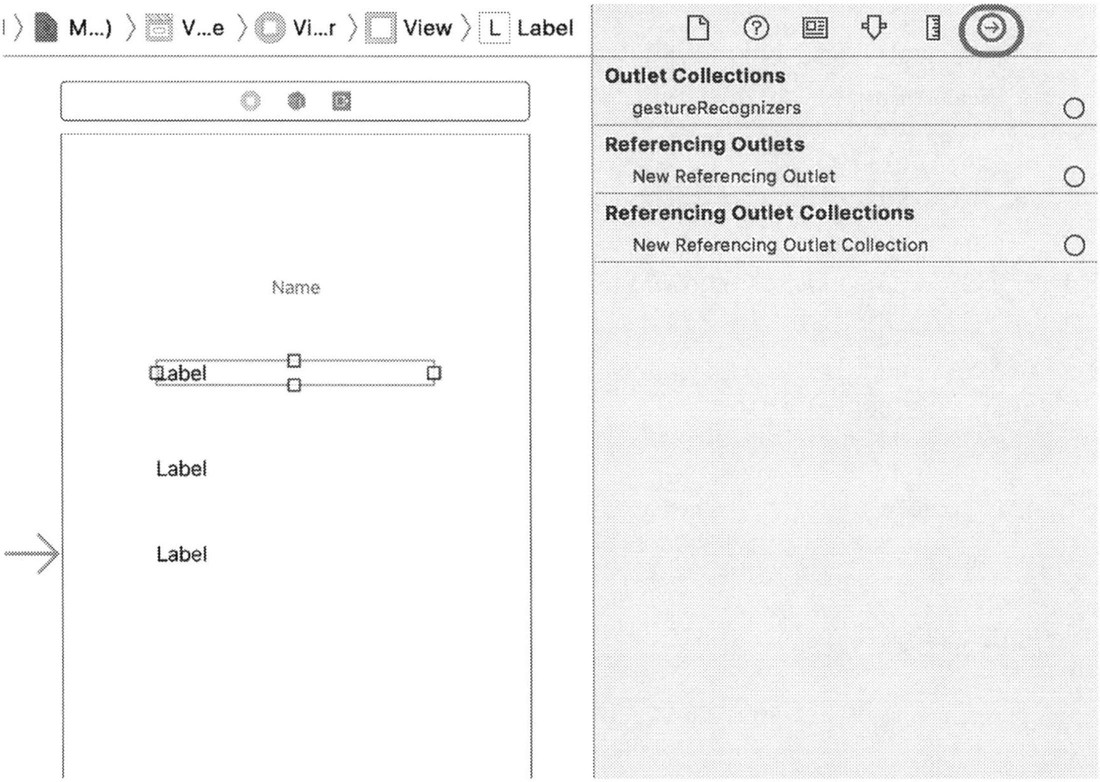

Figure 7-15. *Preparing the connection*

5. Once the first label is selected, drag a line from the New
    Referencing Outlet in the Referencing Outlets section and then
    drop it on the View Controller object (represented by the small
    yellow square at the top of the view), as shown in Figure 7-16.
    Once you drop it, a small menu will display asking what variable
    to connect the label to. For this example, you're going to select
    firstLabel, as shown in Figure 7-17.

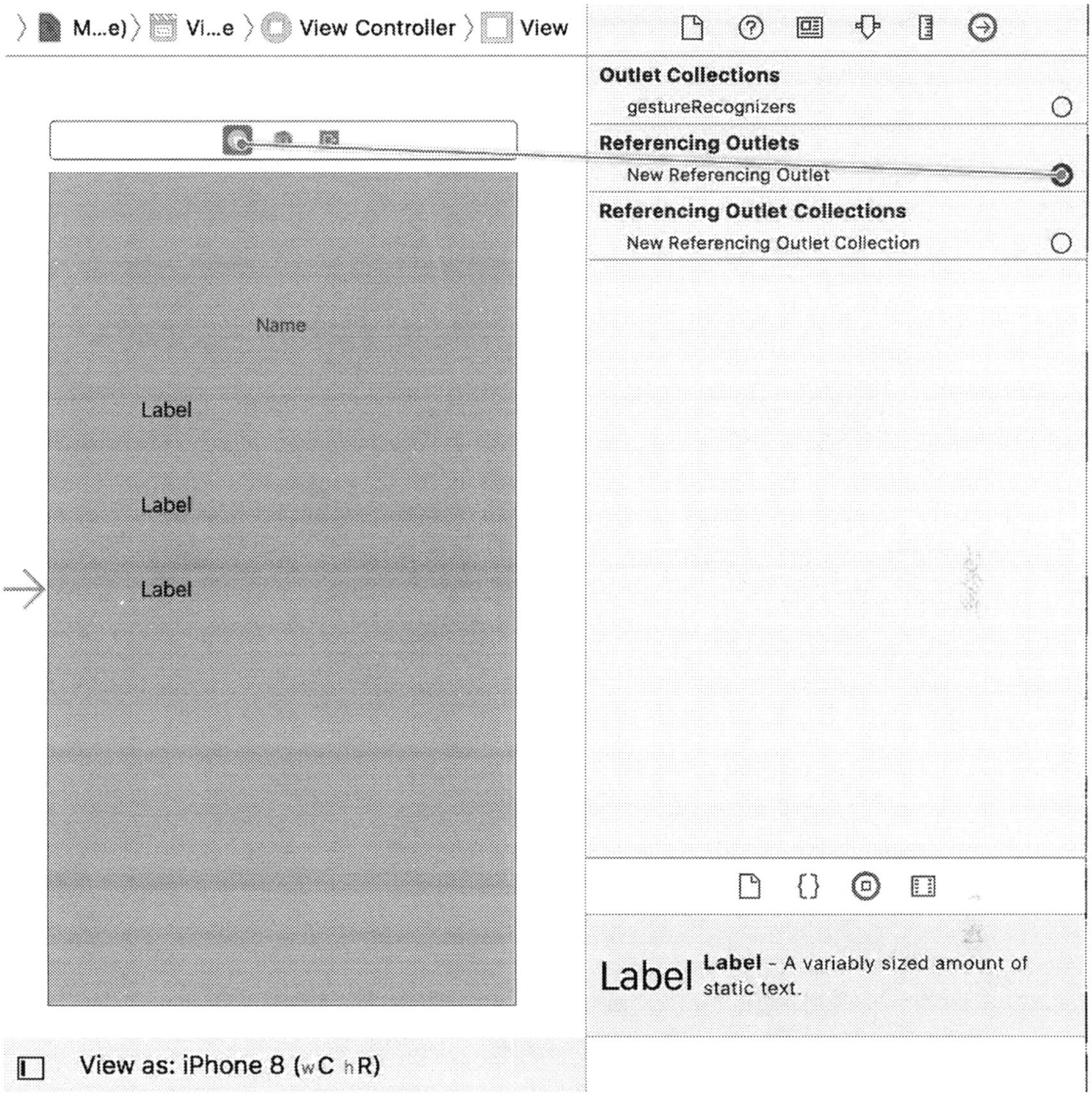

***Figure 7-16.** Creating a connection*

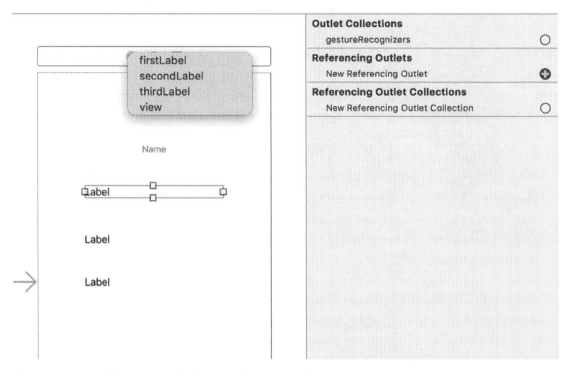

Figure 7-17. *Showing which possible variables you can connect to*

6. Repeat steps 4 and 5 for the second and third labels. Of course, the second label will connect to the variable secondLabel and so on.

7. Next, you're going to add some new code that will create three SimpleLabelData objects and then place that data into the labels. Start by selecting ViewController.m, deleting some old code, and adding some new. Start by deleting line 28 in the ViewController.m file. When you open the file, you'll notice an error on line 28. This error is basically letting you know that the nameLabel is not a valid variable name because you changed nameLabel to firstLabel. At this point, it doesn't matter; delete line 28 since you're going to rewrite this method. See Figure 7-18.

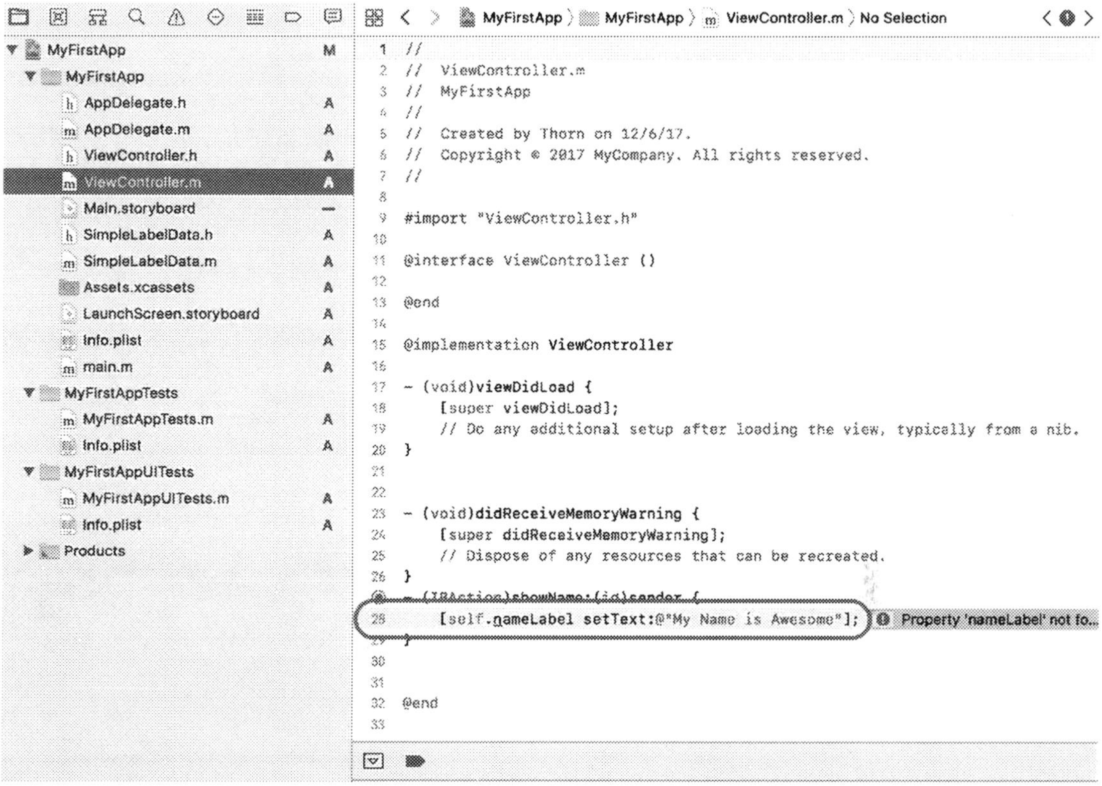

Figure 7-18. *Cleaning up the old code*

8. You can add the new code now; refer to Figure 7-19. The first thing you need to do is add an import of the SimpleLabelData class so that the ViewController class knows about it. This is done on line 10.

9. Now that the ViewController knows about the SimpleLabelData class, you can use it in the showName: method. Lines 29 and 30 define a SimpleLabelData variable called simply one. Also, the class method you defined in Figure 7-2 (line 13) is called to create a new instance of the SimpleLabelData class. The object (or instance) is then stored in the one variable.

10. Line 31 calls the combinedString instance method, which combines the title and value and returns it as a new NSString. That new string is stored directly into the self.firstLabel.text property. This property sets the text of the label so you can then see it in the view.

```
1   //
2   //  ViewController.m
3   //  MyFirstApp
4   //
5   //  Created by Thorn on 12/6/17.
6   //  Copyright © 2017 MyCompany. All rights reserved.
7   //
8
9   #import "ViewController.h"
10  #import "SimpleLabelData.h"
11
12  @interface ViewController ()
13
14  @end
15
16  @implementation ViewController
17
18  - (void)viewDidLoad {
19      [super viewDidLoad];
20      // Do any additional setup after loading the view, typically from a nib.
21  }
22
23
24  - (void)didReceiveMemoryWarning {
25      [super didReceiveMemoryWarning];
26      // Dispose of any resources that can be recreated.
27  }
28  - (IBAction)showName:(id)sender {
29      SimpleLabelData *one = [SimpleLabelData simpleLabelDataWithTitle:@"First Name"
30                                                             andValue:@"John"];
31      self.firstLabel.text = [one combinedString];
32  }
33
34
35  @end
36
```

Figure 7-19. *Using the SimpleLabelData class*

11. Repeat steps 9 and 10 for the remaining two labels. You can put your own values in or use what is in the example. Figure 7-20 shows the completed ViewController.m implementation that sets all three labels.

```
     - (IBAction)showName:(id)sender {
29       SimpleLabelData *one = [SimpleLabelData simpleLabelDataWithTitle:@"First Name"
30                                                           andValue:@"John"];
31       self.firstLabel.text = [one combinedString];
32
33
34       SimpleLabelData *two = [SimpleLabelData simpleLabelDataWithTitle:@"Last Name"
35                                                           andValue:@"Snow"];
36       self.secondLabel.text = [two combinedString];
37
38
39       SimpleLabelData *three = [SimpleLabelData simpleLabelDataWithTitle:@"Age"
40                                                            andValue:@"Unknown"];
41       self.thirdLabel.text = [three combinedString];
42   }
```

Figure 7-20. *The completed method*

12. Now you can run your app and see what happens! Click the Build
     and Run icon (▶) at the top left of the Xcode window, and you
     should see something like Figure 7-21. Click the Name button and
     you should see the View change to Figure 7-22.

Figure 7-21. *Running the newly updated app*

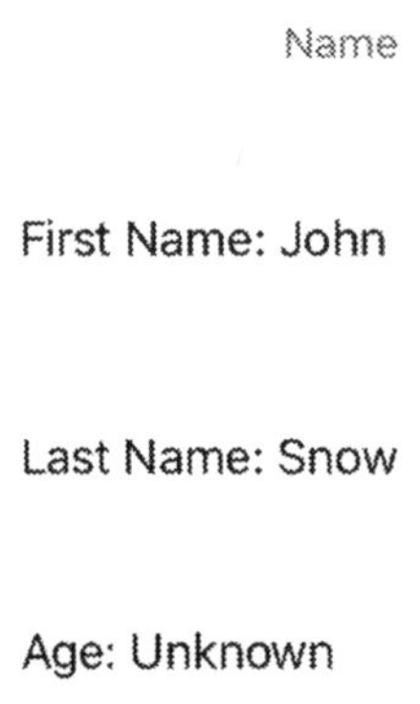

Name

First Name: John

Last Name: Snow

Age: Unknown

Figure 7-22. *Click the button!*

Now you have a running app that uses a new class (`SimpleLabelData`) and stores that data into a label on the screen. While it doesn't seem like much, this is how a lot of applications start: very simple and then improved upon. Don't be afraid to make changes!

Accessing the Xcode Documentation

We cannot emphasize enough the wealth of information provided in the Xcode **Developer Documentation** dialog. When a new project is created or an existing project opened, Xcode shows a Help menu, as shown in Figure 7-23.

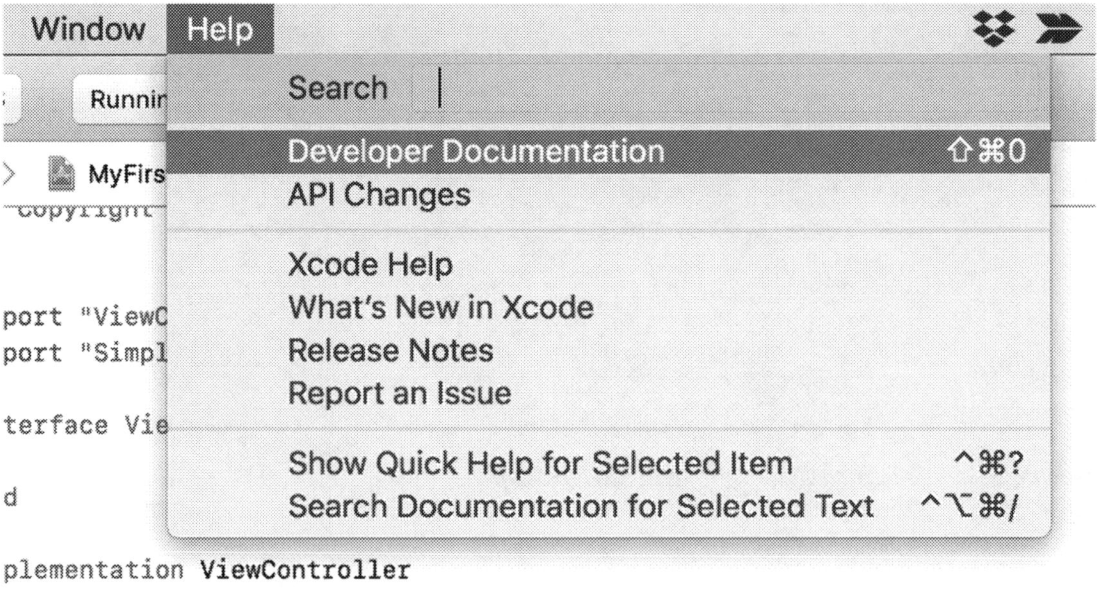

Figure 7-23. *The Xcode Help menu*

Once you open the Help documentation, you can use the search window to look up any of the classes you've used in this chapter, including the NSString class documentation, as shown in Figure 7-24.

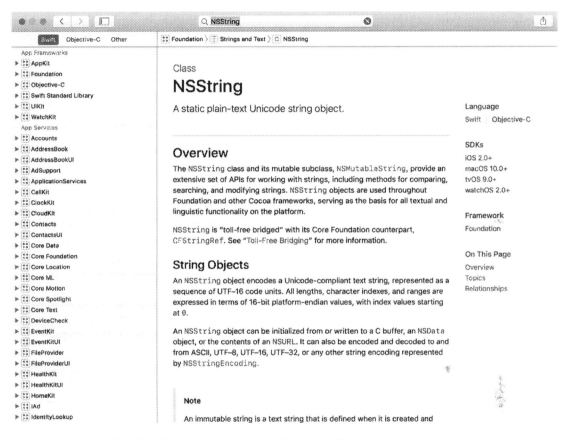

Figure 7-24. *The developer documentation window*

There are several different things to discover about the NSString class shown in Figure 7-24. Go through the documentation and the various companion guides that Apple provides. This will give you a more thorough understanding of the various classes and the various methods supported by them.

Summary

Here you are at the end of another chapter. Once again, congratulate yourself for being able to single-handedly stuff your brain with a lot of information! Here is a summary of what was covered in this chapter:

- Objective-C classes review
- Interface files
  - Properties
  - Class methods
  - Instance methods
- Implementation files
  - Defining the method's interface in the interface file and putting code to that interface in the implementation file
  - Limitations of using class methods vs. instance methods
  - Initializing the class and making use of its properties
- Making use of your new `SimpleLabelData` object
  - Building an iPhone app that uses your new object
  - Connecting interface classes to properties
  - Connecting user interface events to methods in your class

Exercises

Perform the following tasks:

- Change the code that creates your `SimpleLabelData` class and make the title and/or value much longer than what can appear on the screen. What happens?
- Modify the `SimpleLabelData` class to have a new method, similar to `combinedString`, that will do something different with the two strings instead of combining the two strings with a `:`.

- Change the `combinedString` method to take an `NSString*` parameter that will be the separator between the two strings (instead of a hard-coded colon).

- Change the text color or font of a label using the Attributes Inspector.

- Clean up the interface a little by making sure that the user doesn't see the text "Label" when the iPhone application first starts. You can either change this in the storyboard (note that you shouldn't completely clear the label or it may be difficult to find it on the screen) or write some new code that will set the .text property of the label to @"".

CHAPTER 8

Programming Basics in Objective-C

Objective-C is an elegant language. It mixes the efficiency of the C language with the object-oriented goodness of Smalltalk. This combination was introduced in the mid-1980s and is still powering the fantastic applications behind the iPhone, iPad, and Mac. How does a language that is more than 20 years old stay relevant and useful after all that time? Well, some of its success is because the two languages that make up Objective-C are well-tested and well-designed. Another reason is less obvious: the various frameworks available for iOS and macOS make developing full-featured applications much easier. These frameworks benefit from the fact that they have been around a long time, which equates to stability and high functionality. Lastly, Objective-C is highly dynamic. While we won't be focusing on that particular feature in this chapter, the dynamic nature of Objective-C provides a flexibility not found in many compiled languages. With all of these great features, Objective-C and the corresponding frameworks provide an excellent palette from which to create a masterpiece!

This chapter will introduce some of the more common concepts of Objective-C, such as properties and collection classes. This chapter will also show how properties are used from within Xcode when dealing with user interface elements. This sounds like a lot to accomplish, but Objective-C, the Foundation framework, and the Xcode tool provide a wealth of objects and methods and a way to build applications with ease.

Collections

Understanding collections is a fundamental part of learning Objective-C. In fact, collection objects are fundamental constructs of nearly every modern object-oriented language library; sometimes they are referred to as **containers**. Simply put, a collection

© Stefan Kaczmarek, Brad Lees, Gary Bennett, Mitch Fisher 2018
S. Kaczmarek et al., *Objective-C for Absolute Beginners*, https://doi.org/10.1007/978-1-4842-3429-7_8

is a type of class that can hold and manage other objects. The whole purpose of a collection is that it provides a common way to store and retrieve a collection of objects efficiently.

There are several different types of collections. While they all fulfill the same purpose of being able to hold other objects, they differ mostly in the way objects are retrieved. Here are the most common collections used in Objective-C:

- NSSet

- NSArray

- NSDictionary

- NSMutableSet

- NSMutableArray

- NSMutableDictionary

Notice that, among the collection classes listed, there are several that contain the word **mutable**. A mutable (versus nonmutable) class allows the collection object to change the order and add or remove items. Collection class names without the word **mutable** are nonmutable, meaning that the contents of the collection cannot change. This means that items cannot be added or removed at all. Because of this restriction, a nonmutable collection, like NSArray, for example, must be initialized with all of its values at once or initialized to point to an existing array.

Another thing to stress is that the collections store only objects and not simple values. So, it's not possible to store the integer value of 10, but it's possible to store a number object that represents 10. The notation for this is @(10); this creates an NSNumber object that represents the number 10.

Using NSSet

The NSSet class is used to store an unordered list of objects. **Unordered** means exactly that: the objects are stored in the set without regard to order. The advantage of the NSSet class is performance; it's the fastest collection class available. Use NSSet when it is necessary to store a collection of objects and the order in which they are stored or retrieved is not crucial.

Here is a typical NSSet initialization method:

```
NSSet *mySet = [NSSet setWithObjects:@"String 1", @"String 2", @"Whatever", nil];
```

As you can see, the set is initialized with a list of objects, in this case a list of strings. The last object must be nil to indicate the end of the list of objects. Also, the example uses strings, but an NSSet can be comprised of any object or even different types of objects, including other collections!

Tip All collection classes have the ability to store and manage any type of object at once. However, in typical cases, most programmers tend to store a single type of object in any one particular collection class to make the code less complicated.

To retrieve data in an NSSet, a few typical methods of accessing the elements within an NSSet are used. One method, shown in Listing 8-1, is to use what is referred to as a **fast enumerator** and retrieve each object one by one. Note that the fast enumeration (in lines 3–5) works on all collection classes.

Listing 8-1. Iterating Through an NSSet via an Enumerator

```
1 NSSet *mySet = [NSSet setWithObjects:@"One", @"Two", @"Three", nil];
2
3 for (id value in mySet) {
4     NSLog(@"%@", value);
5 }
```

Note On line 3, the class of the value is id. Recall that an id is a generic type that represents any Objective-C class. The reason that id is used is that the value that you store in the NSSet can be of any type. For example, if the NSSet were to contain a class called Animal and another class called Zoo, the code would fail because you don't have a class that is both a Zoo and an Animal type. On the other hand, if the NSSet always had the same class, you could substitute that class for the id on line 3.

Another common method of accessing an NSSet, especially when programming for an iOS device capturing touches, is to use the code in Listing 8-2.

Listing 8-2. Selecting Any of the Objects in the NSSet Collection

```
1 NSSet *mySet = [NSSet setWithObjects:@"One", @"Two", @"Three", nil];
2
3 NSString *value = [mySet anyObject];
```

Line 3 calls the method `anyObject`. This does exactly as it says; it returns any object from the set. The object returned is determined at the set's convenience, so there can be no guarantee that the first item will be returned. Of course, using the `anyObject` method assumes that any object will do. As mentioned, when dealing with touches on an iOS device, sometimes all that's necessary is to know that at least one finger has touched the screen. Each touch to the screen is stored as an entry in the `NSSet`, one for each finger. Using `anyObject` will return any one of the touches.

There are many other ways to actually get objects from an `NSSet`, far too many to cover in this chapter.[1] However, there is one particular method that involves the next collection: the `NSArray` class.

Using NSArray

The `NSArray` class is like any other collection, in that it allows the programmer to manage a group of objects. `NSArray` differs from `NSSet` in that `NSArray` is ordered, allowing an object to be retrieved by its *index* into the array. An index is the numeric position that an object would occupy in the `NSArray`. For example, if there are three elements in the `NSArray`, the objects can be referenced by an index from 0 to 2. As with most things in the C and Objective-C languages, an index starts at 0.

With `NSArray` (and `NSDictionary` covered next), there is a nice feature called a **collection literal**. A collection literal allows a collection to be represented by simple syntax. For `NSArray`, this syntax is simply @[..., ...]. While it's still possible to initialize the `NSArray` class the older, original way, it's best to use the new collection literal instead. See examples in Listing 8-3.

---

[1] https://developer.apple.com/documentation/foundation/nsset

Listing 8-3. Creating an NSArray Object

```
1    // Old out-of-fashion way of doing things.
2    NSArray *oldStyle = [NSArray arrayWithObjects: @"Zero", @"One",
     @"Two", nil];
3    // New way is much better:
4    NSArray *newStyle = @[@"Zero", @"One", @"Two"];
5
6    // Old way of accessing an element of an NSArray
7    NSLog([oldStyle objectAtIndex:0]);
8    NSLog([oldStyle objectAtIndex:1]);
9    NSLog([oldStyle objectAtIndex:2]);
10
11   // New way of accessing an element of an NSArray
12   NSLog(newStyle[0]);
13   NSLog(newStyle[1]);
14   NSLog(newStyle[2]);
```

As you can see, objects within the NSArray can be retrieved via the index. The index starts at 0 and can't exceed the size of the array—1. You can find the size of the array by accessing the count property of the NSArray object.

```
int entries = myArray.count;
```

Another thing that is important to know about an array is that it stores the objects added to the array in the order they were added. This is what's called an **ordered collection**. So, using the example in Listing 8-3, the NSArray object at the index of 1 (that is, newStyle[1]) will always be the value of @"One". Collection classes that don't specifically mention that they are an ordered collection are unordered collections. NSDictionary in the next section is an example.

Before you look at NSDictionary, it's important to take a quick look at how you can use the NSArray collection literal to initialize an NSSet (Listing 8-4).

195

Listing 8-4. Using an NSArray to Create an NSSet

```
1    // Not using an NSArray Collection Literal
2    NSSet *mySet = [NSSet setWithObjects:@"One", @"Two", @"Three", nil];
3
4    // Using an NSArray Collection Literal
5    NSSet *anotherSet = [NSSet setWithArray:@[@"One", @"Two", @"Three"]];
```

NSDictionary

The NSDictionary class is also a useful type of collection class. It allows the storage of objects, just like NSSet and NSArray, but NSDictionary is different in that it allows a *key* to be associated with any value. For example, an NSDictionary could be created to store a list of Animal objects. A list of animals could be stored in an NSArray, but it's accessed by index. Somehow you would, for example, have to know that the Monkey object is stored in index 2.

With NSDictionary, you are able to store the monkey with some key that is more descriptive. Because of this, an entry in NSDictionary consists of a key and a value. You can "look up" the value by simply providing a key. While this **seems** like just a different way of simply using an index into an array, it's actually something completely different because the **key** used can be any object that makes sense, like a string. So, you could store your Monkey object in a dictionary with the key of Monkey instead of an index into an array. If the monkey were in the array, the program would have to go through each element of the array searching for the monkey, and the problem becomes even more complicated if there are tens of thousands of animals.

An NSDictionary Example

Just as with NSArray, there is a way to define (and access) an NSDictionary using a collection literal. Remember that a dictionary entry consists of a key and a value and is represented as shown in Listing 8-5.

Listing 8-5. Defining an NSDictionary

```
@{@"Key": @"Value",
  @"Key2": @"Value2"};
```

It's a little different from the NSArray literal. It uses curly braces, { }, instead of square brackets. Also, the key is separated from the value by a colon, :. Again, this is much simpler and cleaner than previous older ways. Because of this, we're only going to show how to use a dictionary with a literal.

NSDictionary Access, Order, and Uniqueness

An NSDictionary object is an unordered collection object, which means that the order in which the elements are stored are not guaranteed to be in the order represented in code. This is generally not a problem since the program will look something up by the key's name, like Monkey. It doesn't matter what *order* Monkey appears in the dictionary, just that it can be found or not.

How is an entry looked for in an NSDictionary? It's resembles how elements are accessed in an NSArray. This similarity makes it easy to remember (Listing 8-6).

Listing 8-6. Accessing an Element of a Dictionary

```
1    // Create a simple dictionary:
2    NSDictionary *animalCountInZoo = @{@"Monkeys": @(10),
3                                       @"Birds": @(1199),
4                                       @"Fish": @(356)};
5
6    // Retrieving a value in the dictionary
7    NSLog(@"%@", animalCountInZoo[@"Birds"]);
8
9    // Prints the value of 1199
```

Using the Mutable Container Classes

Up to this point, we've only discussed collection objects that are initialized once and can never change. While there are definitely places where this is useful, what's even more useful is a collection class that can be modified. Each of the collection classes has a **mutable** version; we've talked only about the **nonmutable** classes. The classes are fundamentally the same except that elements can be added and removed from the mutable versions.

NSMutableSet

NSMutableSet can be initialized the same as NSSet or can be initialized without any values and then values added. Consider the code in Listing 8-7.

Listing 8-7. Adding Objects to an NSMutableSet

```
1   NSMutableSet *mySet = [NSMutableSet new];
2
3   [mySet addObject:@"One"];
4   [mySet addObject:@"Two"];
5   [mySet addObject:@"Three"];
6
7   for (id val in mySet) {
8       NSLog(@"%@", val);
9   }
```

The nice thing about any of the mutable classes is that elements can be added and removed programmatically instead of having to declare the class with all the values at once. All objects in a set can be removed with the following line:

```
[mySet removeAllObjects];
```

A specific object can also be removed from a mutable set, as shown in Listing 8-8.

Listing 8-8. Removing a Specific Object in an NSMutableSet

```
10  NSString *testString = @"Zero";
11
12  [mySet addObject: testString];
13  [mySet addObject: testString];  // Just a test
14
15  for (id val in mySet) {
16      NSLog(@"%@", val);
17  }
18
19  [mySet removeObject:testString];
20
```

```
21   for (id val in mySet) {
22       NSLog(@"%@", val);
23   }
```

In Listing 8-8, line 19 will remove the string "Zero". This brings up another good point: NSSet and NSMutableSet will store only *unique* objects. Two objects that are the same (that is, identical) cannot be added more than once. For example, line 13 effectively does nothing since the testString is added on line 12.

NSMutableArray

As with NSMutableSet, NSMutableArray is similar to its parent, NSArray. In fact, an object can be added to the NSMutableArray object exactly as it's done in NSMutableSet, which is by using the addObject: method. However, unlike NSMutableSet, NSMutableArray can also insert elements into the array; NSMutableSet can add only objects to the set. Take a look at Listing 8-9.

Listing 8-9. Adding and Inserting Values into an NSMutableArray

```
1    NSMutableArray *myArray = [NSMutableArray new];
2
3    [myArray addObject:@"One"];
4    [myArray addObject:@"Two"];
5    [myArray addObject:@"Three"];
6
7    for (id val in myArray) {
8        NSLog(@"%@", val);
9    }
10
11   [myArray insertObject:@"One and a Half" atIndex:1];
12
13   for (id val in myArray) {
14       NSLog(@"%@", val);
15   }
```

In Listing 8-9 a new array is created similarly to NSMutableSet. However, on line 11 a new element is being inserted into the array at position 1. Remember, position 0 is the first element of the array. The contents of the array after the insert would look like this:

Index	Value
0	One
1	One and a Half
2	Two
3	Three

Line 11 inserted a new element; the remaining elements were moved up in the array to make room. This is critical to know, especially if there is a code assumption that a particular index into an array will have a specific value.

With NSMutableArray, there are several ways to remove an object. The following are a few of the more commonly used methods:

- removeAllObjects: This method does exactly as advertised. It removes all objects from a given NSMutableArray.

- removeLastObject: This method removes the last object at the end of the array. The array size is reduced by one.

- removeObjectAtIndex:(NSUInteger)index: This method removes an object at a given index. The index can be from 0 to the length of the array—1.

NSMutableDictionary

By this point, it must be pretty obvious to you how the mutable versions of the collection classes work, and NSMutableDictionary is no different. NSMutableDictionary provides all the capabilities of NSDictionary, but, of course, elements can be added and removed, as shown in Listing 8-10.

Listing 8-10. Adding Objects to an NSMutableDictionary

```
1    NSMutableDictionary *myDict = [NSMutableDictionary new];
2
3    myDict[@"1"] = @"Number One";
4    myDict[@"2"] = @"Number Two";
5    myDict[@"3"] = @"Number Three";
6
7    for (id val in myDict) {
8        NSLog(@"key=%@ value=%@", val, [myDict objectForKey:val]);
9    }
10
11   myDict[@"1.5"] = @"One and a Half";
12
13   for (id val in myDict) {
14       NSLog(@"key=%@ value=%@", val, [myDict objectForKey:val]);
15   }
```

In this example, the object @"One and a Half" is being added to the dictionary. It's different from an array since an object can't be inserted into the dictionary at a specific position, as can be done with NSMutableArray.

Creating the Bookstore Application

Let's start by creating the base application project. You start by opening Xcode and creating a new project with the Single View template. In this project, you will create a few simple objects for what is to become a bookstore application: a Book object and the Bookstore object itself. You'll visit properties again and see how to get and set the value of one during this project. Lastly, you'll put your bookstore objects to use, and you'll learn how to make use of objects once you've created them.

1. Fire up Xcode, and start by creating a new project, as shown in Figure 8-1.

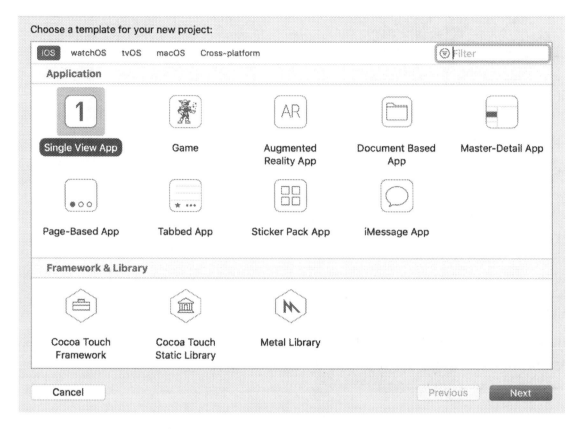

Figure 8-1. *Creating the initial project*

2. Click the **Next** button, and name the project **MyBookstore**,
    as shown in Figure 8-2. The company name is required; any
    company name, real or otherwise, can be used. The example uses
    com.mycompany, which is perfectly fine.

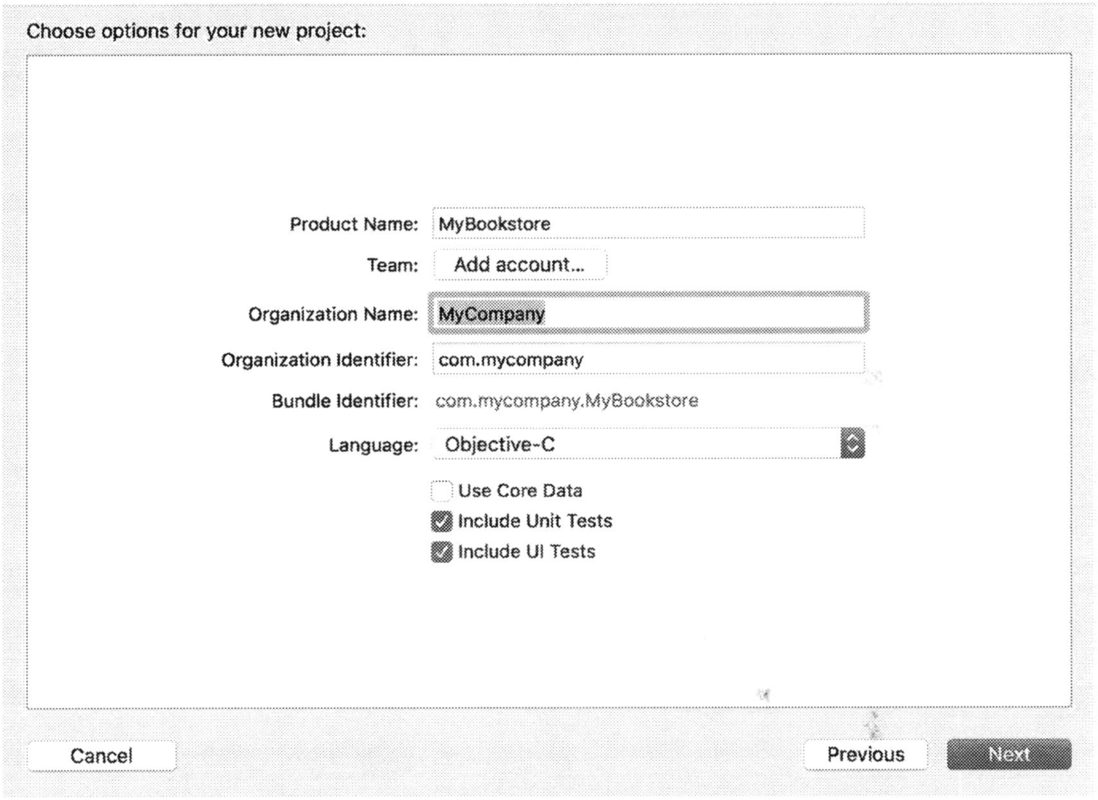

Choose options for your new project:

Product Name:	MyBookstore
Team:	Add account...
Organization Name:	MyCompany
Organization Identifier:	com.mycompany
Bundle Identifier:	com.mycompany.MyBookstore
Language:	Objective-C

☐ Use Core Data
☑ Include Unit Tests
☑ Include UI Tests

Cancel   Previous   Next

Figure 8-2. *Selecting the product (application) name and options*

3. Once everything is filled out, click the **Next** button. Xcode will
    prompt you to specify a place to save the project. Anywhere you
    can remember is fine; the desktop is a good place too.

4. Once you decide on a location, click the **Create** button to create the new project. This will create the boilerplate bookstore project, as shown in Figure 8-3.

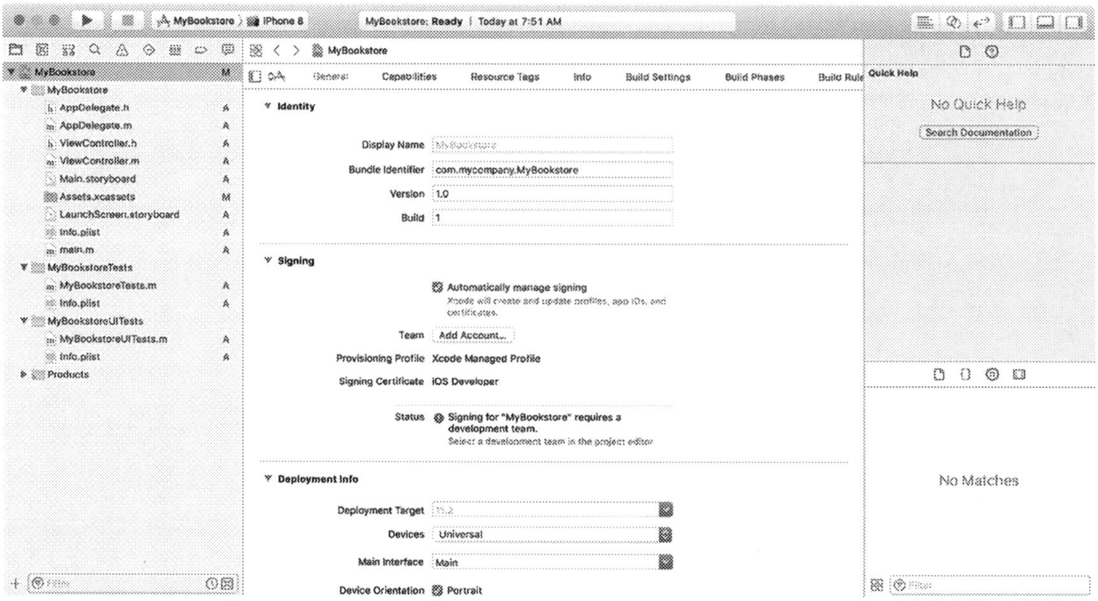

Figure 8-3. *The source listing of the boilerplate project*

5. Click the MyBookstore Folder on the left. Click the plus (+) sign
    in the lower left of the screen in the Navigation pane to add a new
    object to the project. Choose **File** and then under the iOS section
    on the top choose **Cocoa Touch Class**, as shown in Figure 8-4. It's
    also possible to right-click in the Navigation area and then select
    the New File menu option. There is no difference between this
    approach and clicking the plus sign, so do whatever feels more
    natural.

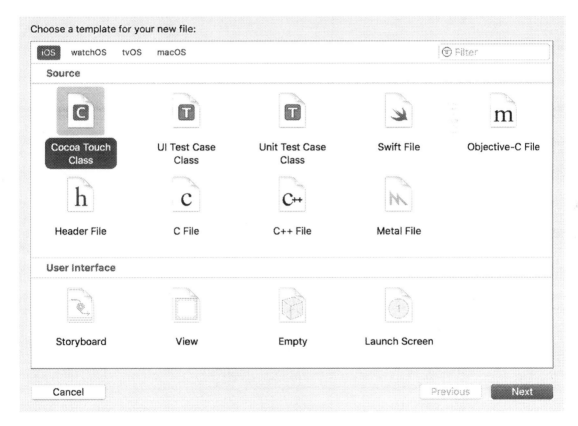

Figure 8-4. *Creating a new Cocoa Touch class*

6. Here you're choosing a plain Cocoa Touch class, which will create a new empty Objective-C object that you're going to use for your Book class. After selecting this, click the **Next** button.

7. Xcode will now prompt for the object name and which class it's going to be a subclass of. Choose the name Book and make Book a subclass of NSObject, as shown in Figure 8-5, and then click the **Next** button.

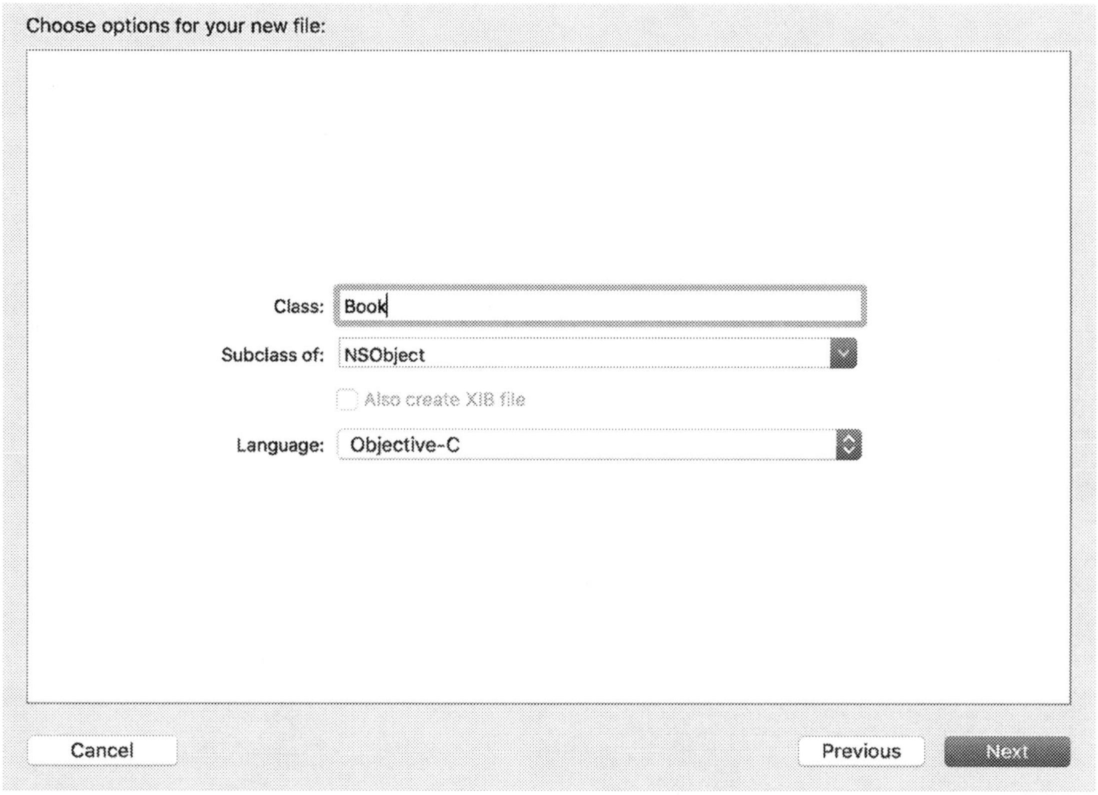

Choose options for your new file:

Class: Book

Subclass of: NSObject

☐ Also create XIB file

Language: Objective-C

Cancel   Previous   Next

Figure 8-5. *Giving your new class a name and parent class*

8. Finally, Xcode will ask to which folder it should save the new class files. To keep things simple, just add the file to the MyBookstore subfolder, as shown in Figure 8-6. This is where all the other class files for the project are stored.

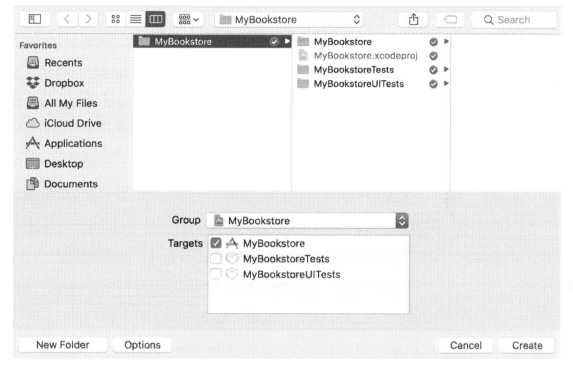

Figure 8-6. *Choosing the place to save your new class files*

Note   The Book and Bookstore classes are what are referred to as **data model** classes. Data model classes are just used to store information and have nothing to do with the interface of the app.

---

9. Click the **Create** button. You'll see the main edit window for Xcode and your new class files, Book.m and Book.h, in the Navigation pane.

10.   Repeat these steps and create a second class called Bookstore.
This will create a Bookstore.m file and a Bookstore.h file, as
shown in Figure 8-7. You'll use this class later in this chapter. For
now, you'll concentrate on the Book class.

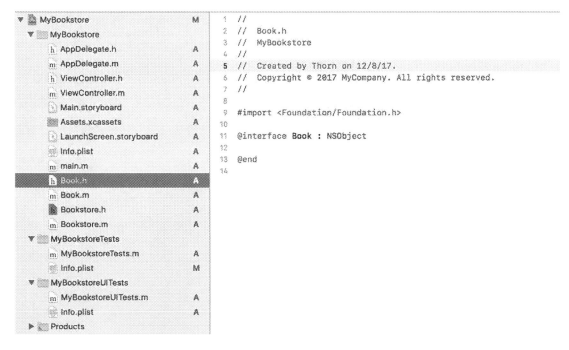

Figure 8-7. *Viewing your new class*

11.   Click the Book.h file and let's start defining your new class!

Introducing Properties

The class is simply called Book and is a subclass of NSObject. True, you have a class, but
it doesn't *store* anything at this point. For this class to be useful, it needs to be able to
hold some information, which is done with properties. When an object is used, it has
to be instantiated. Once the object is instantiated, it has access to its properties. These
variables are available to the object as long as the object stays in scope. As you know
from Chapter 7, scope defines the context in which an object exists. In some cases, an
object's scope may be the life of the program. In other cases, the scope might be just a
function or method. It all depends on where the object is declared and how it's used.

Scope will be discussed more later. For now, let's add some properties to your Book class to make it more useful. See Listing 8-11.

Listing 8-11. Adding Properties to the Book.h File

```
1    //
2    //   Book.h
3    //   MyBookstore
4    //
5    //   Created by Thorn on 12/8/17.
6    //   Copyright © 2016 MyCompany. All rights reserved.
7    //
8    #import <Foundation/Foundation.h>
9    @interface Book : NSObject
10   @property (nonatomic) NSString *title;
11   @property (nonatomic) NSString *author;
12   @property (nonatomic) NSString *bookDescription;
13   @end
```

This is the same Book object from before, but now there are three new properties placed inside the interface, lines 10–12. These are all NSString objects, which means that they can hold text information for the Book object. So, the Book object now has a place to store the title, the author, and the book's description information.

Lines 10–12 may not look familiar. These **properties** are constructs in Objective-C uses to store data, in this case NSStrings. Properties are available to the class only once it's **instantiated** as an object. Instantiating an object is the same as creating an object: Book *myBook = [Book new];.

Accessing Properties

Now that you have some properties, how can you use them? How are they accessed? As you learned in previous chapters, Objective-C objects respond to messages. There are two ways to access these properties:

- One way is, of course, within the Book object.

- The second way is from outside of the object—that is, another part of the program that uses the Book object.

If you are writing the code for a method within your Book object, accessing a property is quite simple. For example, you could simply write the following:

```
self.title = @"Test Title";
```

The preceding line is written within the Book class. The variable self represents the instance of the class (a.k.a. object). When accessed outside of the class instead of self, you use the variable that holds the object.

```
1    Book *theBook = [Book new];
2    theBook.title = @"Test Title";
```

This code pattern should look a little familiar. Line 1 creates a new Book object and stores it in the variable theBook. Line 2 then uses the variable theBook to access the title property.

Note   You may have noticed that the properties take on a naming convention called **camel case** (or camelCase) that uses an uppercase letter to distinguish different words in a method, variable, or class name. The text is suggestive of a camel, since the uppercase letters tend to form humps. It makes the label easier to read. For example, `stringWithContentsOfURL` is much easier to read than `stringwithcontentsofurl`.

Once a property has been specified in the interface file, using the properties is straightforward and simple.

```
myBookObject.title = newTitle; // Setting the property to a value. In this
case the newTitle variable.
```

Something important to note is that the object access is not within brackets ([...]). Accessing a property does not require them. On the surface, the property seems just like a variable attached to the object. Internally, it's a little different. In fact, the compiler automatically creates two internal methods to manage the property. One method is called the *setter* and the other is the *getter*. Under most circumstances, it's not necessary to even have to deal with the getter or setter. But, sometimes it may be necessary to perform something like validation on what the property is being set to.

Custom Getter and Setter

As mentioned, a property consists of two methods that are normally hidden. But, it's possible to override the default behavior of the getter or setter. If you haven't guessed by now, a getter returns (or gets) a value from the property. A setter stores (or sets) a value in the property. Listing 8-12 provides an example of a setter and why it may be necessary. As an example, in the custom setter shown in Listing 8-12, you cut off the title of a book if it's more than 20 letters long.

Listing 8-12. A Custom Setter

```
1 - (void)setTitle:(NSString *)newTitle
2 {
3     if (newTitle.length > 20) {
4         _title = [newTitle substringToIndex:20];
5     } else {
6         _title = newTitle;
7     }
8 }
```

In Listing 8-12, you create a setter method that overrides the default one. A setter always starts with the word set and then is followed by the property name with the first character capitalized. So, the method setTitle: means that you are overriding the setter for the property title. Another thing to note is the instance variable _title. This is important to understand. The "real" property is internally stored in a variable named the same as the property but with an underscore (_). You might be wondering why you simply don't just write self.title = newTitle on lines 4 and 6. If you remember, the setter is the internal method used to set the property. Calling self.title will then call the custom setter. So, calling self.title will continue to call the setter until the app crashes. Using _title avoids this problem.

```
1   Book *theBook = [Book new];
2   theBook.title = @"This is a really long book title.";
```

These lines will call your own custom setter instead of the standard one. The same would be true had you written your own getter method. So, given that new setter, when you set the theBook title to something that long, the actual book title is shortened (line 4) to be only 20 characters long. So,

```
"This is a really long book title."
```

becomes

```
"This is a really lon"
```

Without using a custom setter, your app may end up with a book title that is longer than you want.

Finishing the MyBookstore Program

With this understanding of instance variables and properties, you are going to now venture forth to create the actual bookstore program. The idea is simple enough: create a class called Bookstore that will be stocked with a few Book objects.

When you first created the initial application, it was a plain single-view application. Choosing that template creates just enough of what you want. The only problem is that you're going to redo the single-view part. So, you're going to delete a few things from the MyBookstore project and then create the initial storyboard. A storyboard is just a collection of views that your app will use. The storyboard allows for all the views to be displayed in one big canvas.

You first need to clean up the template so you can build your app.

1. You start the cleanup by deleting the ViewController.h and .m files. This is done by highlighting them in the Project Navigator, as shown in Figure 8-8, and then pressing the **Delete** key.

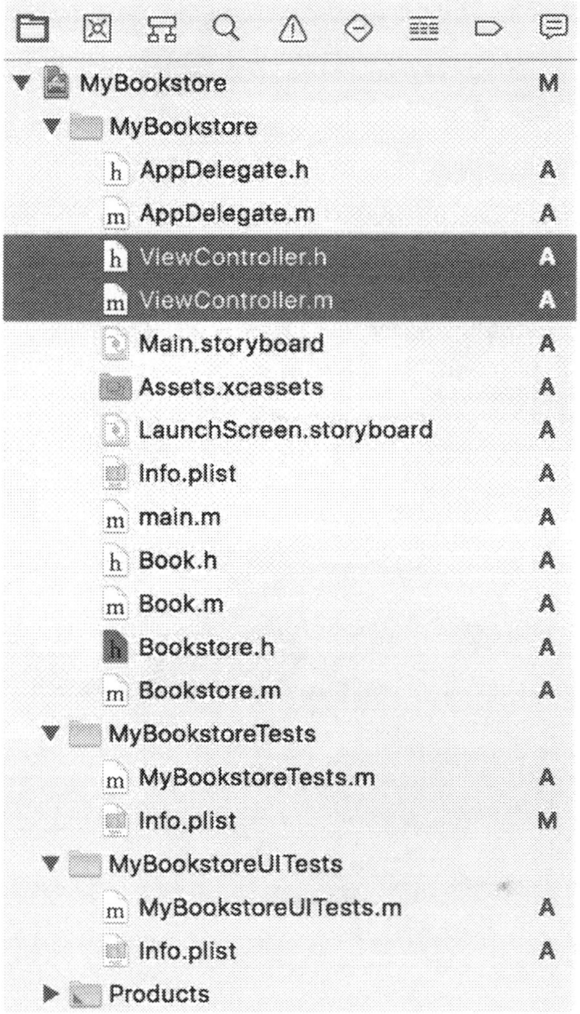

Figure 8-8. *Deleting the old ViewController files*

2. Once the Delete key is pressed, Xcode will put up a message that asks if the files should be moved to the trash or if you just want to remove their references. In this case, it's OK to click the Move to Trash button since you really don't want these files anymore, as shown in Figure 8-9.

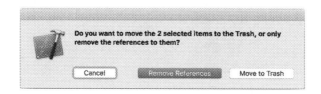

Figure 8-9. *Prompt to move to trash*

3. Next, you want to change the Main.storyboard file. A storyboard
    is basically a collection of views that your app consists of. In this
    case, you're going to delete the view controller that was created by
    the Single View template used when the project was first created.
    So, select the Main.storyboard file in the Project Navigator, as
    shown in Figure 8-10. Once you've selected it, you will see the
    blank View Controller.

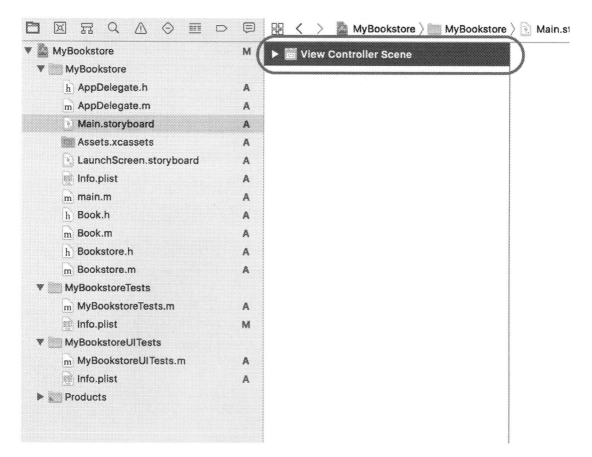

Figure 8-10. *The selected Main.storyboard file*

4. From here, select the **View Controller Scene** and press the **Delete**
    key, as shown in Figure 8-10. Now you'll have a blank `Main.`
    `storyboard` from which you can begin your app. Click the **Show/**
    Hide Utilities Pane button so you can add a new view control, as
    shown in Figure 8-11.

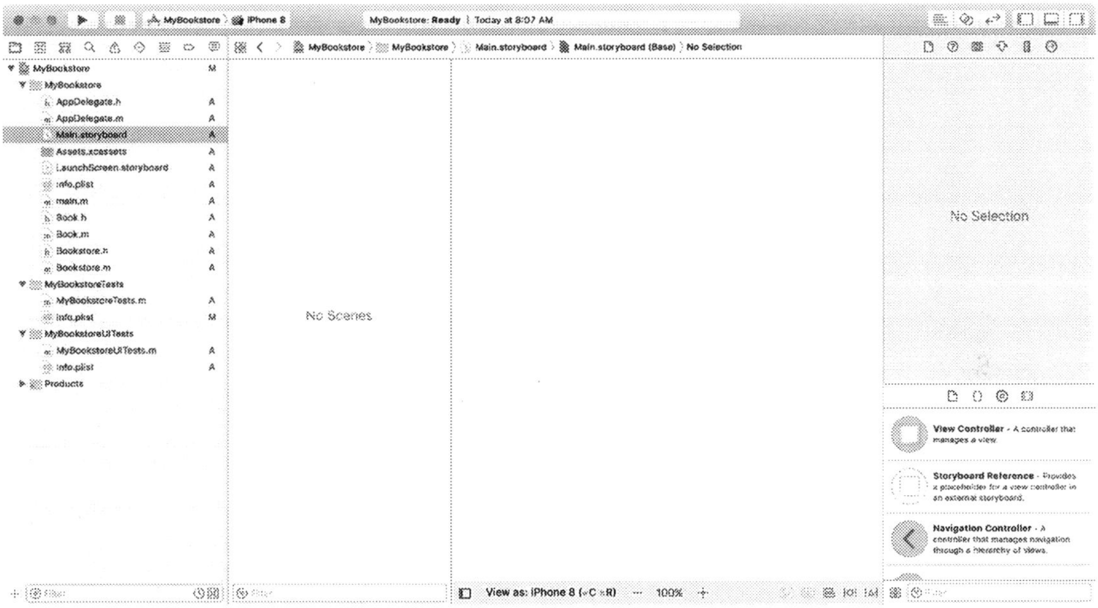

Figure 8-11. *A clean slate and the Utilities pane displayed*

5. Next, you're going to add a new controller scene with what is
    called a **Navigation Controller**. A Navigation Controller allows
    the user to navigate from one view controller to another. Just click
    and drag the Navigation Controller object from the Utilities pane
    to the empty storyboard canvas, as shown in Figure 8-12. While
    you drag and drop, the little icon with an arrow will expand to two
    views: one is the base Navigation Controller, and the second one
    is an empty View Controller. It can be placed anywhere on the
    storyboard window.

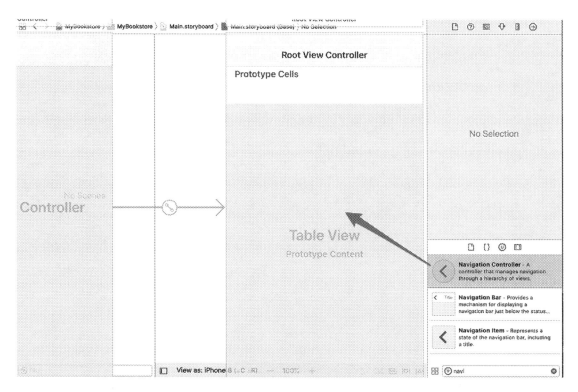

Figure 8-12. *Adding the Navigation Controller object from the Utilities pane to the empty storyboard canvas*

6. This step isn't necessary, but it simplifies things because it makes the views in your storyboard fit on the screen. To do this, simply highlight the Navigation Controller. At the bottom of the screen, make sure iPhone 8 is selected, as show in Figure 8-13.

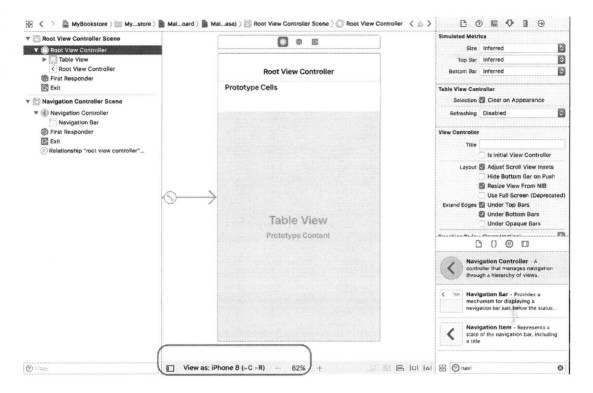

Figure 8-13. *(Optional) Shrinking the views*

7. Next, click the Root View Controller scene, which will then switch over to that view, as shown in Figure 8-14. This is the view where you will be starting all your work. You now have something called a Root View Controller, which is the first screen that will show up in your app. Initially, this View Controller is completely set up as the default, meaning that it's not connected to any of your code. In the next section you will create a new View Controller class and associate it with this new view.

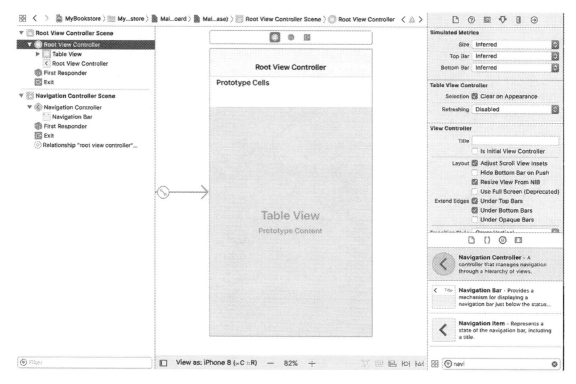

Figure 8-14. *Start all your work with this view*

Creating the Initial View

The first view you will be creating is the view that will contain your list of books. This is a view called a Table View, and it displays rows of information in a single column. You have your view in the storyboard, but you now need to create your controller class. The controller class is responsible for taking information, in this case the list of books, and placing it into the Table View.

First, you need to create the `MainViewController` class. Do this by highlighting the MyBookstore group in the Project Navigator and then clicking the + button to add a new file, as shown in Figure 8-15. Then, select **Cocoa Touch Class**, as shown in Figure 8-16, and click **Next**.

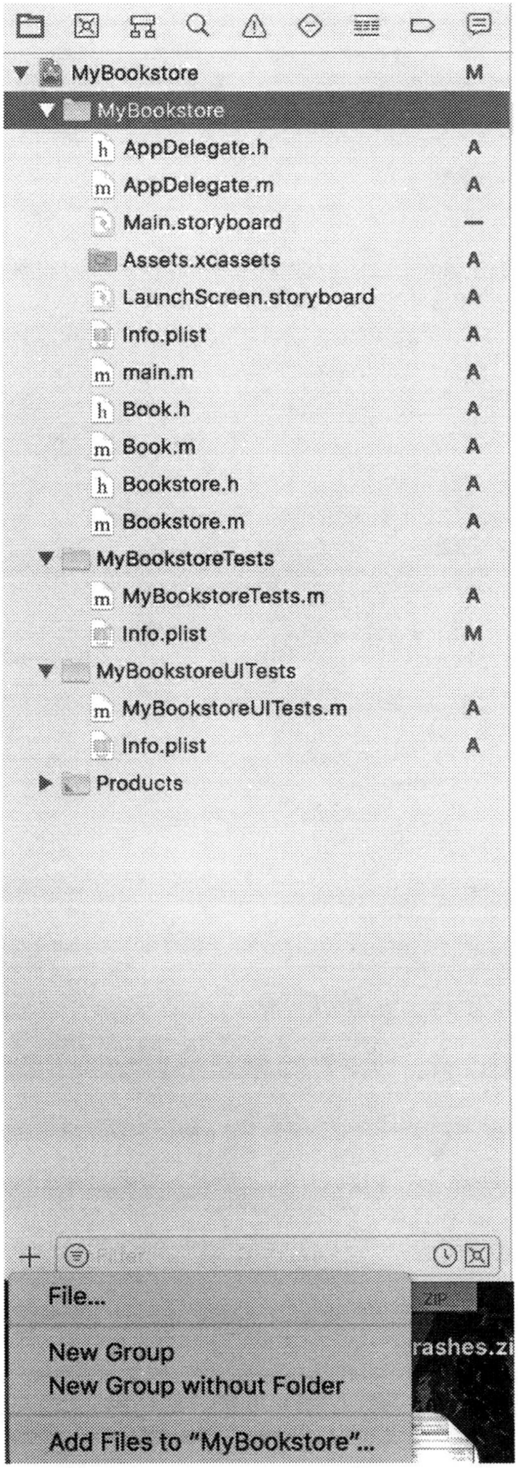

Figure 8-15. *Adding a new file*

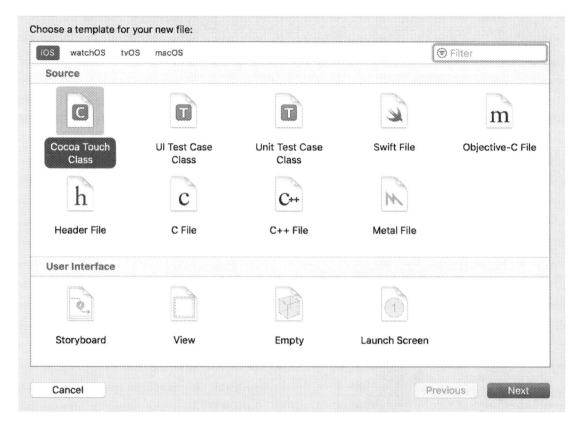

Figure 8-16. *Selecting Cocoa Touch Class*

Next, Xcode will prompt you for a file to create. Type **MainViewController** as the class name, with this being a subclass of UITableViewController, as shown in Figure 8-17. From here, click **Next**. Xcode will then ask you where to save the file. Just click **Create** from here.

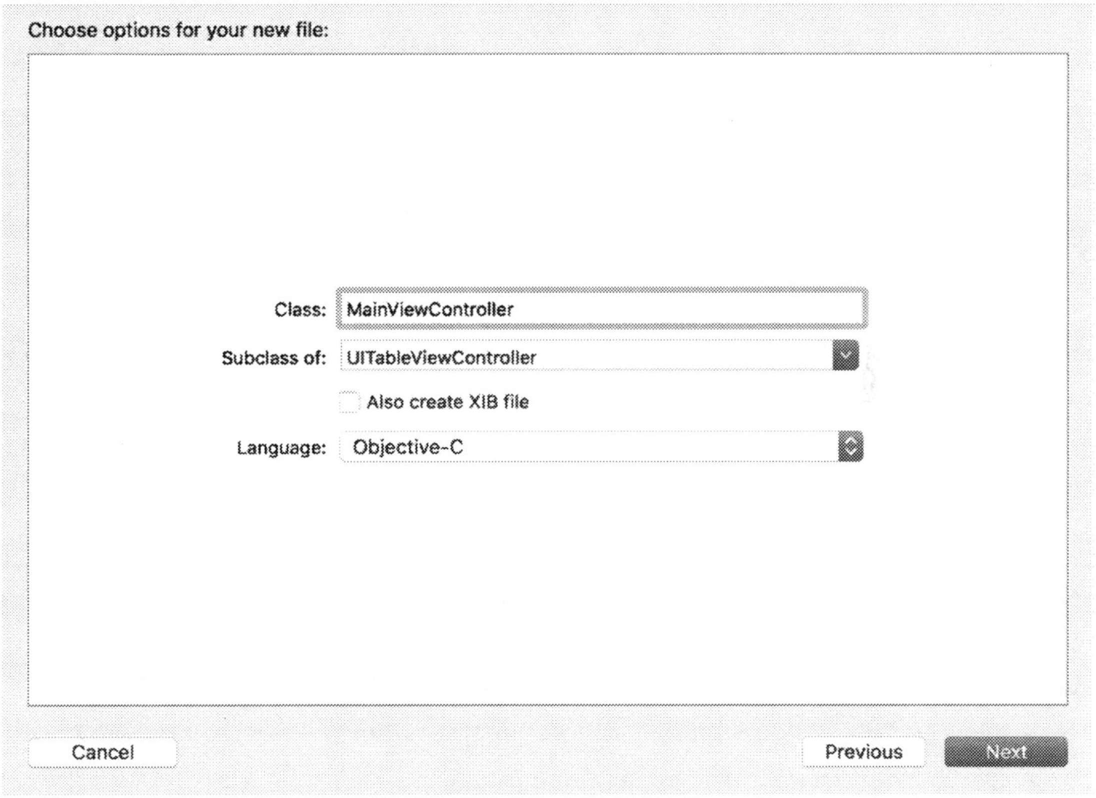

Choose options for your new file:

Class:	MainViewController
Subclass of:	UITableViewController
	Also create XIB file
Language:	Objective-C

Cancel   Previous   Next

Figure 8-17. *Creating the MainViewController class*

Now that the new file has been created, the Xcode screen should look something like Figure 8-18. You can ignore the warnings for now. By default, Xcode adds these warnings because these methods need to be completed.

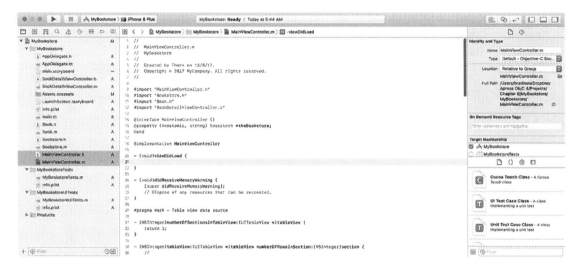

Figure 8-18. *The Xcode screen for the MainViewController class*

Note   View Controller classes are common and are used to control the flow of information from the data model to the actual view. They're also responsible for handling any view-specific actions, like a user selecting a row in your Table View. It's important to keep the data model separate from the View Controller only because it's a better way of partitioning programs.

There is a *lot* of commented-out code in this class because it's a template. It will actually work but doesn't display anything. Before you continue, you need to first let your storyboard Root View Controller know about this new class. This is done back in the storyboard. So, select the Main.storyboard file and make sure that the Root View Controller scene is selected. You should see something like Figure 8-19.

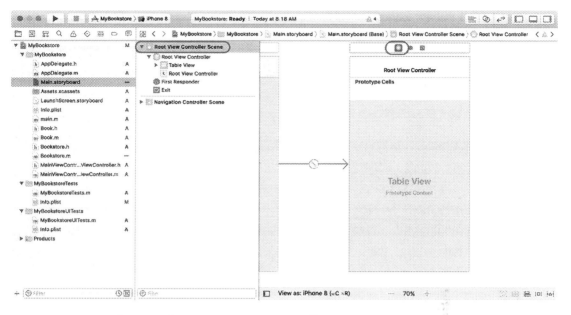

Figure 8-19. *Selecting the Root View Controller*

Next, change the custom class to be the `MainViewController` class, as shown in Figure 8-20.

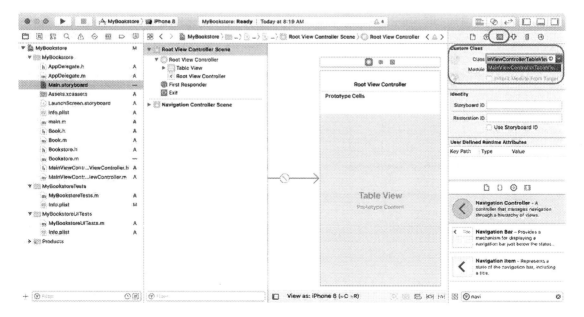

Figure 8-20. *Setting your class as the custom class*

Now your new class, MainViewController, is the controller for the Root View Controller. In the next section, you can add the data model to your new Table View Controller and get it ready to display something.

The Bookstore Object

Before you can display anything on your new view, you will need to create the data model. In this case, this is the Bookstore object. You've already built the Book object; you can find it back in the section that introduced properties.

The Bookstore object is a simple data model that is used to store a list of Book objects. Each Book object contains a title, the author (or the authors), and a brief description. So, let's take a look at the heart of the Bookstore object. Note that the line numbers represent the line number from the source file Bookstore.m in the source code provided with this book. See Listing 8-13.

Listing 8-13. Setting Up the Bookstore Object

```
13   -(instancetype)init
14   {
15       self = [super init];
16       if (self) {
17           self.books = [NSMutableArray new];
18
19           //
20           // Add book requires an array of dictionaries. Each element of the
21           // array contains a dictionary that describes a book.
22           //
23           NSArray *arrayOfBooks = @[   // This starts the array
24
25               //
26               // This is the first book as a dictionary.
27               // It's the first element in the array
28               //
29               @{@"title": @"Objective-C for Absolute Beginners",
30                   @"author": @"Bennett, Fisher and Lees",
31                   @"description": @"iOS Programming made easy."},
```

```
32
33              //
34              // Now we're creating the second dictionary as
35              // the second element of the array.
36              //
37              @{@"title": @"A Farewell To Arms",
38                @"author": @"Ernest Hemingway",
39                @"description": @"The story of an affair between"
40                                   "an English nurse and an"
41                                   "American soldier on the Italian"
42                                   "front during World War I."}
43
44          ]; // End of the array
45
46          [self addBooks:arrayOfBooks];
47      }
48
49      return self;
50  }
```

This method of the Bookstore.m file is called when the Bookstore object is created. In this method, you set up the data for the model; in this case, you are creating two books and storing them in an NSArray. Please refer to the "Collections" section if you need a refresh.

Line 23 begins by creating the NSArray and using the collection literal syntax for an NSArray, which is @[...];. The NSArray contains two NSDictionary objects. These objects are created with the NSDictionary collection literal syntax, which is @{ ... };. Lines 29–31 represent the first book, and lines 37–42 are the second book. Remember that an NSDictionary is stored as a **key: value** pair.

Line 46 is the call to a method named addBooks: that accepts the newly created array. Let's look at that method now; see Listing 8-14.

Listing 8-14. The addBooks: Method

```
57   - (void)addBooks:(NSArray *)bookArray
58   {
59       for (NSDictionary *bookInfo in bookArray) {
60           Book *newBook;
61
62           // Create a new book object.
63           newBook = [Book new];
64           newBook.title = bookInfo[@"title"];
65           newBook.author = bookInfo[@"author"];
66           newBook.bookDescription = bookInfo[@"description"];
67
68           [self.books addObject:newBook];
69       }
70   }
```

This method will go through the array that was created in the init method and create the number of Book objects that are in the array. While you know that there are only two in the init method, the addBooks: method is designed to take in as many as are in the array, making it flexible if more books are added in the init method.

Line 59 is what is called a **for-in** enumerator in that it goes through the array one element at a time. You know that the NSArray that is passed to this method is an array of dictionaries with each dictionary containing information for a book.

```
for (NSDictionary *bookInfo in bookArray)
```

The first argument here is an NSDictionary object. This object is assigned the NSDictionary that is in each element of the array. So, the first element in the array will be the dictionary containing the *Objective-C for Absolute Beginners* book information.

Now that you have the dictionary, lines 63–66 create the Book object and set the Book object's properties to the values from the dictionary.

Line 68 takes the newly created Book object and adds it to the self.books property, which is an NSMutableArray. Remember a mutable object is one that can be modified. In this case, you're adding new elements to what is initially an empty array. Once the for-in enumerator has gone through all the elements in the array, the addBooks: method finishes and returns. In this case, it returns to line 46 in the init method of the Bookstore class.

The last part of this class is the method shown in Listing 8-15.

Listing 8-15. The numberOfBooks Method

```
52   - (NSInteger)numberOfBooks
53   {
54       return self.books.count;
55   }
```

This method simply returns the number of books stored in the self.books array.

Using the Bookstore Object

Now that you have a view set up, you can start adding in your data model. As mentioned, the data model manages your data: the bookstore and the books in that bookstore. In Listing 8-16, you add a property to hold the Bookstore object. The numbers to the side represent the line numbers that can be found in the MainViewController.m file provided in the source code for this book.

Listing 8-16. Setting Up the Bookstore Object

```
 9   #import "MainViewController.h"
10   #import "Bookstore.h"   // <-- This is our Bookstore object include file.
11   #import "BookDetailViewController.h"
12
13   @interface MainViewController ()
14   @property (nonatomic) Bookstore *theBookstore;
15   @end
```

This snippet of code is at the top of the MainViewContoller.m file. Line 10 imports the information for your Bookstore class. That allows MainViewController to use the Bookstore class. If it's not included, Xcode will flag line 13 in error. Speaking of line 13, this line is where you create a property to hold the Bookstore object.

Listing 8-17 shows the viewDidLoad method. This method is called whenever the view is starting up and loaded by iOS.

Listing 8-17. Setting Up the Bookstore Object

```
18  - (void)viewDidLoad {
19      [super viewDidLoad];
20      self.theBookstore = [Bookstore new];
21      self.title = @"My Bookstore"; // This is the title of our main view.
22  }
```

Line 20 creates a new `Bookstore` object and stores it in the property that you defined on line 13. After this method is done, you're all set. Another method that's important to your Table View is to return the number of rows you have to display. The method `tableView:numberOfRowsInSection:` is called by the Table View to get this number (Listing 8-18). This number becomes more important in the following section.

Listing 8-18. Returning the Number of Rows to Display

```
39  - (NSInteger)tableView:(UITableView *)tableView numberOfRowsInSection:(
    NSInteger)section
40  {
41      //
42      // you want to return the number of books we have in the bookstore.
43      // you don't care about the section since there is only one!
44      //
    return self.theBookstore.numberOfBooks;
45  ..}
```

Preparing the Table View

One thing that you need to do is to set up the Table View in the storyboard. In this case, you're going to give a row in the Table View an identifier. In the storyboard, the Table View has just a single row shown. This is a template row that will be used for each row in the Table View. To help manage multiple rows, the Table View uses this identifier, as shown in Figure 8-21.

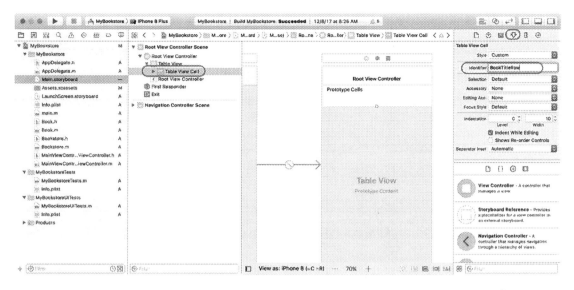

Figure 8-21. *Setting up the Table View Row*

This identifier, `BookTitleRow`, now needs to be added in the `MainViewController` class so that the Table View knows what identifier to look for.

In Listing 8-19, lines 60–61 **dequeue** the cell. This is the way that the Table View manages and reuses rows. The important part of this line is the `BookTitleRow` identifier being used. It's important that the name that is use here is the same as the one added to the Table View Row in the storyboard, as shown in Figure 8-21.

Listing 8-19. Reusing the Row and Getting a Book Title

```
48    - (UITableViewCell *)tableView:(UITableView *)tableView
49             cellForRowAtIndexPath:(NSIndexPath *)indexPath
50    {
51        //
52        // A UITableViewCell is a row in the UITableView. We want to display
53        // a book title in each row. This method is called for every book
54        // in the bookstore (see tableView:numberOfRowsInSection:). That method
55        // returns the number of rows that the UITableView should show - this
56        // is the number of books in the Bookstore object.
57        //
58        // We start by getting the cell from our Main.storyboard file. This is
59        // the UITableViewCell "Identifier" found in the Storyboard.
```

```
60      UITableViewCell *cell =
61          [tableView dequeueReusableCellWithIdentifier:@"BookTitleRow"];
62
63      //
64      // Get the book in the Bookstore. The indexPath.row is set to the
row
65      // we are going to display.
66      Book *book = self.theBookstore.books[indexPath.row];
67
68      //
69      // Once we have the book, we want to show its title in the
        UITableViewCell.
70      // There is a titleLabel already built in to the UITableViewCell so
        we use
71      // that. The titleLabel has a text attribute we can set to an NSString.
72      cell.textLabel.text = book.title;
73
74      //
75      // Return the cell that has been setup for this row.
76      return cell;
77  }
```

Line 66 gets a Book object from the Bookstore object stored in the self. theBookstore property. The Bookstore object has a property named books that represents the NSArray of Book objects that were created when you loaded your Table View. If you look back at Listing 8-15, you can see that the Table View knows the number of rows to display based upon the number of books in your Bookstore object. This count applies directly here. In the method from Listing 8-16, the NSIndexPath object will contain a row number. This row number will be from 0 to self.theBookstore. numberOfBooks-1 (refer to Listing 8-15). This makes indexPath.row a direct correlation between a row in the Table View and a row in the Bookstore object.

Line 72 sets the title of the cell (which is a row in a Table View) to the title of the book.

The Book Detail View

Now that you have the list of books in the Table View complete, it's time to go to the next step and create the Detail View. This is a view that displays more information about the book when the user taps it.

1. The first step is to add a new view controller to the storyboard (Figure 8-22).

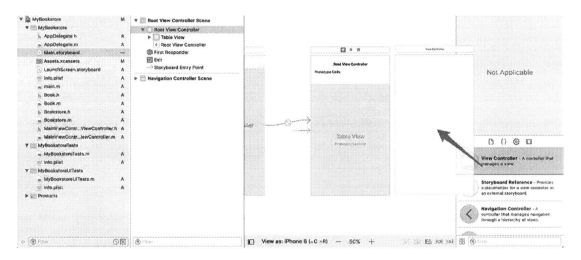

Figure 8-22. *Adding in the details view controller*

2. Drag the new **View Controller** around the canvas until things look like Figure 8-23.

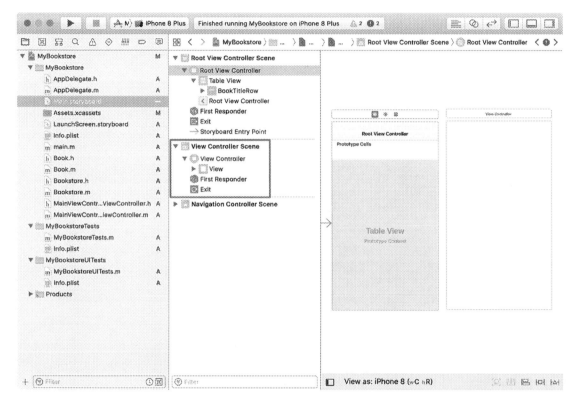

Figure 8-23. *The newly added View Controller*

3. You will notice that there is a new scene in the storyboard; it's just called the View Controller scene, and it represents the view you just added to the storyboard. The next step for you to do is to link this new View Controller to be displayed whenever you click the Table View Row. You do this by Control-dragging from the BookTitleRow to the blank area of the new View Controller, as shown in Figure 8-24. This means you press and hold the Control key on the keyboard and click and drag the mouse from the BookTitleRow to anywhere on the empty area of the new View Controller.

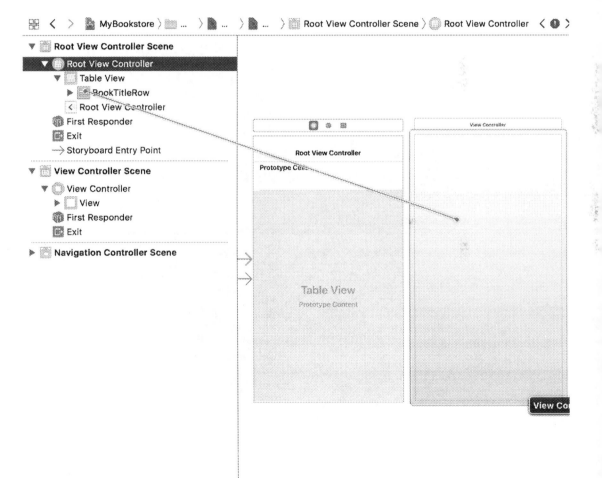

Figure 8-24. *Connecting the Table View to the Detail View*

4. Once the mouse reaches the new area, release it. What you're doing here is creating a link between the Table View Row to the new View Controller, which will become your Book Details View. This link will make it so that when the user taps one of the books from the main view, the details view will be shown.

5. Once the drop on the view occurs, a menu will be displayed. This menu contains, among other things, items for what is called the **selection segue**, as shown in Figure 8-25. First, a **segue** is basically a transition from one thing to another. In this case, it's a transition from the main Root View Controller Scene to the View Controller Scene.

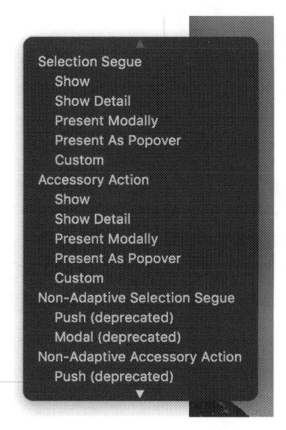

Figure 8-25. *The Selection Segue menu*

6. The Selection Segue menu is the only thing you are concerned
    with here. It deals with transitioning between two scenes because
    of a selection. In this case, it's the user selecting a row in the Table
    View. Click the **Show** option in the Selection Segue menu, and
    you will see something like Figure 8-26. You can move the View
    Controller around so that it matches Figure 8-26 just to keep the
    lines straight, but this is completely optional.

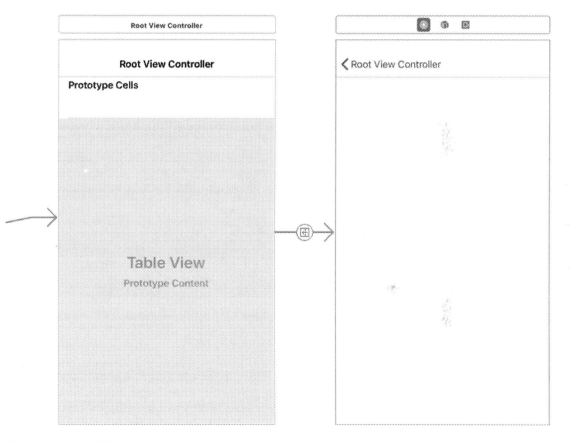

Figure 8-26. *The segue is now connecting the two views*

7. At this point, you can run the application to see how things are
    shaping up. Just click the **Run** button (or press Command-R)
    to build and run the application. It should look something like
    Figure 8-27. And by tapping one of the titles, the view should
    transition from the main view to what is now a blank view.

Carrier 🛜   8:04 AM   ▬▬

Objective-C for Abso

A Farewell To Arms

Figure 8-27. *A first look at your app*

8. So, the next step is to make the details view actually do a little more work. First, you need to give the segue you created earlier an identifier. Before you do this, make sure the application that is running is stopped. To do this, just click the **Stop** button in the Xcode window. Next, click the segue so the identifier can be added.

9. Name the segue identifier **BookDetailsSegue**, as shown in Figure 8-28. The identifier can be anything, but it's best to make the segue identifier meaningful. While you have just one segue in this example, you can create an app that has many segues. Naming is very important.

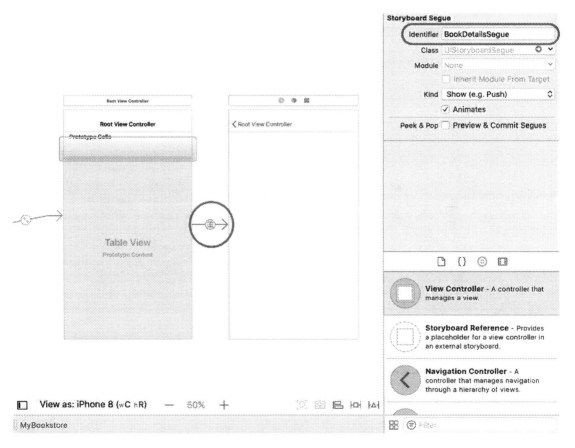

Figure 8-28. *Setting the segue identifier*

10.   Next, you need to create a new ViewController class that will be used for the details view, which is the blank View Controller. To do this, click the + in the Project Navigator and add a new Cocoa Touch class to the project named BookDetailViewController, as shown in Figure 8-29.

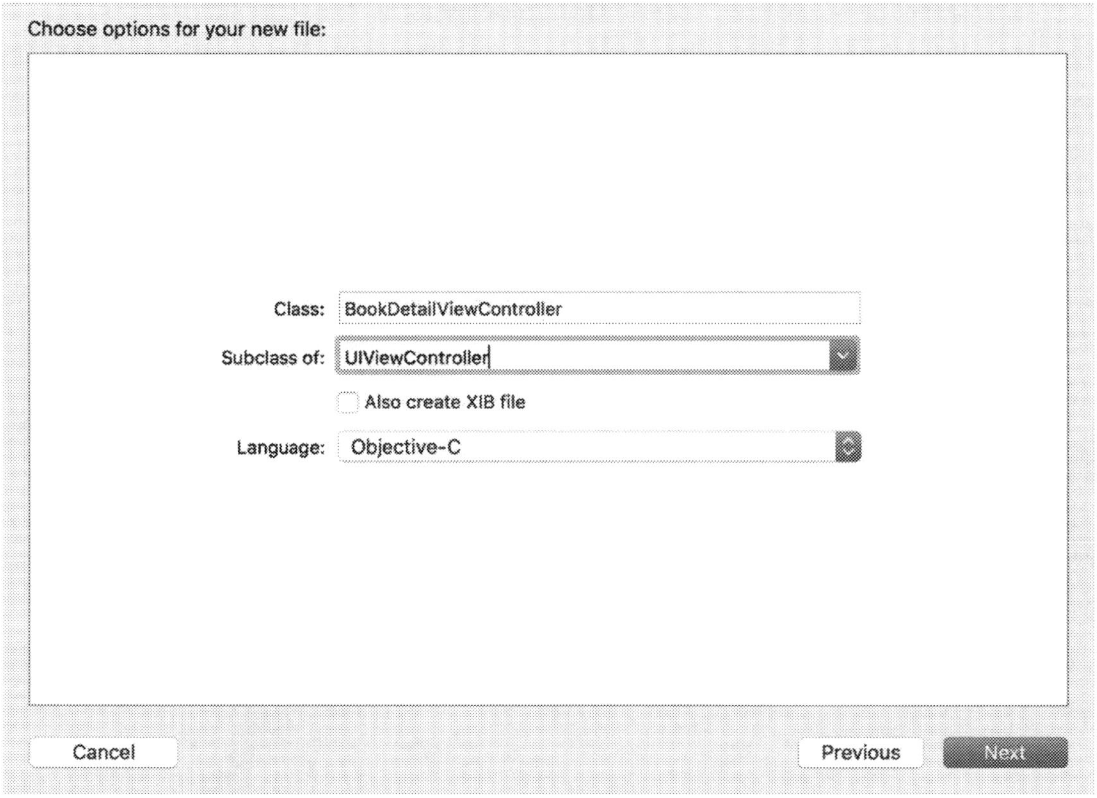

Choose options for your new file:

Class:	BookDetailViewController
Subclass of:	UIViewController
	☐ Also create XIB file
Language:	Objective-C

Cancel   Previous   Next

Figure 8-29. *Adding the BookDetailViewController class*

11. Make sure that the new file is a subclass of `UIViewController`.

12. Next, you are going to add some Label views to your detail view so you can see more of the information of the book. But, before you can do this, the detail View Controller needs to be set to use the new `BookDetailViewController` class, as shown in Figure 8-30. Make sure that the `Main.storyboard` file is selected in the Project Navigator.

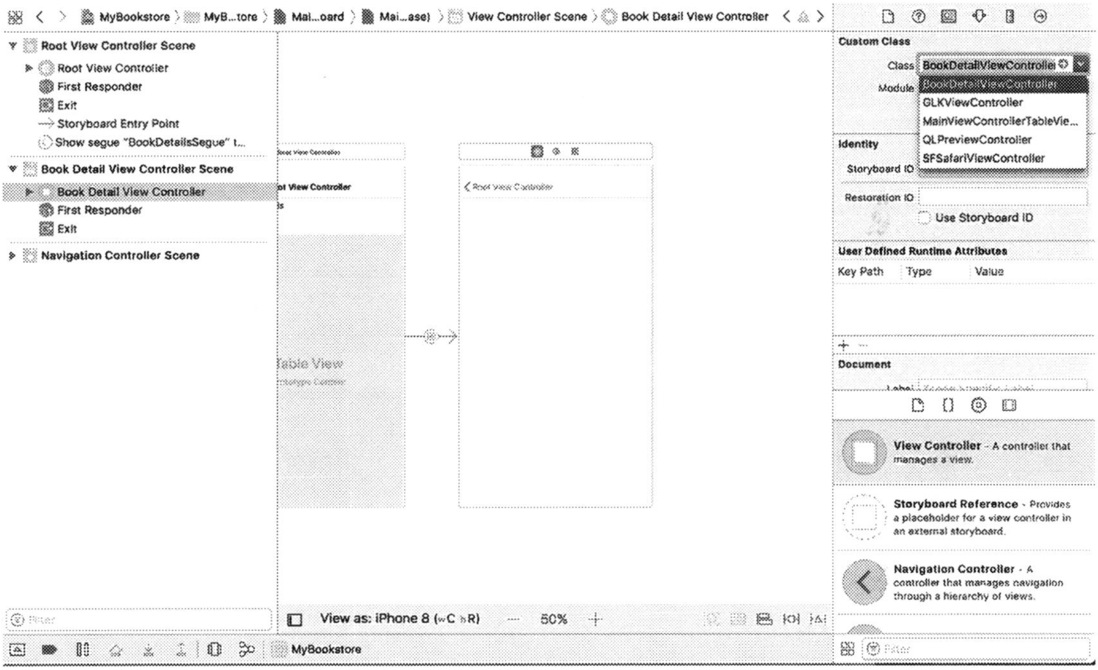

Figure 8-30. *Setting the BookDetailViewController*

13. Now that you have the class assigned, you need to add some
     labels so that you can display the title, authors, and description of
     the book. To start this, drag and drop some **Label** views from the
     Object Library to the Book Details View Controller, as shown in
     Figure 8-31.

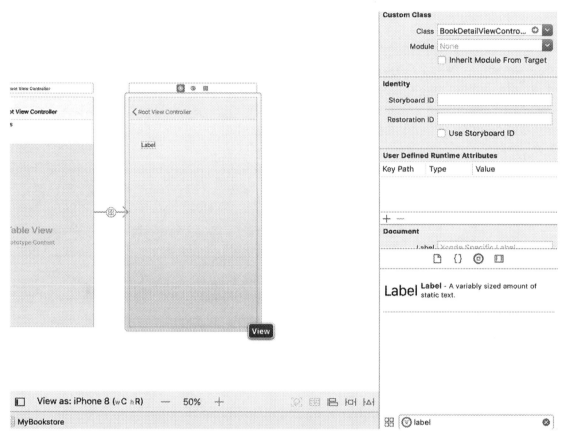

Figure 8-31. *Adding your first label*

14. Expand the label's size by dragging the "handles" so that it is
roughly 3/4 the width of the view, as shown in Figure 8-32.

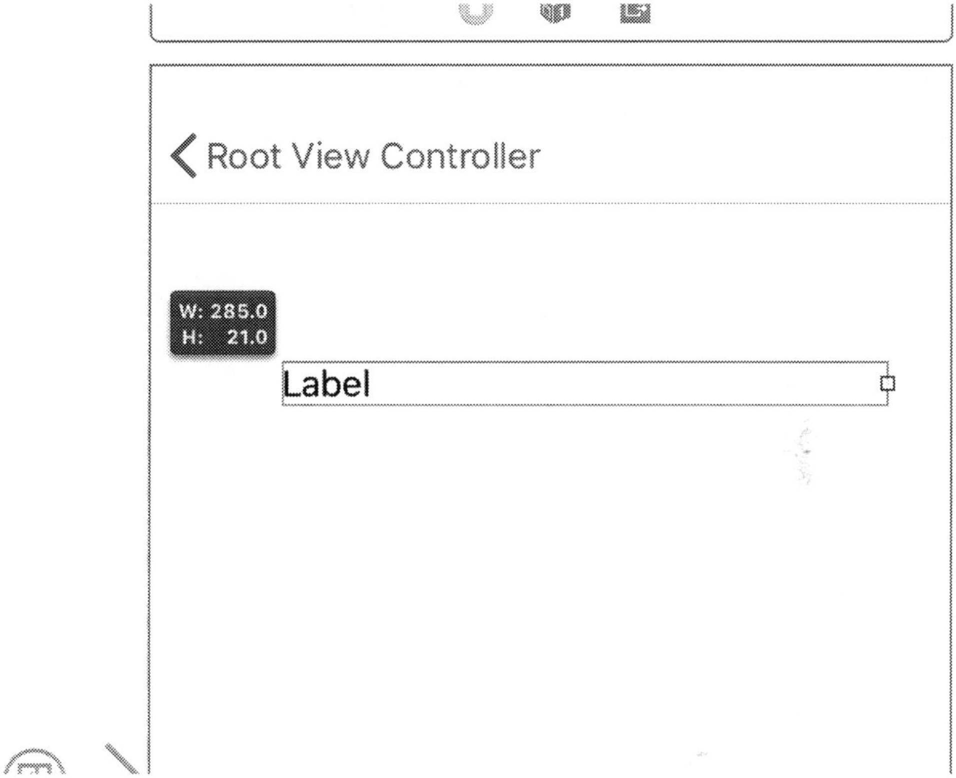

Figure 8-32. *Expanding the label*

15.   This will provide enough room for the titles of the fields. Repeat this process until your view looks like Figure 8-33.

Figure 8-33. *Three labels*

16. Next, change the titles of these labels to be **Title**, **Author(s)**, and **Description**. To do this, click a label and change the text, as shown in Figure 8-34.

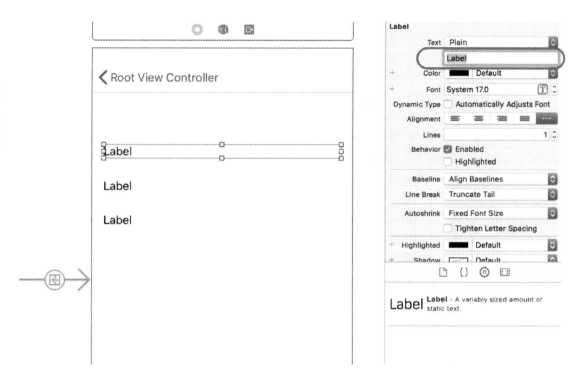

Figure 8-34. *Changing the label text*

17. After changing all the labels, they should now contain all of the titles (Title, Author(s), and Description), as shown in Figure 8-35.

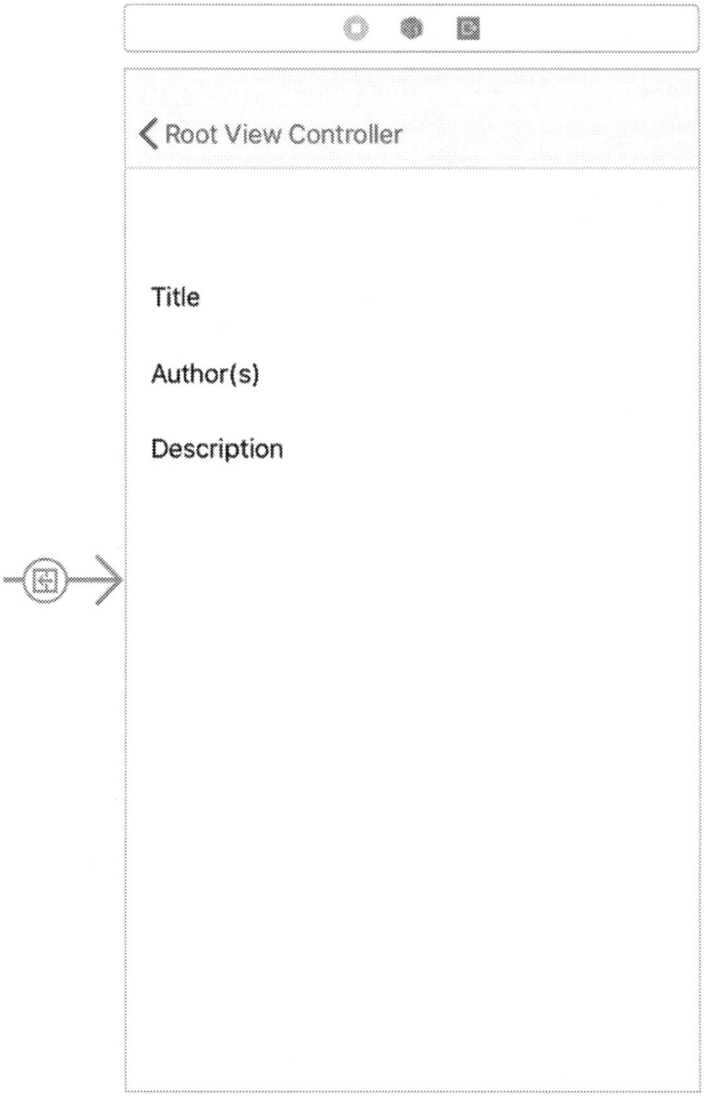

Figure 8-35. *Changing the label text*

18. Repeat the steps of creating and sizing labels and add them to the view so there are three more labels that are sized as shown in Figure 8-36. You also want to expand the bottom label to be slightly larger, as shown in Figure 8-37.

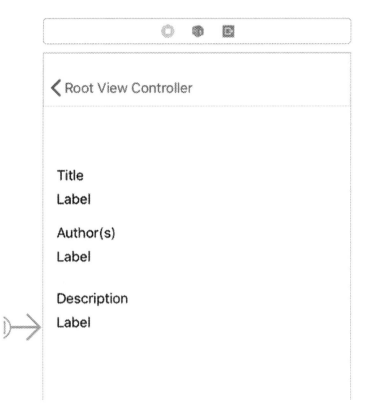

Figure 8-36. *Adding the remaining labels*

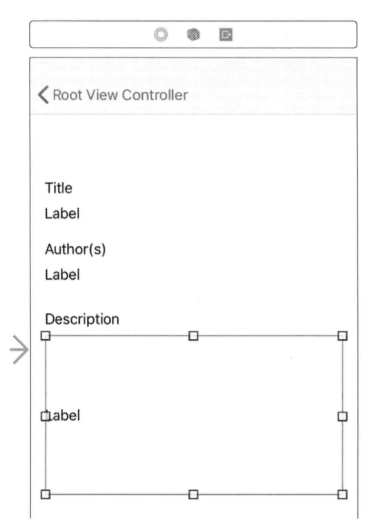

Figure 8-37. *Making the description label larger*

Setting Up the Outlets

Now that the view is all set up, it needs to have real book data. It just has a bunch of placeholder labels. To do this, you need to dive back into the code. Go into the Project Navigator and select the BookDetailViewController.h file. You are going to add three properties that will hold the book details but also show this detail information (Listing 8-20).

Listing 8-20. Adding Outlets to Show the Information

```
1   //
2   //   BookDetailViewController.h
3   //   MyBookstore
4   //
5   //   Created by Thorn on 12/10/17.
6   //   Copyright © 2017 MyCompany. All rights reserved.
7   //
8
9   #import <UIKit/UIKit.h>
10
11  @interface BookDetailViewController : UIViewController
12
13  @property (nonatomic, weak) IBOutlet UILabel *bookTitle;
14  @property (nonatomic, weak) IBOutlet UILabel *bookAuthor;
15  @property (nonatomic, weak) IBOutlet UILabel *bookInfo;
16
17  @end
```

BookDetailViewController doesn't contain much at this point, but you need to add something that will link the actual book data with the labels that are shown on the screen. To do this, you add three new properties, as shown in Listing 8-20's lines 12–14.

These properties look **almost** like other properties that you have created except for two items: IBOutlet and UILabel. Put simply, the IBOutlet lets Xcode know that this property is an **outlet** for an element on the view. The UILabel is the class that represents a Label object; you're really only concerned with three labels that you added to the Book Details View Controller.

Also, when looking at Xcode, there are three empty circles to the left of the property declarations, as shown in Figure 8-38. These circles represent that these are items that can be hooked up to something on the storyboard. Since they're empty, it means they haven't been connected to anything. Let's do that next.

```
11   @interface BookDetailViewController : UIViewController
12
○    @property (nonatomic, weak) IBOutlet UILabel *bookTitle;
○    @property (nonatomic, weak) IBOutlet UILabel *bookAuthor;
○    @property (nonatomic, weak) IBOutlet UILabel *bookInfo;
16
17   @end
18
```

Figure 8-38. *Empty outlet circles*

From the Book Detail View Controller, Control-drag from the first icon (which represents the BookDetailViewController class) to the first label, as shown in Figure 8-39. When dropped, the outlet menu is displayed as shown in Figure 8-40. For the label under "Title," choose the bookTitle outlet. Repeat this same process for the other labels, choosing bookAuthor for the second label and bookInfo for the third label.

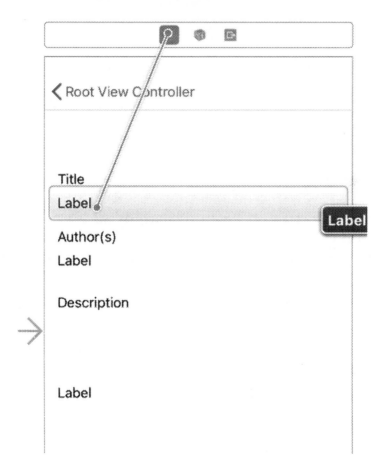

Figure 8-39. *Connecting up the first label*

Figure 8-40. *Available outlets*

Going back to the `BookDetailViewController.h` file, the connection circles should now be filled in, as shown in Figure 8-41.

```
11   @interface BookDetailViewController : UIViewController
12
     @property (nonatomic, weak) IBOutlet UILabel *bookTitle;
     @property (nonatomic, weak) IBOutlet UILabel *bookAuthor;
     @property (nonatomic, weak) IBOutlet UILabel *bookInfo;
16
17   @end
```

Figure 8-41. *The outlets are now connected.*

Plugging in the Book Details

Now that the outlets are all connected, you can add the necessary code that will put the book information into the labels you added in the previous steps. To start, go to the Project Navigator and select the `MainViewController.m` file.

You need to add the code that will determine which book the user selected and then store that into the details view. To accomplish this, you implement a method called `prepareForSegue:`. This method is called whenever a segue is chosen (Listing 8-21).

Listing 8-21. Plugging in the Book Details

```
80  - (void)prepareForSegue:(UIStoryboardSegue *)segue sender:(id)sender
81  {
82      if ([segue.identifier isEqualToString:@"BookDetailsSegue"]) {
83      BookDetailViewController *detailViewController = segue.
        destinationViewController;
84      [detailViewController view];
85      NSIndexPath *selectedRow = [self.tableView indexPathForSelectedRow];
86
87      Book *selectedBook = self.theBookstore.books[selectedRow.row];
88
89      detailViewController.bookTitle.text = selectedBook.title;
90      detailViewController.bookAuthor.text = selectedBook.author;
91      detailViewController.bookInfo.text = selectedBook.bookDescription;
92
93      detailViewController.bookInfo.numberOfLines = 0;
94      }
95  }
```

The lines of importance are really lines 89–91. These lines put the fields from the
Book object to the labels on the details view via the outlets you created earlier. When you
see detailViewController.bookTitle.text, the .text represents the property of the
UILabel that you need to set in order to see the value in the actual label on the view. You
assign the label's text property to selectedBook.title, author, or bookDescription.

Line 93 is used to let the UILabel know that it can span multiple lines. This is
necessary so you can see the information of a book that is too long. Otherwise, the label
will simply keep it to one line and not display the remainder of the information.

So now, when the app is run, you should see Figure 8-42 and then Figure 8-43. Selecting a row will transition to the detail view as seen in Figure 8-43.

Figure 8-42. *The main view*

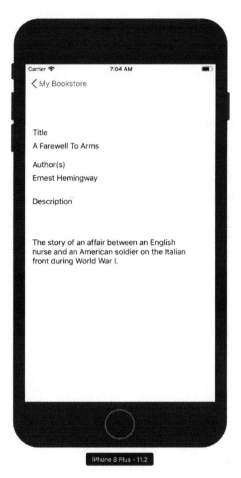

Figure 8-43. *A Farewell to Arms detail*

Summary

You've finally reached the end of this chapter! Here is a summary of the things we covered:

- *Understanding collection classes:* Collection classes are a powerful set of classes that come with the Foundation and allow you to store and retrieve information efficiently.

- *Using properties*: Properties are variables that are defined in the interface file of the class and are accessible once the class has been instantiated.

- *Working with properties*: Properties are short ways of creating getters and/or setters. Getters and setters get or set the values of the underlying instance variable.

- *Looping with* `for-in`*:* This feature offers a new way to iterate through an enumerated list of items.

- *Using a storyboard to build an interface:* The storyboard is nothing more than a collection of views that makes it easy to create an app.

- *A simple data model:* Using the `Collection` classes you learned about, you used an `NSMutableArray` to construct a `Bookstore` object and used it as a data source in your bookstore program.

- *Connect data to the view:* You connected your `Book` object's data to the interface fields using Xcode.

Exercises

Perform the following tasks:

- Add more books to the bookstore using the original program as a guide.

- Enhance the `Book` class so it can store another attribute, such as a price or ISBN number.

- Modify `BookDetailViewController` so that the new fields are displayed. Remember to connect an interface control to an outlet.

- Change the `Bookstore` object so that a separate method is called to initialize the list of `Book` objects (instead of putting them all in the `init` method).

- There is another attribute of a `UITableViewCell` called the `detailTextLabel`. Make use of this by setting its `text` property to something.

- Using Xcode to modify the interface, play with changing the background color of the `DetailViewController.xib` file.

For a tougher challenge:

- Sort the books in the `Bookstore` object so they appear in ascending order on the `MasterDetailView`.

CHAPTER 9

Comparing Data

In this chapter, we will discuss one of the most basic and frequent operations you will perform as you program: comparing data. In the bookstore example, you may need to compare book titles if your clients are looking for specific books. You may also need to compare authors if your clients are interested in purchasing books by specific authors. Comparing data is a common task performed by developers. Many of the loops you learned about in the previous chapter will require you to compare data so that you know when your code should stop looping.

Comparing data in programming is like using a scale. You have one value on one side and another value on the other side. In the middle is an operator. The operator determines what kind of comparison is being done. Examples of operators are "greater than," "less than," and "equal to."

The values on either side of the scale are usually variables. You learned about the different types of variables in Chapter 3. In general, the comparison functions for different variables will be slightly different. It is imperative that you become familiar with the functions and syntax to compare data, as this will form a basis for your development.

For the purpose of this chapter, we'll use the bookstore application. This application will allow users to log into the application, search for books, and purchase them. We will relate the different ways of comparing data to show how they would be used in this type of application.

Revisiting Boolean Logic

In a previous chapter, we introduced Boolean logic. Because of its prevalence in programming, we will revisit this subject in this chapter and go into more detail.

© Stefan Kaczmarek, Brad Lees, Gary Bennett, Mitch Fisher 2018
S. Kaczmarek et al., *Objective-C for Absolute Beginners*, https://doi.org/10.1007/978-1-4842-3429-7_9

The most common comparison that you will program your application to perform is Boolean logic. Boolean logic usually comes in the form of if then statements. Boolean logic can have only one of two answers: yes or no. The following are some good examples of Boolean questions that you will use in your applications:

- Is 5 larger than 3?

- Does "now" have more than five letters?

- Is 6/1/2010 later than today?

Notice that there are only two possible answers to these questions: yes and no. If you are asking a question that could have more than two answers, that question will need to be worded differently for programming.

Each of these questions will be represented by an if then statement (for example, if 5 is greater than 3, then print a message to the user). Each if statement is required to have some sort of relational operator. A relational operator can be something like "is greater than" or "is equal to."

To start using these types of questions in your programs, you will first need to become familiar with the different relational operators available to you in the C and Objective-C languages. We will cover them first. After that, we will look into how different variables can behave with these operators.

Using Relational Operators

Objective-C uses six standard relational operators. These are the standard algebraic operators with only one real change: in the Objective-C language, as in most other programming languages, the "equal to" operator is made by two equal signs (==). In Chapter 4, Table 4-7, we described the different operators available to you as a developer.

Note   A single equal sign (=) is used to assign a value to a variable. Two equal signs (==) are needed to compare two values. For example, if(x=9) will assign the value of 9 to the variable x and return "yes" if 9 is successfully assigned to x, which will be in most, if not all, of the cases. if(x==9) will actually do a comparison to see if x equals 9.

Comparing Numbers

One of the difficulties developers had in the past was dealing with different data types in comparisons. Earlier in this book, we discussed the different types of variables. You may remember that 1 is an integer. If you want to compare an integer with a float such as 1.2, this could cause some issues. Thankfully, Objective-C helps with this. In Objective-C, you can compare any two numeric data types without having to typecast (typecasting is still sometimes needed when dealing with other data types, and we cover this later in the chapter). This allows you to write code without worrying about the numeric data types that need to be compared.

Note   Typecasting is the conversion of a variable from one type to another.

In the bookstore application, you will need to compare numbers in many ways. For example, let's say that the bookstore offers a discount for people who spend more than $30 in a single transaction. You will need to add the total amount the person is spending and then compare this to $30. If the amount spent is larger than $30, you will need to calculate the discount. See the following example:

```
float totalSpent;
int discountThreshold;
int discountPercent;

discountThreshold = 30;
discountPercent = 0;
totalSpent = calculateTotalSpent();

if (totalSpent > discountThreshold) {
    discountPercent = 10;
}
```

Let's walk through the code. First, you declare the variables (totalSpent, discountThreshold, and discountPercent). As discussed in Chapter 3, if the number can contain decimals, you should declare it as a float rather than as an int. You know that discountThreshold and the discountPercent will not contain decimals, so you can declare these as ints. In this example, let's assume that you have a function called calculateTotalSpent, which will calculate the total spent in this current order. You then simply check to see whether the total spent is larger than the discount threshold; if it is, you set the discount percent. Also notice that it was not necessary to tell the code to convert the data when comparing the different numeric data types. As mentioned, this is all handled by Objective-C.

Another action that requires the comparison of numbers is looping. As discussed in Chapter 4, looping is a core action in development, and many loop types require some sort of comparison to determine when to stop. Let's take a look at a for loop:

```
int numberOfBooks;
numberOfBooks = 50;

for (int y = 1; y <= numberOfBooks; y++) {
    doSomething();
}
```

In this example, you iterate, or loop, through the total number of books that you have in the bookstore. The for statement is where the interesting stuff starts to happen. Let's break it down.

```
int y = 1;
```

This portion of the code is declaring y as an int and then assigning it a starting value of 1.

```
y <= numberOfBooks;
```

This portion is telling the computer to check to see whether the counting variable y is less than or equal to the total number of books you have in the store. If y becomes larger than the number of books, the loop will no longer run.

```
y++
```

This portion of code increases y by 1 every time the loop is run.

Creating an Example Xcode App

Now let's create an Xcode application so that you can start comparing numeric data.

1. Launch Xcode. From Finder, go to the Applications folder.

2. Click **Create a New Xcode project** to open a new window. On the left side of that window, under **iOS**, select **Single View App**. Click **Next** (Figure 9-1).

Note   The Single View App template is the most generic and basic of the iOS application types.

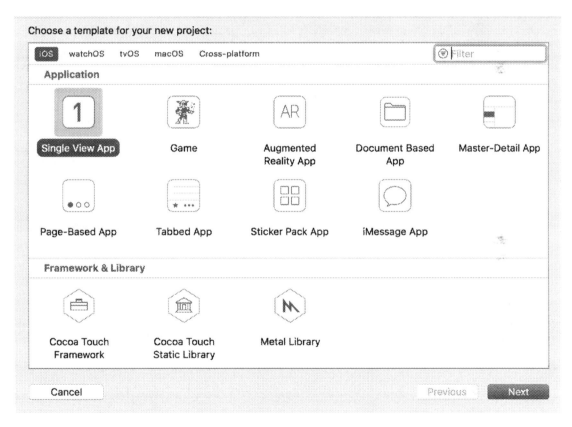

Figure 9-1.   *Creating a new project*

3. On the next page, enter the name of your application. We used
    Comparison as the name, but you can choose any name you like.
    See Figure 9-2.

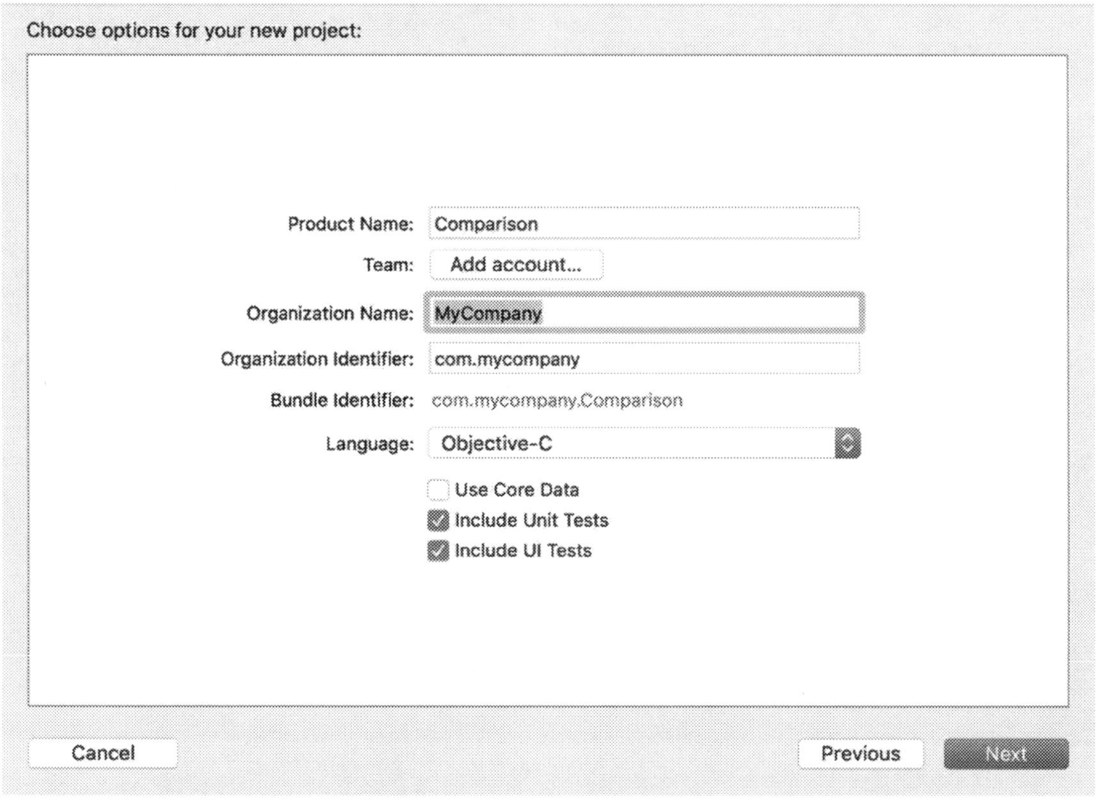

Figure 9-2. *Entering the project name*

Note   Xcode projects, by default, are saved in the Documents folder in your
user home.

---

4. Click **Next** and choose a location to save your project. Once the
    new project is created, you will see the standard Xcode window.
    In the Comparison folder, you will see several files including
    AppDelegate.m and AppDelegate.h. The .h file is a header file,
    and you will not be changing anything in that file at this moment.
    For these examples, you will focus on the AppDelegate.m file.

5. Click the AppDelegate.m file and you will see the following code:

```
#import "AppDelegate.h"

@interface AppDelegate ()

@end

@implementation AppDelegate

- (BOOL)application:(UIApplication *)application didFinishLaunching
WithOptions:(NSDictionary *)launchOptions {
    // Override point for customization after application launch.
    return YES;
}
```

6. At this point, the application will just launch and display a
    window. You are going to add a little "Hello World" to your
    application. After the line // Override point for customization
    after application launch, add the following code:

```
NSLog(@"Hello World");
```

This line creates a new NSString with the contents "Hello World" and passes it to the NSLog function that is used for debugging.

Let's run the application to see how it works.

1. Click the **Run** button in the default toolbar.

2. The iOS simulator will launch. This will just display a window.
    Back in Xcode, a debug window will appear at the bottom of the
    screen, as shown in Figure 9-3. You can always toggle this window
    by selecting **View ➤ Debug Area ➤ Activate Console**.

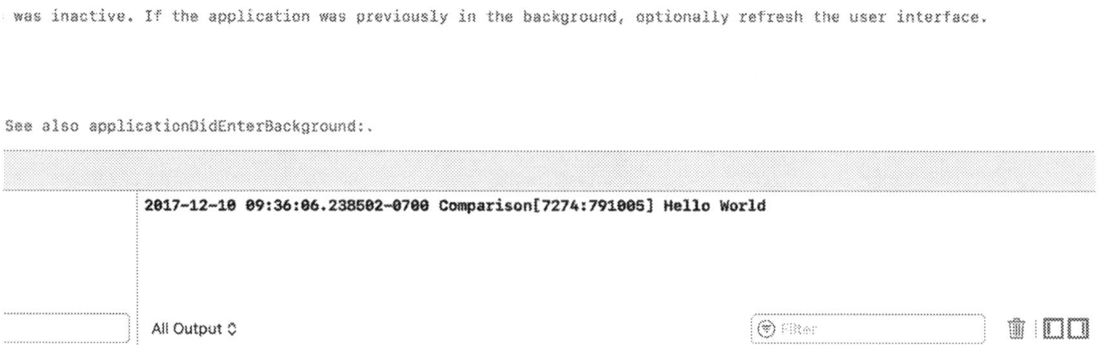

```
was inactive. If the application was previously in the background, optionally refresh the user interface.
```

```
See also applicationDidEnterBackground:.
```

```
2017-12-10 09:36:06.238502-0700 Comparison[7274:791005] Hello World
```

All Output ◇   ⊛ Filter   🗑 | ⬜⬜

Figure 9-3. Debugger window

Most of the information in this window will mean very little to you. The most important line is the bold section that shows the output of your application. The first part of the line shows the date, time, and name of the application. The "Hello World" part was generated by the NSLog line that you added before.

1. Go back to the AppDelegate.m file.

2. Go to the beginning of the line that begins with NSLog. This is the line that is responsible for printing the "Hello World" section. You are going to comment out this line by placing two forward slashes (//) in front of the line of code. Commenting out code tells Xcode to ignore it when it builds and runs the application. Code that is commented out will not run.

3. Once you comment out the line of code, you will no longer see the line in bold if you run the program because the application is no longer outputting that text.

4. For the application to output the results of the comparisons, you will have to add one line:

```
NSLog(@"The result is %@", (6>5 ? @"True" : @"False"));
```

Note   The code snippet of (6>5 ? @"True" : @"False"); is called a **ternary** operation. It is essentially just a simplified way of writing an if/else statement.

---

5. Place this line into your code. This line is telling your application to print out "The result is." Then it will print "True" if 6 is greater than 5, or "False" if 5 is greater than 6. Because 6 is greater than 5, it will print out "True."

You can change this line to test any of the examples you have put together thus far in this chapter, or any of the examples you will see later.

Let's try another example:

```
int i = 5;
int y = 6;
NSLog(@"The result is %@", (y>i ? @"True" : @"False"));
```

In this example, you create an integer variable and assigned its value to 5. You then create another integer variable and assigned the value to 6. You then changed the NSLog example to compare the variables i and y instead of using actual numbers. When you run this example, you will get the result shown in Figure 9-4.

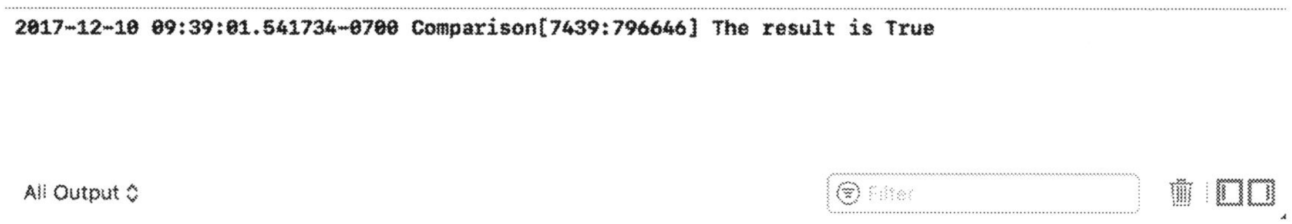

```
2017-12-10 09:39:01.541734-0700 Comparison[7439:796646] The result is True
```

All Output ◇   ⊛ Filter   🗑 ⃒ ☐☐

Figure 9-4. *NSLog output*

Let's explore other kinds of comparisons, and then you will come back to the application and test some of them.

Using Boolean Expressions

A Boolean expression is the easiest of all comparisons. Boolean expressions are used to determine whether a value is true or false. False is defined as 0 and true as non-zero. Here's an example:

```
int j = 5;
if (j) {
    some_code();
}
```

The if statement will always evaluate to true because the variable j is not equal to zero. Because of that, the program will run the some_code() method:

```
int j = 0;
if (j) {
    some_code();
}
```

If you change the value of j, the statement will evaluate to false because j is now 0. This can be used with BOOL and number variables.

```
int j = 0;
if (!j) {
    some_code();
}
```

Placing an exclamation point in front of a Boolean expression will change it to the opposite value (a false becomes a true and a true becomes a false). This line now asks "if not j," which, in this case, is true because j is equal to 0. This is an example of using an integer to act as a Boolean variable. As discussed earlier, Objective-C also has variables called BOOL that have only two possible values: YES or NO.

Note   Many programming languages use the terms TRUE and FALSE instead of YES and NO used by Objective-C.

Let's look at an example related to the bookstore. Say you have a frequent buyers club that entitles all members to a 15 percent discount on all books they purchase. This is easy to check. You simply set the variable clubMember to YES if they are a member and NO if they are not. The following code will apply the discount only to club members:

```
int discountPercent;
BOOL clubMember;

clubMember = NO;
discountPercent = 0;
if (clubMember) {
    discountPercent = 15;
}
```

Comparing Strings

Strings are a difficult data type for most C languages. In ANSI C (or standard C), a string is just an array of characters. Objective-C has taken the development of the string even further and made it an object called the NSString. Many more properties and methods are available when working with an object. Fortunately, NSString has many methods for comparing data, which makes your job much easier.

While developing for the Mac, iPad, Apple TV, and iPhone, you will be able to use both NSStrings and standard C strings. For the purposes of this book, you will focus on comparing the NSString objects. If you have C type strings in your application, they will need to be converted to NSStrings in order to use the code included in this book. Fortunately, this conversion is simple:

```
char *myCString;
NSString *myNSString;

myCString = "testing a string";
myNSString = [NSString stringWithUTF8String: myCString];
```

The first two lines are code you have seen before. They are your variable declarations. You are declaring a standard C string called myCString and an NSString called myNSString. The third line is just a simple initialization of your standard C string. You are assigning a value to it.

The last line is where everything happens. You are assigning your NSString object to be equal to creating a new NSString object, with the value coming from the standard C string you created. Once you have converted all of your standard C strings to NSStrings, you can take advantage of the powerful comparison features provided by the class.

Let's look at another example. This is a much easier and cleaner way to create an NSString. Here, you will compare passwords to see whether you should allow a user to log in:

```
NSString *enteredPassword, *myPassword;

myPassword = @"duck";
enteredPassword = @"Duck";
BOOL continueLogin = NO;

if ([enteredPassword isEqualToString:myPassword]) {
    continueLogin = YES;
}
```

The first line just declares two NSStrings. The next two lines initialize the strings. Remember, before you use any objects, they need to be initialized. In your actual code, you will need to get the enteredPassword string from the user. These lines use a shortcut. Notice the @ symbol before the C-style string. The @ symbol creates a new NSString from the C-style string that follows it.

The next line is the part of the code that actually does the work. You are sending a message to the enteredPassword object asking it if it is equal to the myPassword string. The method always needs to have an NSString passed to it. The example code will always be false because of the capital *D* on the enteredPassword versus the lowercase *d* on the myPassword.

Note   If you need to compare two NSStrings, regardless of case, you simply use the caseInsensitiveCompare method instead of the isEqualToString to see if the result of this method is NSOrderedSame.

There are many other different comparisons you might have to perform on strings. For example, you may want to check the length of a certain string. This is easily done, like so:

```
NSString *enteredPassword;
NSString *myPassword;
myPassword = @"duck";
enteredPassword = @"Duck";
BOOL continueLogin = NO;

if ([enteredPassword length] > 5) {
        continueLogin = YES;
}
```

This code checks to see whether the entered password is longer than five characters.

There will be other times when you will have to search within a string for some data. Fortunately, Objective-C makes this easy to do. NSString provides a function called rangeOfString, which allows you to search within a string for another string. The function rangeOfString takes only one argument, which is the string for which you are searching.

```
NSString *searchTitle, *bookTitle;
searchTitle = @"Sea";
bookTitle = @"2000 Leagues Under the Sea";

if ([bookTitle rangeOfString:searchTitle].location != NSNotFound) {
    // Calling a method to add it to results
    //Do Something Here
}
```

This code is similar to other examples you have examined. This example takes a search term and checks to see whether the book title has that same search term in it. If it does, it adds the book to the results. This can be adapted to allow users to search for specific terms in book titles, authors, or even descriptions.

Note   All string searches are case sensitive by default. If you want to search inside of a string, regardless of the case, you can change the preceding call from

```
[bookTitle rangeOfString:searchTitle];
```

to

```
[bookTitle rangeOfString:searchTitle options:NSCaseInsensitiv
eSearch];
```

For a complete listing of the methods supported by NSString, see the Apple documentation at https://developer.apple.com/documentation/foundation/nsstring.

Comparing Dates

Dates are a fairly complicated variable type in any language; unfortunately, depending on the type of application you are writing, they are common. Objective-C previously used the NSCalendarDate class, but it has been replaced with the more up-to-date NSDate. The NSDate has a lot of nice methods that make comparing dates easy. We will focus on the compare function. The compare function returns an NSComparisonResult, which has three possible values: NSOrderedSame, NSOrderedDescending, or NSOrderedAscending. See Listing 9-1 for an example.

Listing 9-1. The Compare Function

```
NSDate *today = [NSDate date];

// Sale Date as of 10/15/2016
NSString *saleDateString = @"2016-10-15";
NSDateFormatter *dateFormatter = [[NSDateFormatter alloc] init];
[dateFormatter setDateFormat:@"yyyy-MM-dd"];
NSDate *saleDate = [dateFormatter dateFromString:saleDateString];

NSComparisonResult result;
BOOL saleStarted;

result = [today compare:saleDate];

if (result == NSOrderedAscending) {
    // Sale Date is in the future
    saleStarted = NO;
} else if (result == NSOrderedDescending) {
    // Sale Date is in the past
    saleStarted = YES;
} else {
    // Sale Date and Today are the same
    saleStarted = YES;
}
```

This may seem like a lot of work just to compare some dates. Let's walk through the code to make sense of it.

```
NSDate *today = [NSDate date];
NSString *saleDateString = @"2016-10-15";
NSDateFormatter *dateFormatter = [[NSDateFormatter alloc] init];
[dateFormatter setDateFormat:@"yyyy-MM-dd"];
NSDate *saleDate = [dateFormatter dateFromString:saleDateString];
```

Here, you declare two different NSDate objects. The first one, named today, is initialized with the system date or your computer or iPad date. (For the purpose of this example, let's pretend today is July 4, 2016.) The second one, named saleDate, is created from an NSDateFormatter with a date sometime in the future. You will use this date to see whether this sale has begun. We will not go into detail about the initialization of NSDates, but they can be initialized using the NSDateFormatter class similar to what you saw previously.

Note   In most programming languages, dates are dealt with in a specific pattern. They usually start out with the four-digit year followed by a hyphen, then a two-digit month followed by a hyphen, then a two-digit day. If you are using a data format with a time, this data is usually presented in a similar manner. Times are usually presented with the hour, minute, and second, each separated by a colon. Objective-C also has time zone support. The -0700 tells Objective-C that the time is seven hours less than Greenwich Mean Time or Mountain Standard Time.

```
NSComparisonResult result;
```

The results of using the compare function of an NSDate object is an NSComparisonResult. You have to declare an NSComparisonResult to capture the output from the compare function.

```
result = [today compare:saleDate];
```

This simple line runs the comparison of the two dates. It places the resulting NSComparisonResult into the variable called result.

```
if(result == NSOrderedAscending) {
    // Sale Date is in the future
    saleStarted = NO;
} else if (result == NSOrderedDescending) {
    // Sale Date is in the past
    saleStarted = YES;
} else {
    // Sale Date and Today are the same
    saleStarted= YES;
}
```

Now you need to find out what value is in the variable result. To accomplish this, you perform an if statement that compares the result to the three different options for the NSComparisonResult. The first line finds out if the sale date is greater than today's date. This means that the sale date is in the future, and thus the sale has not started. You then set the variable saleStarted to NO. The next line finds out whether the sale date is less than today. If it is, then the sale has started and you set the saleStarted variable to YES. The next line just says else. This captures all other options. You know, though, that the only other option is NSOrderedSame. This means that the two dates are the same, and thus the sale is just beginning.

There are other methods that you can use to compare NSDate objects. Each of these methods will be more efficient at certain tasks. We chose the compare method because it can handle most of your basic date comparison needs.

Note   Remember that an NSDate holds both a date and a time. This can affect your comparisons with dates because it not only compares the date but the time.

Combining Comparisons

As discussed in Chapter 4, sometimes something more complex than a single comparison is needed. This is where logical operators come in. Logical operators enable you to check for more than one different requirement. For example, if you have a special discount for people who are members of your book club and who spend more than $30, you can write one statement to check this, like so:

```
float totalSpent;
int discountThreshold;
int discountPercent;
BOOL clubMember = YES;

discountThreshold = 30;
discountPercent = 0;
totalSpent = calculateTotalSpent();

if (totalSpent > discountThreshold && clubMember) {
    discountPercent = 15;
}
```

This is a combination of two of the examples from earlier. The new comparison line reads as follows: if totalSpent is greater than discountThreshold AND clubMember is true, then you set the `discountPercent` to 15. For this `if` statement to return YES, both items need to be true. `||` can be used instead of `&&` to signify "or." You can change the earlier line to this:

```
if (totalSpent > discountThreshhold || clubMember) {
        discountPercent=15;
}
```

Now this reads as follows: if `totalSpent` is greater than `discountThreshold` **OR** `clubMember` is `true`, then set the discount percent. This will return YES if either of the options is `true`.

You can continue to use the logical operations to string as many comparisons together as you need. In some cases, you may need to group comparisons together using parentheses. This can be more complicated and is beyond the scope of this book.

Using the switch Statement

Up to this point, you've seen several examples of comparing data by simply using the `if` statement or the `if/else` statements:

```
if (someValue == SOME_CONSTANT) {
    ...
} else if (someValue == SOME_OTHER_CONSTANT) {
    ...
} else if (someValue == YET_SOME_OTHER_CONSTANT) {
    ...
}
```

If you need to compare a specific ordinal type to several constant values, you can use a different method that can simplify the comparison code: the `switch` statement.

Note   An ordinal type is a built-in C data type that can be ordered. Examples are `int`, `long`, `char`, and BOOL.

The `switch` statement allows the comparison of one or more constant values against the ordinal data type. This is important to understand. The `switch` statement does not allow the comparison of the ordinal type to a variable. Listing 9-2 shows an example of a proper switch statement.

Listing 9-2. A Proper switch Statement

```
char value;
value = 'd';

switch (value)
{         // The switch statement followed by a begin brace
case 'a':  // Equivalent to if (value == 'a')
    ...       // Call functions and put any other statements here after the
              case.

    ...
    break;  // This indicates that this is the end of the "case 'a':"
case 'b':
    ...

    ...

    break;
case 'c':  // If there is a case without a break, the program continues.
case 'd':  //  If value is a 'c' or a 'd', this code will be executed.
    ...

    ...
break;
default:   // Default is optional and is only used if there is no case
              statement
    ...       // for 'value'. So, if value was equal to 'x', the default part
              of the switch
    ...       // statement will be executed since there is no "case 'x':"
              present.
break;
}  // End of the switch statement.
```

The switch statement is powerful, and it simplifies and streamlines comparisons of an ordinal type to several possible constants. That said, this is also the limiting factor of the switch statement. It is not possible, for example, to use the switch statement to compare an NSString variable to a series of string constants. This is because an

NSString value is not an ordinal type. The switch statement also must compare an ordinal type to a constant. Therefore, it is not possible to write this:

```
switch (value) {
    case variable: // case must be a constant, not a variable.
        ...
        break;
}
```

While it does seem that these are severe limitations to the switch statement, the switch statement is still a powerful statement that can be used to simplify certain if/else statements.

Summary

You've reached the end of the chapter! Here is a summary of the key things that were covered:

- *Comparisons*: Comparing data is an integral part of any application.

- *Integers*: Integers are the easiest pieces of information to compare. You learned how comparison of integers will be used in your programs and how to implement it.

- *Examples*: You created a sample application where you could test your comparisons and make sure that you are correct in your logic. You also learned how to change the application to add different types of comparisons.

- *Boolean*: You learned how to check Boolean values.

- *Strings*: You learned how strings behave differently from other pieces of information you have tested. You learned some of the pitfalls of comparing strings.

Exercises

Perform the following tasks:

- Modify the example application to compare some string information. This can be in the form of either a variable or a literal.

- Create a loop in your application to display a number using the methods you learned in the Boolean portion of the chapter.

- Write an Objective-C app that determines whether the following years are leap years: 1800, 1801, 1899, 1900, 2000, 2001, 2003, and 2010. Output should be written to the console in the following format: "The year 2000 is a leap year." or "The year 2001 is not a leap year."

CHAPTER 10

Creating User Interfaces

Interface Builder is the part of the Xcode application that enables iOS and macOS developers to easily create their user interfaces. It provides the ability to build user interfaces by simply dragging objects from Interface Builder's library to use within your app.

Interface Builder stores your user interface design in one or more resource files. The two types of user interface resource files are **storyboards** and **XIBs**. These resource files represent your app's interface objects and their relationships.

To build a user interface, simply drag objects from Interface Builder's Library pane onto your views. To connect these user interface objects to your app's code, you will use two key components of Interface Builder that help you streamline the development processes: **actions** and **outlets**.

Actions are events (like button clicks) that your view objects trigger that are connected to methods in your app's code. **Outlets** (data pointers) declared in your object's interface file are connected to specific property data members. See Figure 10-1.

© Stefan Kaczmarek, Brad Lees, Gary Bennett, Mitch Fisher 2018
S. Kaczmarek et al., *Objective-C for Absolute Beginners*, https://doi.org/10.1007/978-1-4842-3429-7_10

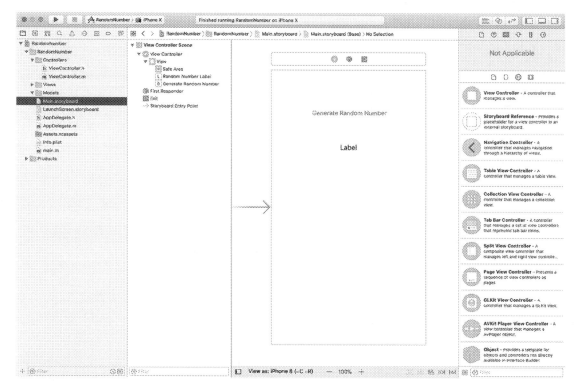

Figure 10-1. *Interface Builder*

Understanding Interface Builder

Interface Builder saves the user interface files as one or more bundles that contain the interface objects and relationships used in the application. These bundles have the file extension .storyboard or .XIB.

Unlike most other graphical user interface applications, storyboards and XIBs are often referred to as "freeze-dried" because they contain the archived objects themselves and are ready to run.

Storyboards and XIBs utilize the XML file format in order to better facilitate storage with source control systems like Subversion and Git.

In the next section, we'll discuss an app design pattern called Model-View-Controller. This design pattern enables developers to easily maintain code and reuse objects over the life of an app.

The Model-View-Controller

Model-View-Controller (MVC) is the most prevalent design pattern used in iOS and macOS development, and learning about it will make your life as a developer much easier. MVC is used in various other types of software development and is known as an **architectural pattern**.

Architectural patterns describe solutions to software design problems that developers can use in their code. The MVC pattern is not unique to Apple OOP developers; it has been adopted by many makers of IDEs, including those running on Windows and Linux platforms.

Software development is considered an expensive and risky venture for businesses. Frequently, apps take longer than expected to write, come in over budget, and don't work as promised. OOP produced a lot of hype and gave the impression that companies would realize savings if they adopted its methodology, primarily because of the reusability of objects and easier maintainability of the code. Initially, this didn't happen.

As engineers looked at why OOP wasn't living up to these expectations, they discovered a key shortcoming with how developers were designing their objects: developers were frequently mixing objects together in such a way that the code became difficult to maintain as the application matured, as the application moved to different platforms, or as hardware displays changed.

Objects were often designed so that, if any of the following changed, it was difficult to isolate the objects that were impacted:

- Business rules
- User interface
- Client-server communication

Objects can be broken down into three task-related categories. It is the responsibility of the developer to ensure that each of these categories keeps their objects from drifting across to other categories.

- *Models*: Data objects
- *Views*: User interface objects
- *Controllers*: Objects that communicate with both the models and the views

As objects are categorized in these groups, apps can be developed and maintained more easily over time. The following are examples of objects and their associated MVC category for an iPhone banking application:

Model:

- Account balances
- User encryption
- Account transfers
- Account login

View:

- Account balances table cell
- Account login spinner control

Controller:

- Account balance view controller
- Account transfer view controller
- Logon view controller

The easiest way to remember and classify your objects in the MVC paradigm is the following:

> *Model*: Unique business or application rules or data that represent the real world

> *View*: Unique user interface code

> *Controller*: Anything that controls or communicates with the model or view objects

Figure 10-2 represents the MVC paradigm.

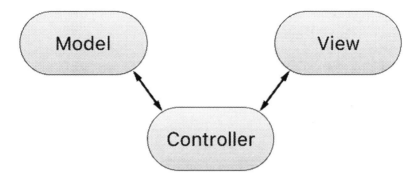

Figure 10-2. *MVC paradigm*

Neither Xcode nor Interface Builder force developers to use the MVC design pattern. It is up to the developer to organize their objects in such a way to use this design pattern.

It is worth mentioning that Apple *strongly* embraces the MVC design pattern and all of the frameworks are designed to work in an MVC world. This means that if you also embrace the MVC design pattern, working with Apple's classes will be much easier. If you don't, you'll be swimming upstream.

Human Interface Guidelines

Before you get too excited and begin designing dynamic user interfaces for your app, you need to learn some of the ground rules. Apple has developed one of the most advanced operating systems in the world with the iOS operating system. Additionally, Apple's products are known for being intuitive and user-friendly. Apple wants users to have the same experience from one app to the next.

To ensure a consistent user experience, Apple provides developers guidelines on how their apps should look and feel. These guidelines, called the Human Interface Guidelines (HIG), are available for iOS, macOS, watchOS, tvOS, and CarPlay. You can download these docs at `https://developer.apple.com/design/`. See Figure 10-3.

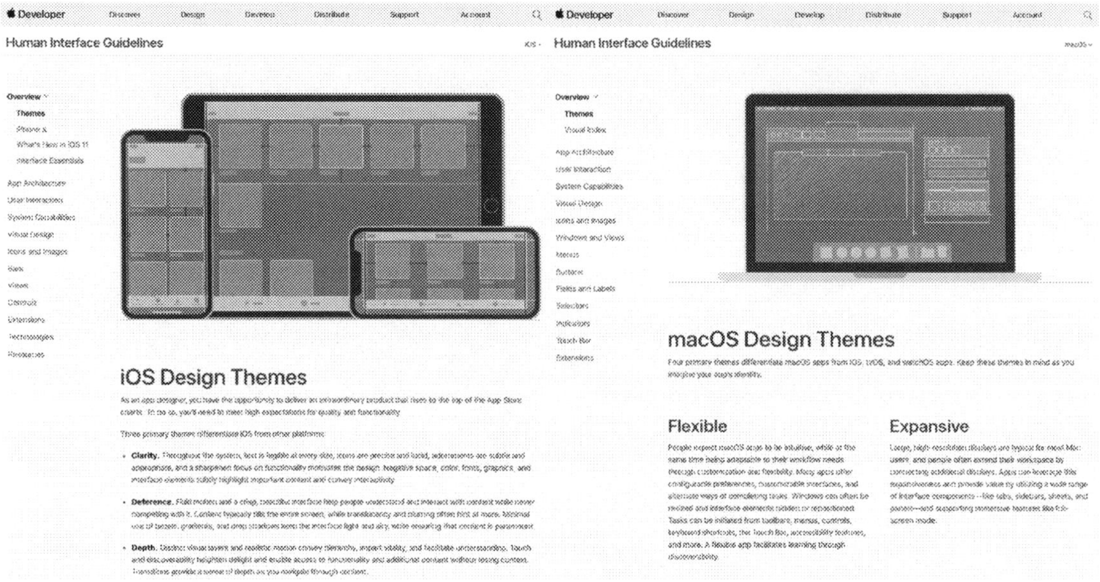

Figure 10-3. *Apple's HIGs for iOS and macOS*

Note   Apple's HIG is more than recommendations or suggestions. Apple takes it very seriously. While the HIG doesn't describe how to implement your user interface designs in code, it is great for understanding the proper way to implement your views and controls.

The following are the top reasons apps are rejected in Apple's iTunes App Store:

- The app crashes.

- *It violates the HIG.*

- It uses Apple's private APIs.

- It doesn't function as advertised on iTunes App Store.

You can read, learn, and follow the HIG before you develop your app, or you can read, learn, and follow the HIG after your app gets rejected by Apple and you have to rewrite part or all of it. Either way, all iOS developers end up becoming familiar with the HIG.

Many new iOS developers find this out the hard way, but if you follow the HIG from day one, your iOS development will be a far more pleasurable experience.

Creating an Example iPhone App with Interface Builder

Let's get started by building an iPhone app that generates and displays a random number. See Figure 10-4. This app will be similar to the app you created in Chapter 4, but you'll see how much more interesting the app becomes with an iOS user interface (UI).

Figure 10-4. *Completed iOS random number generator app*

1. Open Xcode and select **Create a new Xcode project**.
    Make sure you select a **Single View App** for iOS. See Figure 10-5.

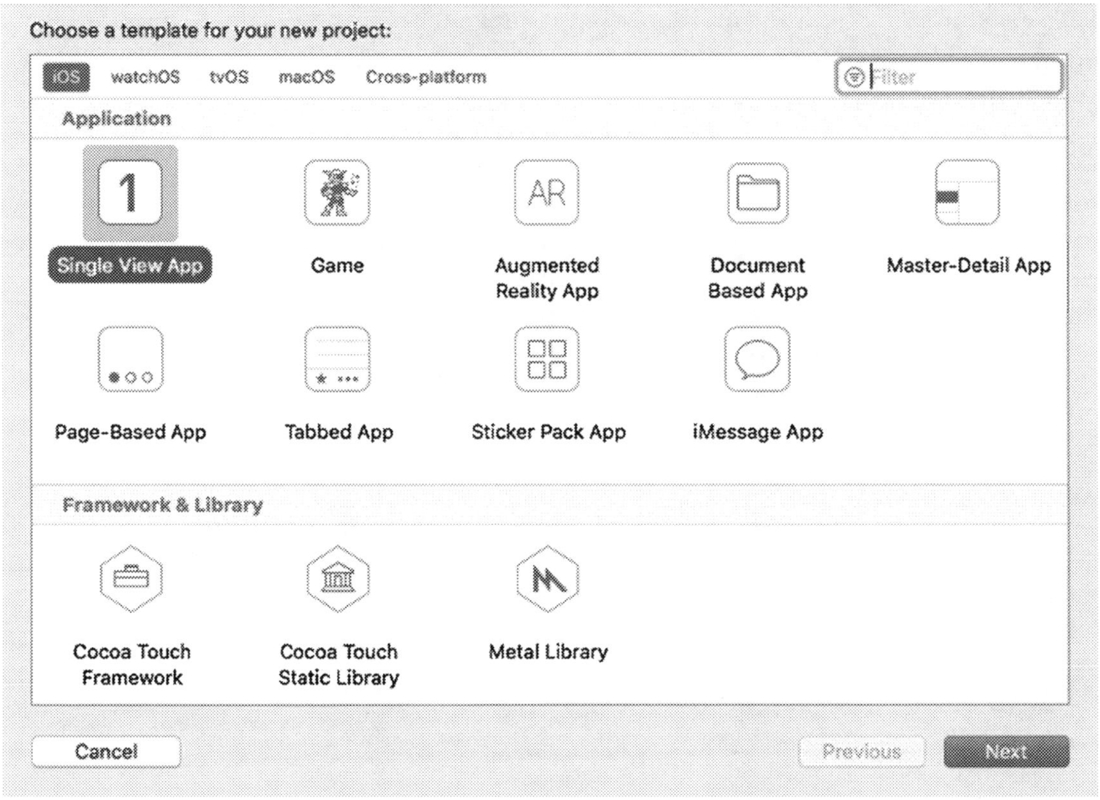

Figure 10-5. *Selecting the iOS Single View App template*

2. Name your project **RandomNumber**, select the language as
    Objective-C, and save the project. See Figure 10-6.

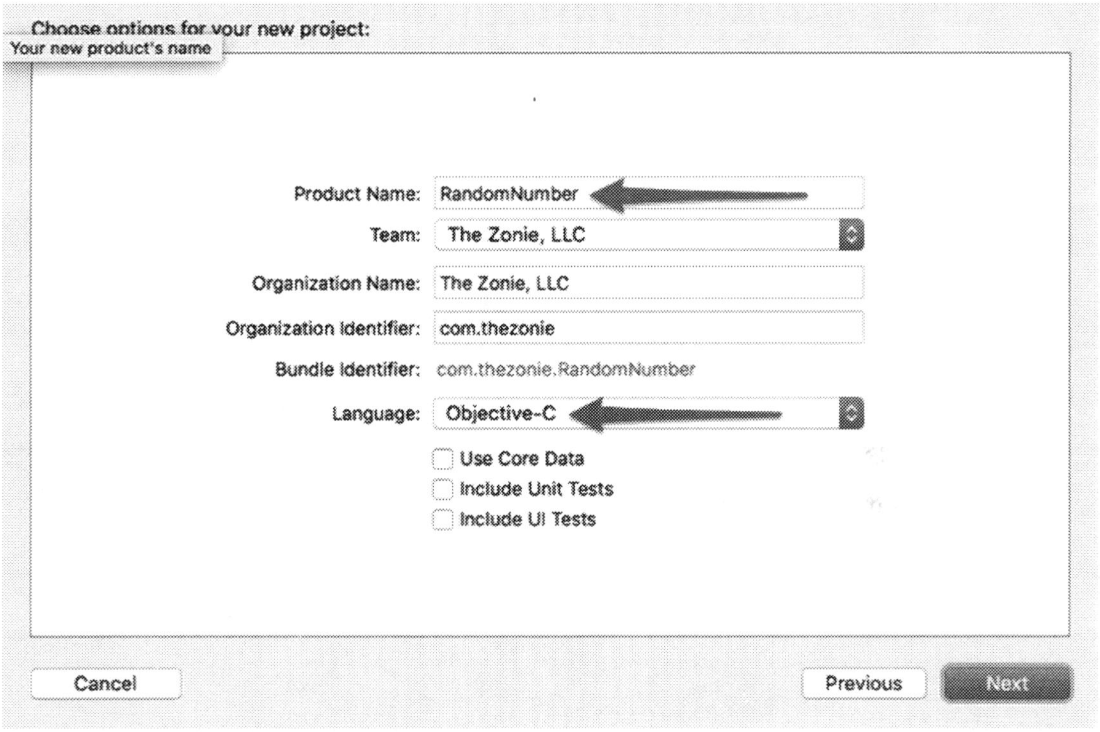

Figure 10-6. Naming your iOS project

3. Your project files and settings are created and displayed. See Figure 10-7.

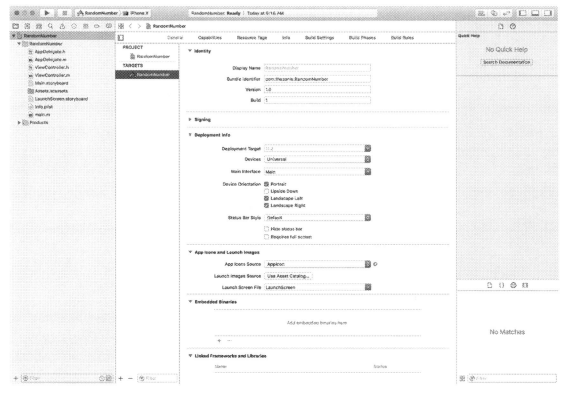

Figure 10-7. *Source files*

Although you have only one controller in this project, it's good programming practice to make your MVC groups at the beginning of your development. This helps remind developers to keep to the MVC paradigm and not put all of their code unnecessarily in their controller.

4. **Right-click** the **RandomNumber** project and then select **New Group**. See Figure 10-8.

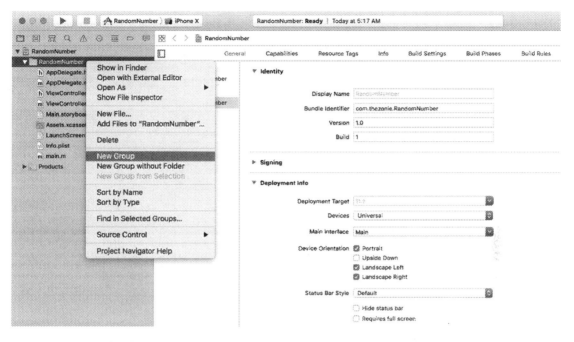

Figure 10-8. *Creating new groups*

5. Create a Models Group, a Views Group, and a Controllers Group.

6. Drag the ViewController.m and .h files into the Controllers Group. See Figure 10-9.

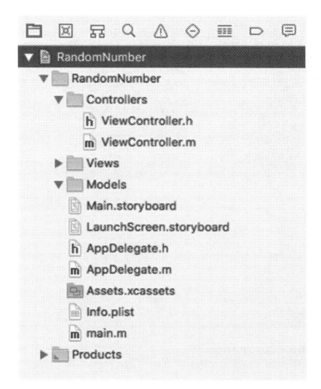

Figure 10-9. *MVC groups with controller and storyboard files organized*

Developers have found it helpful to keep their storyboard and XIB files with their controllers as their projects grow. It is not uncommon to have dozens of controllers, storyboards, and XIB files in your project. Keeping them together helps keep everything organized.

7. Click the Main.storyboard file to open Interface Builder.

Using Interface Builder

The most common way to launch Interface Builder and begin working on your view is to click the storyboard or XIB file related to the view. See Figure 10-10.

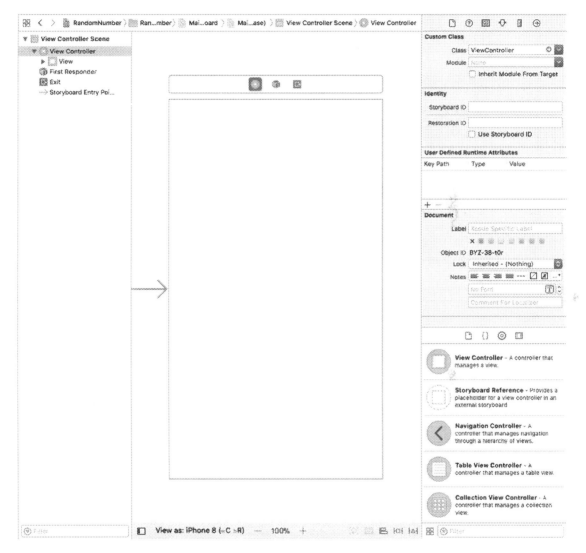

Figure 10-10. *Interface Builder window*

When Interface Builder opens, you can see your view displayed in the canvas. You are now able to design your user interface. First, you must understand some of the subwindows within Interface Builder.

The Document Outline

The Document window shows all the objects that your view contains. Here are some examples of these objects:

- Buttons
- Labels
- Text fields
- Web views
- Map views
- Picker views
- Table views

Note   You can expand the width of the Document Outline to see a detailed list of all your objects. See Figure 10-11. To get more real estate for the canvas, you can shrink or remove your file list window.

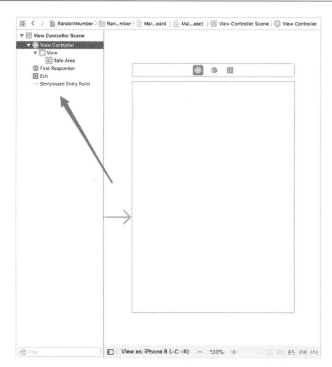

Figure 10-11. *The Document window's width is expanded to show a detailed view of all the objects in your scene*

The Object Library

The Object Library is where you can exploit your creativity. It's a smorgasbord of objects that you can drag and drop into the view window. Note that the Object Library pane can grow and shrink by moving the window splitter. See Figure 10-12.

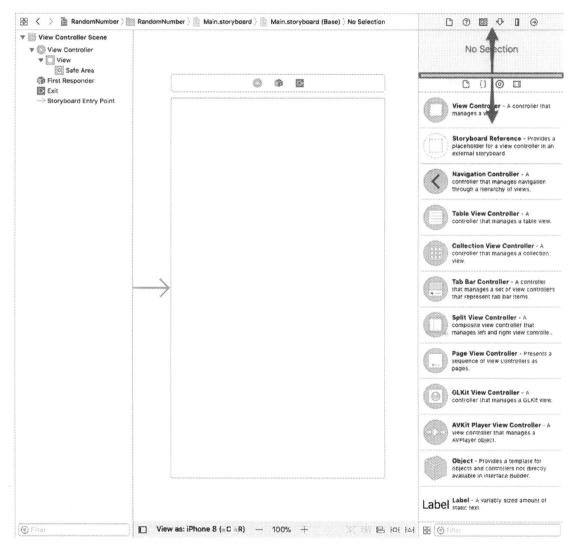

Figure 10-12. *Expand the Object Library pane to see more controls. Slide the splitter with the mouse to resize the window.*

Creating the View

The random number generator will have two objects in the view: one Label object and one Button object. The button will generate the random number, and the label will show the random number generated by the app.

1. Drag a **Label** object from the Object Library pane to the View window.

2. Drag a **Button** object from the Object Library pane to the View window.

3. Double-click the button and change the name of it to **Generate Random Number**. See Figure 10-13.

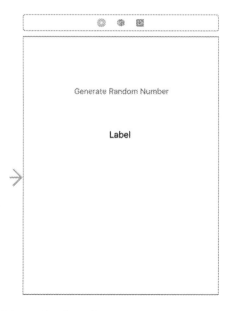

Figure 10-13. *Placing objects in the view*

You now have the ability to quickly and easy connect your outlets and actions to your code. All you have to do is drag and drop.

4.   Click the Assistant Editor icon at the top right of the screen.
     This will display the .m file for the scene you are working on.
     See Figure 10-14.

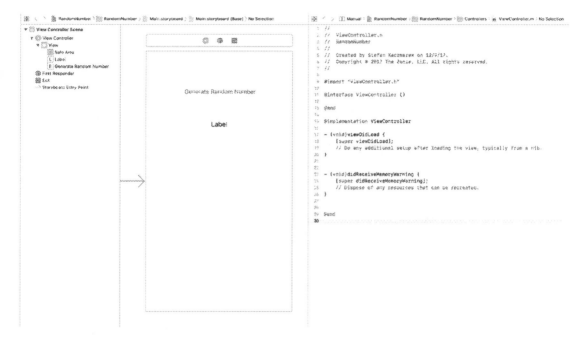

Figure 10-14.   *Using the Assistant Editor to display the .m file for the scene you are working with.*

Using Outlets

Now you can connect your label to your code by creating an outlet.

1.   Control-drag from the label in the view to inside the @interface.
     See Figure 10-15.

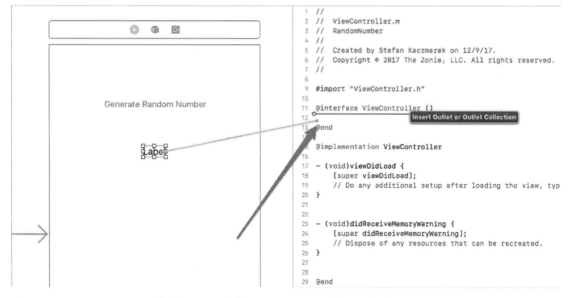

Figure 10-15. *Control-drag and drop to create the code for the* *randomNumberLabel outlet*

A pop-up window will appear. This enables you to name and specify the type of outlet.

2. Complete the pop-up as shown in Figure 10-16 and click the Connect button.

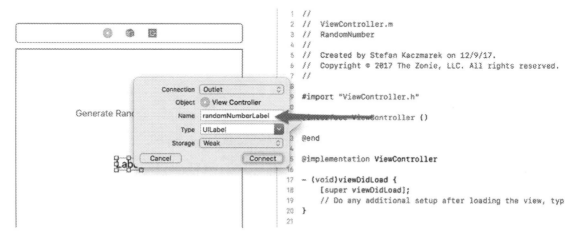

Figure 10-16. *Pop-up for randomNumber outlet*

This creates a private property, accessible from only the class.

The code is now created for the outlet, and the outlet is now connected to the Label object in the storyboard file. The shaded circle next to line number 12 indicates the outlet is connected to an object in the storyboard file. See Figure 10-17.

Figure 10-17. *Outlet property code generated and connected to the Label object*

There is also a declaration that may be new to you called an `IBOutlet`, commonly referred to as an outlet. **Outlets** signal to your controller that this property is a pointer to another object that is set up in Interface Builder. `IBOutlet` will enable Interface Builder to see the outlet and enable you to connect the property to the object in Interface Builder.

Using the analogy of an electrical wall outlet, these outlets are connected to objects. Using Interface Builder, you can connect these properties to the appropriate object.

Connecting Actions and Objects

User interface object events, also known as **actions**, trigger methods.
Now you need to connect the object actions to the buttons.

1. Control-drag from the Generate Random Number button to above the @end and drop. Complete the pop-up as indicated in Figure 10-18 and click the **Connect** button.

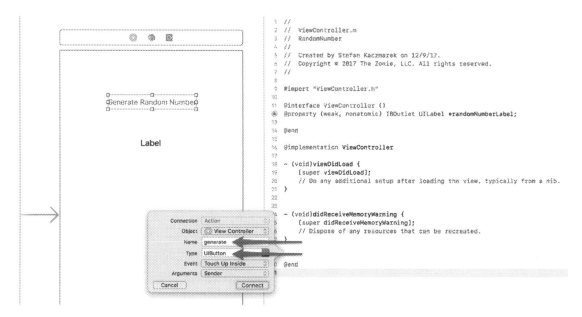

Figure 10-18. *Complete the pop-up for the generate: method.*

Implementation File

All that is left is to complete the code for your outlet and actions in the implementation file for the controller.

Open the ViewController.m file and complete the generate: method. See Figure 10-19.

```
28
⊚    - (IBAction)generate:(UIButton *)sender {
30        int randomNumber = (arc4random() % 100) + 1;
31        self.randomNumberLabel.text = [NSString stringWithFormat:@"%i", randomNumber];
32    }
```

Figure 10-19. *The generate: method is complete*

The generate: method generates a random number between 1 and 101 inclusive.

The method setText: sets the UILabel text in your view. The connections you established in Interface Builder from your outlet to the Label object do all the work for you.

That's it!

To run your iPhone app, click the **Run** button, and your app should launch in the simulator. See Figure 10-20.

Figure 10-20. *The completed random number generator app running in the iPhone simulator*

To generate the random number, tap **Generate Random Number**.

Summary

Great job! Interface Builder saves you a lot of time when creating user interfaces. You have a powerful set of objects to use in your application and are responsible for a minimal amount of coding. Interface Builder handles many of the details you would normally have to deal with.

You should be familiar with the following terms:

- Storyboard files

- Model-View-Controller

- Architectural pattern

- Human Interface Guidelines

- Outlets

- Actions

Exercises

Perform the following tasks:

- Extend the random number generator app to show a date and time in a Label object when the app starts.

- After showing a date and time label, add a button to update the data and time label with the new time.

CHAPTER 11

Storing Information

As a developer, there will be many different situations in which you will need to store data. Users will expect your application to remember preferences and other information each time they launch it. Previous chapters discussed the MyBookstore app. With this app, users will expect your application to remember all of the books in the bookstore. Your application will need a way to store this information, retrieve it, and possibly search and sort this data. Working with data can sometimes be difficult. Fortunately, Apple provides methods and frameworks to make this process easier.

This chapter will discuss two different formats in which data will need to be stored. It will discuss how to save a preference file for an iOS device and then discuss how to use a SQLite database in your application to store and retrieve data.

Storage Considerations

There are some major storage differences between the Mac and the iPhone, and these differences will affect how you work with data. Let's start by discussing the Mac and how you will need to develop for it.

On the Mac, by default, applications are stored in the `Applications` folder. Each user has their own home folder where preferences and information related to that user are stored. Not all of the users will have access to write to the `Applications` folder or to the application bundle itself.

On the iPhone and iPad, developers do not need to deal with different users. Every person who uses the iPhone has the same permissions and the same folders. There are some other factors to consider with the iPhone, though. Every application on an iOS device is in its own *sandbox*. This means that files written by an application can be seen and used only by that individual application. This makes for a more secure environment for the iPhone, but it also presents some changes in the way you work with data storage.

© Stefan Kaczmarek, Brad Lees, Gary Bennett, Mitch Fisher 2018
S. Kaczmarek et al., *Objective-C for Absolute Beginners*, https://doi.org/10.1007/978-1-4842-3429-7_11

Preferences

There are some things to consider when deciding where to store certain kinds of information. The easiest way to store information is within the preferences file, but this method has some downsides.

- All of the data is both read and written at the same time. If you are going to be writing often or writing and reading large amounts of data, this could take time and slow down your application. As a general rule, your preferences file should never be larger than 100KB. If your preferences file starts to become larger than 100KB, consider using Core Data as a way to store your information.

- The preferences file does not provide many options when it comes to searching and ordering information.

The preferences file is really nothing more than a standardized XML file with accompanying classes and methods to store application-specific information. A preference would be, for example, the sorting column and direction (ascending/descending) of a list. Anything that is generally customizable within an app should be stored in a preferences file.

Note   Sensitive data should not be stored in the preferences file or in a database without additional encryption. Luckily, Apple does provide a way to store sensitive information. It is called the **keychain**. Securing data in the keychain is beyond the scope of this book.

Writing Preferences

Apple has provided developers with the NSUserDefaults class; this class makes it easy to read and write preferences for iOS and macOS. The great thing is that, in this case, you can use the same code for iOS and macOS. The only difference between the two implementations is the location of the preferences file.

Note   For macOS, the preferences file is named `com.yourcompany.`
`applicationname.plist` and is located in the `/Users/username/Library/`
`Preferences` folder. On iOS, the preferences file is located in your application
bundle in the `/Library/Preferences` folder.

All you need to do to write preferences is to create an `NSUserDefaults` object. This is done with the following line:

`NSUserDefaults *prefs = [NSUserDefaults standardUserDefaults];`

This instantiates the `prefs` object so you can use it to set preference values. Once you have instantiated the `prefs` object, you need to set the preference keys for the values that you want to save. The MyBookstore app example will be used to demonstrate specific instructions throughout this chapter. When running a bookstore, you might want to save a username in the preferences. You also might want to save things such as a default book category or recent searches. The preferences file is a great place to store this type of information because this is the kind of information that needs to be read-only when the application is launched.

Also, on iOS, it is often necessary to save your current state. If a person is using your application and then gets a phone call, you want to be able to bring them back to the exact place they were in your application when they are done with their phone call. This is less necessary now with the implementation of multitasking, but your users will still appreciate it if your application remembers what they were doing the next time they launch it.

Once you have instantiated the object, you can just call `setObject:forKey:` to set an object. If you want to save the username of `sherlock.holmes`, you call the following line of code:

`[prefs setObject:@"sherlock.holmes" forKey:@"username"];`

You can use `setInteger`, `setDouble`, `setBool`, `setFloat`, and `setURL` instead of `setObject`, depending on the type of information you are storing in the preferences file. Let's say you store the number of books a user wants to see in the list. Here is an example of using `setInteger` to store this preference:

`[prefs setInteger:10 forKey:@"booksInList"];`

After a certain period of time, your app will automatically write changes to the preferences file. You can force your app to save the preferences by calling the synchronize method, but this is not necessary in most cases. To call the synchronize method, you write the following line:

```
[prefs synchronize];
```

With just three lines of code, you are able to create a preference object, set two preference values, and write the preferences file. It is an easy and clean process. Here is all of the code:

```
NSUserDefaults *prefs = [NSUserDefaults standardUserDefaults];
[prefs setObject:@"sherlock.holmes" forKey:@"username"];
[prefs setInteger:10 forKey:@"booksInList"];
```

Reading Preferences

Reading preferences is similar to writing preferences. Just like with writing, the first step is to obtain the NSUserDefaults object. This is done in the same way as it was done in the writing process:

```
NSUserDefaults *prefs = [NSUserDefaults standardUserDefaults];
```

Now that you have the object, you are able to access the preference values that are set. For writing, you use the setObject syntax; for reading, you use the stringForKey method. You use the stringForKey method because the value you put in the preference was an NSString. In the writing example, you set preferences for the username and for the number of books in the list to display. You can read those preferences by using the following simple lines of code:

```
NSString *username = [prefs stringForKey:@"username"];
NSInteger booksInList = [prefs integerForKey:@"booksInList"];
```

Pay close attention to what is happening in each of these lines. You start by declaring the variable username, which is an NSString. This variable will be used to store the preference value of the username you stored in the preferences. Then, you just assign it to the value of the preference username. You will notice that in the read example you do not use the synchronize function. This is because you have not changed the values of the preferences; therefore, you do not need to make sure they are written to a disk.

Databases

You learned how to store some small pieces of information and retrieve them at a later point. What if you have more information that needs to be stored? What if you need to conduct a search within this information or put it in some sort of order? These kinds of situations call for a database.

A database is a tool for storing a significant amount of information in a way that it can be easily searched or retrieved. When using a database, usually small chunks of the data are retrieved at a time rather than the entire file. Many applications you use in your daily life are based on databases of some sort. Your online banking application retrieves your account activity from a database. Your supermarket uses a database to retrieve prices for different items.

A simple example of a database is a spreadsheet. You may have many columns and many rows in your spreadsheet. The columns in your spreadsheet represent different types of information you want to store. In a database, these are considered **attributes**. The rows in your spreadsheet would be considered different **records** in your database.

Storing Information in a Database

Databases are usually an intimidating subject for a developer; most developers associate databases with enterprise database servers such as Microsoft SQL Server or Oracle. These applications can take time to set up and require constant management. For most developers, a database system like Oracle would be too much to handle. Luckily, Apple has included a small database engine called SQLite in iOS and macOS. This allows you to gain many of the features of complex database servers without the overhead.

SQLite provides you with a lot of flexibility in storing information for your application. It stores the entire database in a single file. It is fast, reliable, and easy to implement in your application. The best thing about the SQLite database is that there is no need to install any software; Apple has taken care of that for you.

However, SQLite does have some limitations that, as a developer, you should be aware of:

- SQLite was designed to be used as a single-user database. You will not want to use SQLite in an environment where more than one person will be accessing the same database. This could lead to data loss or corruption.

- In the business world, databases can grow to become very large. It is not surprising for a database manager to handle databases as large as half a terabyte, and in some cases databases can become much larger than that. SQLite should be able to handle smaller databases without any issues, but you will begin to see performance issues if your database starts to get too large.

- SQLite lacks some of the backup and data restore features of the enterprise database solutions.

For the purposes of this chapter, you will use SQLite as your database engine. If any of the mentioned limitations are present in the application you are developing, you may need to look into an enterprise database solution, which is beyond the scope of this book.

Note   SQLite (pronounced "sequel-lite") gets its name from Structured Query Language (SQL, pronounced "sequel"). SQL is the language used to enter, search, and retrieve data from a database.

Apple has worked hard to iron out a lot of the challenges of database development. As a developer, you will not need to become familiar with SQL because Apple has taken care of the direct database interaction for you through a framework called Core Data that makes interacting with the database much easier. Core Data has been adapted by Apple from a NeXT product called Enterprise Object Framework, and working with Core Data is a lot easier than interfacing directly with the SQLite database. Directly accessing a database via SQL is beyond the scope of this book.

Getting Started with Core Data

Let's start by creating a new Core Data project.

1. Open Xcode and select **File ➤ New ➤ Project**. To create an iOS
    Core Data project, select **Single View App** under **iOS**, as shown in
    Figure 11-1.

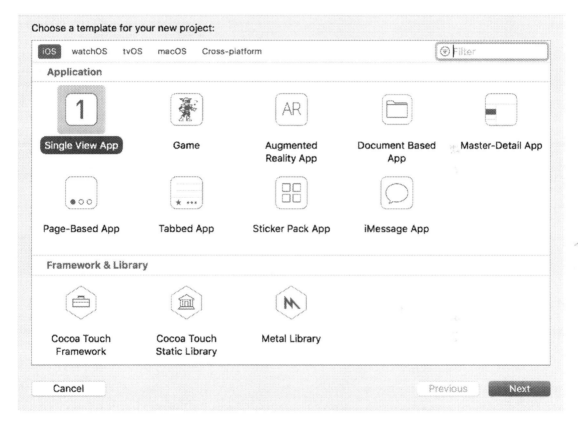

Figure 11-1. *Creating a new project*

2. Click the **Next** button when done. The next screen will allow
    you to enter the name you want to use. For the purposes of this
    chapter, you will use the name **BookStore**.

3. Make sure the Language field is set to **Objective-C**. Near the
    bottom, you will see the **Use Core Data check box**. Make sure this
    is checked and then click **Next**, as shown in Figure 11-2.

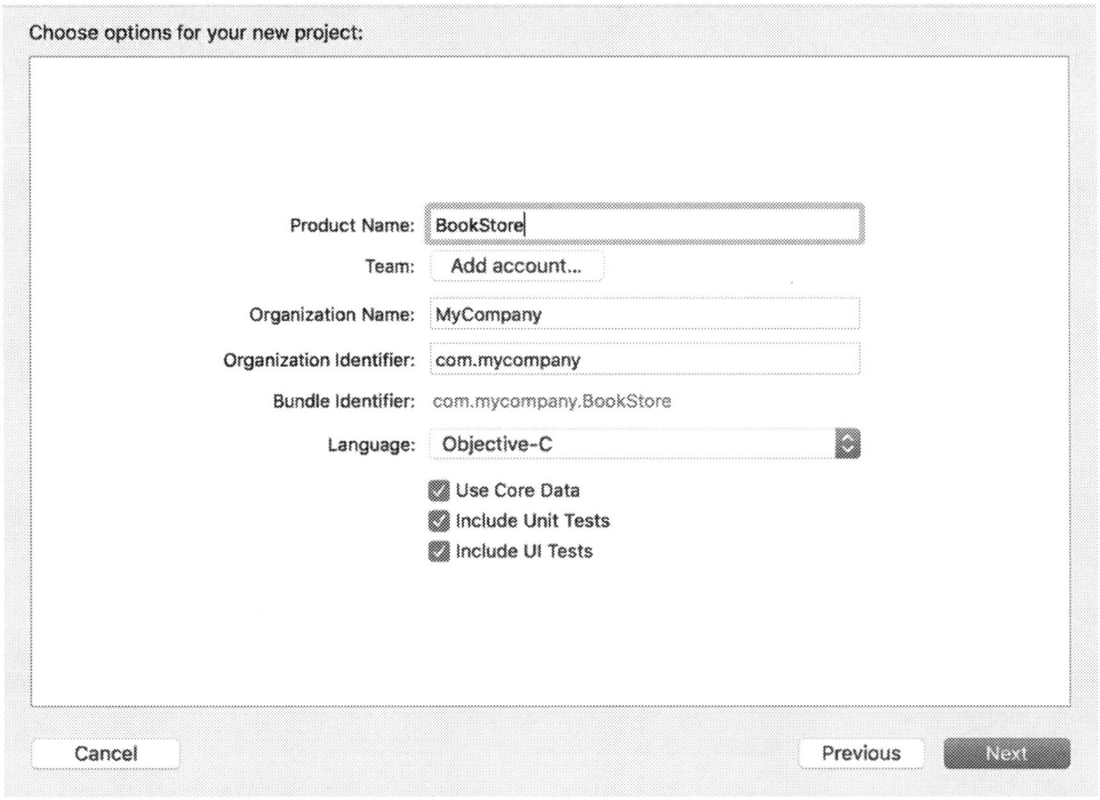

Choose options for your new project:

Product Name:	BookStore
Team:	Add account...
Organization Name:	MyCompany
Organization Identifier:	com.mycompany
Bundle Identifier:	com.mycompany.BookStore
Language:	Objective-C

☑ Use Core Data
☑ Include Unit Tests
☑ Include UI Tests

Cancel   Previous   Next

Figure 11-2. *Including Core Data*

Note   Core Data can be added to any project at any point. Checking that box
when creating a project will add the Core Data frameworks and a default data
model to your application.

---

4. Select a location to save the project and click **Create**.

Once you are done with that, your new project will open. It will look similar to a
standard application, except now you will have a BookStore.xcdatamodeld file. This file
is called a **data model** and will contain the information about the data that you will be
storing in Core Data.

The Model

In your BookStore folder on the left, you will see a file called BookStore.xcdatamodeld. This file will contain information about the data you want stored in the database. Click the model file to open it. You will see a window similar to the one shown in Figure 11-3.

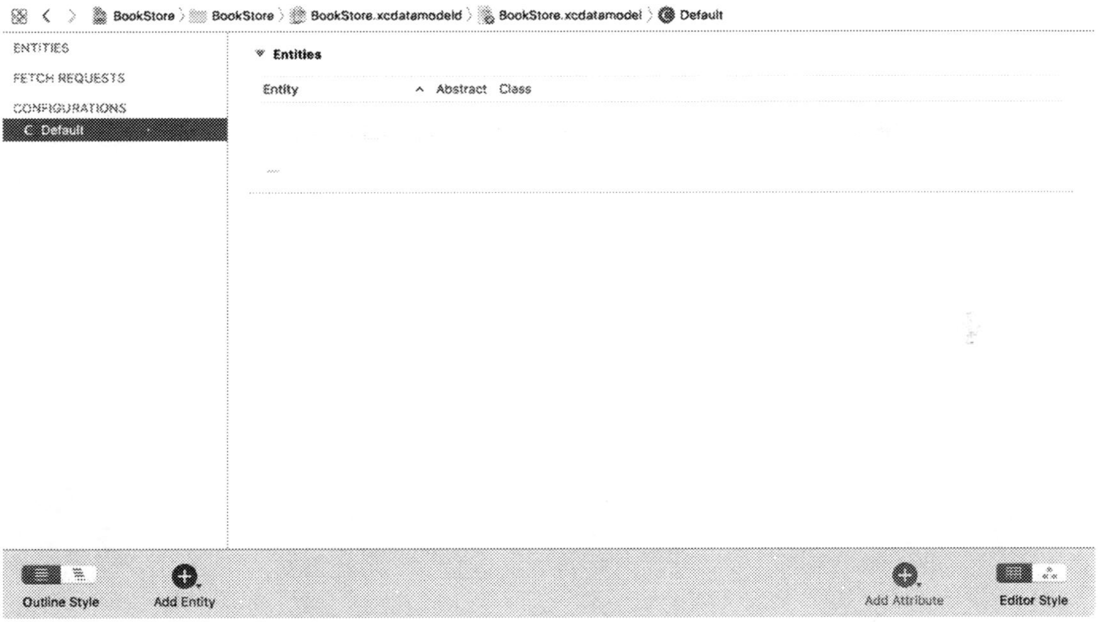

Figure 11-3. The blank model

Let's create an entity.

1. Click the plus sign in the bottom-left corner of the window, or select **Editor ➤ Add Entity** from the menu, as shown in Figure 11-4.

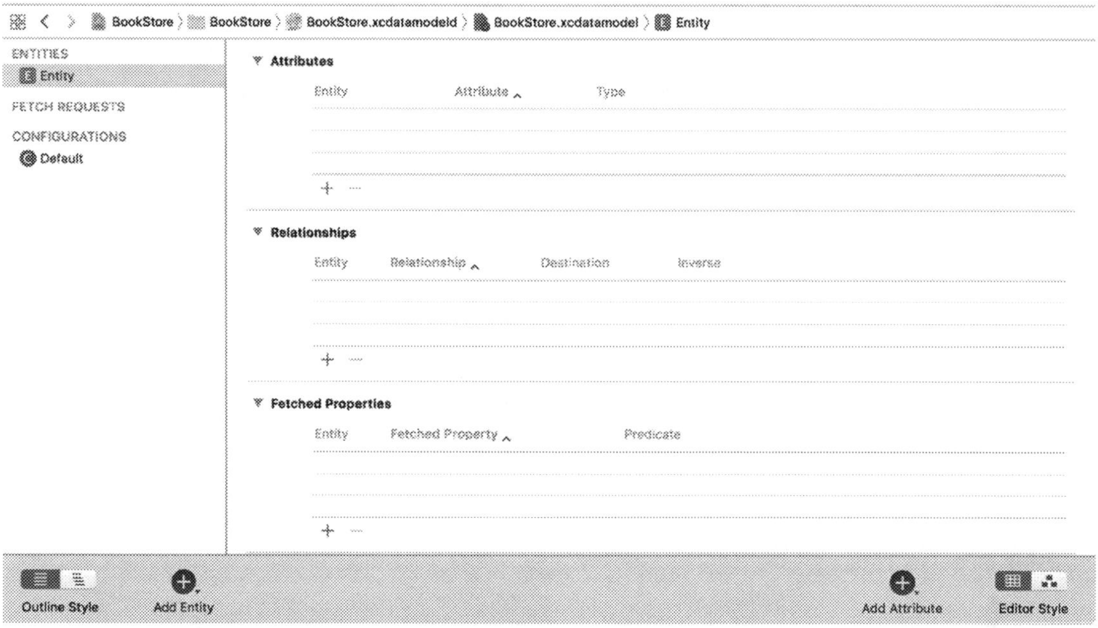

Figure 11-4. *Adding a new entity*

The window is divided into four sections. On the left are your entities. In more common terms, these are the objects or items that you want to store in the database.

The top-right window contains the attributes. Attributes are pieces of information about the entities. For example, a book would be an entity, and the title of the book would be an attribute of that entity.

Note   In database terms, entities are your **tables** and the attributes of the entities are called **columns**. The objects created from those entities are referred to as **rows**.

The other sections of the Data Model view will only be visible once you have an entity defined. The middle window on the right will show you all the relationships of an entity. A relationship connects one entity to another. For example, you will create a Book entity and an Author entity. You will then relate them so that every book can have an author. The bottom-right portion of the screen deals with fetched properties. Fetched properties are beyond the scope of this book, but they allow you to create filters for your data.

2.   On the left side, double-click your new entity and rename it **Book**.

Note   It is required to capitalize the names of your entities.

---

3.   Now let's add some attributes. Attributes would be considered the details of a book, so you will store the title, author, price, and year the book was published. Obviously, in your own applications, you may want to store more information, such as the publisher, page count, and genre, but let's start simple here. Select the Book entity and click the Add Attribute plus sign at the bottom right of the window, or select **Editor ➤ Add Attribute**, and a new attribute will be created, as shown in Figure 11-5.

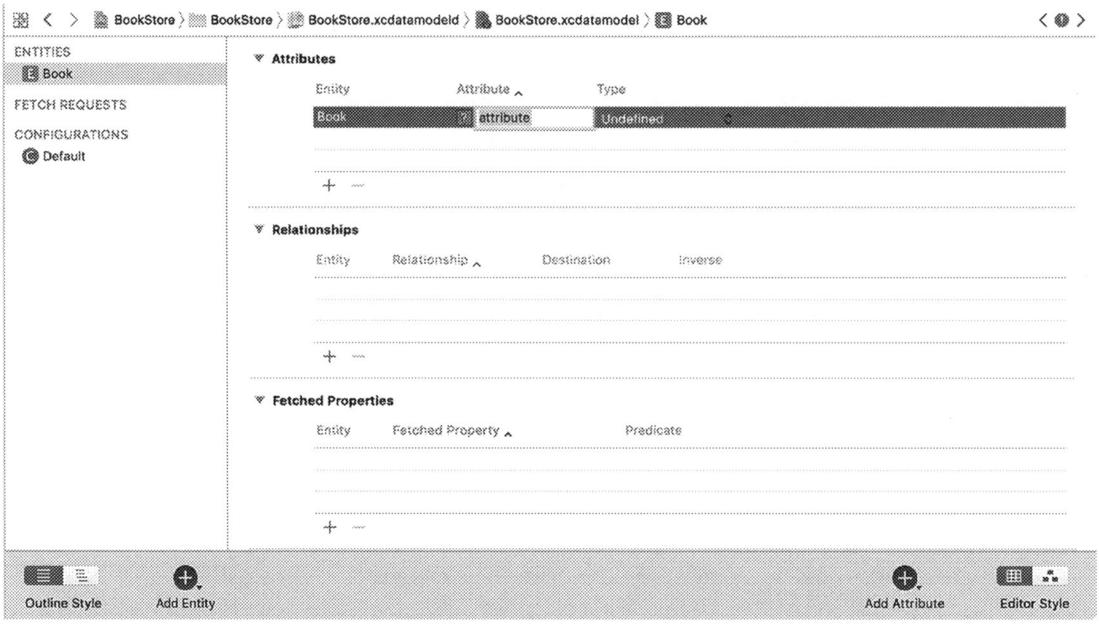

Figure 11-5. *Adding a new attribute*

4. You will be given only two options for your attribute: the name and the data type. Let's call this attribute **title**. Unlike entities, attribute names must start with a lowercase letter.

5. Now, you will need to select a data type. Selecting the correct data type is important. It will affect how your data is stored and retrieved from the database. The list has 14 items in it and can be daunting. We will discuss the most common options and, as you become more familiar with Core Data, you can experiment with the other options. The most common options are String, Integer 32, Decimal, and Date. For the title of the book, select **String**.

String: This is the type of attribute used to store text. This generally should be used to store any kind of information that is not a number or a date. In this example, the book title and author will be strings.

Integer 32: There are three different integer values possible for an attribute. Each of the integer types differs only in the minimum and maximum values possible. Integer 32 should cover most of your needs when storing an integer. An integer is a number without a decimal. If you try to save a decimal in an integer attribute, the decimal portion will be truncated. In this example, the year published will be an integer.

Decimal: A decimal is a type of attribute that can store numbers with decimals. A decimal is similar to a double attribute, but they differ in their minimum and maximum values and precision. A decimal should be able to handle any currency values. In this example, you will use a decimal to store the price of the book.

Date: A date attribute is exactly what it sounds like. It allows you to store a date and time and then performs searches and lookups based on these values. You will not use this type in this example.

6. Let's create the rest of the attributes for the book. Now, add price. It should be a decimal type. Add the year the book was published. For two-word attributes, it is standard to make the first word lowercase and the second word start with a capital letter. For example, an ideal name for the attribute for the year the book was published would be `yearPublished`. Select Integer 32 as the attribute type. Once you have added all of your attributes, your screen should look like Figure 11-6.

Note   Attribute names cannot contain spaces.

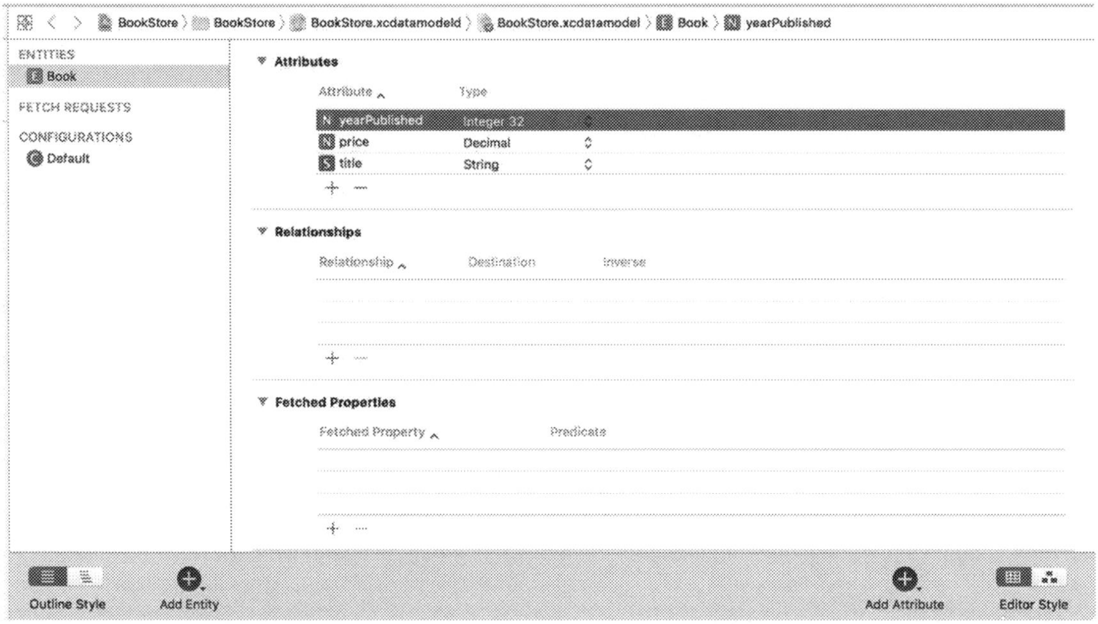

Figure 11-6. *The finished Book entity*

Note   If you are used to working with databases, you will notice that you did not add a primary key. A primary key is a field (usually a number) that is used to uniquely identify each record in a database. In Core Data databases, there is no need to create primary keys. The framework will manage all of that for you.

Now that you have finished the Book entity, let's add an Author entity.

1. Add a new entity and call it Author.

2. To this entity, add lastName and firstName as attributes, both of which are strings.

Once this is done, you should have two entities in your attributes list. Now you need to add the relationships.

1. Click the Book entity, and then click and hold on the plus sign that is located on the bottom right of the screen. Select **Add Relationship** and a new relationship will be created, as shown in Figure 11-7. (You can also click the plus under the Relationships section of the Core Data model.)

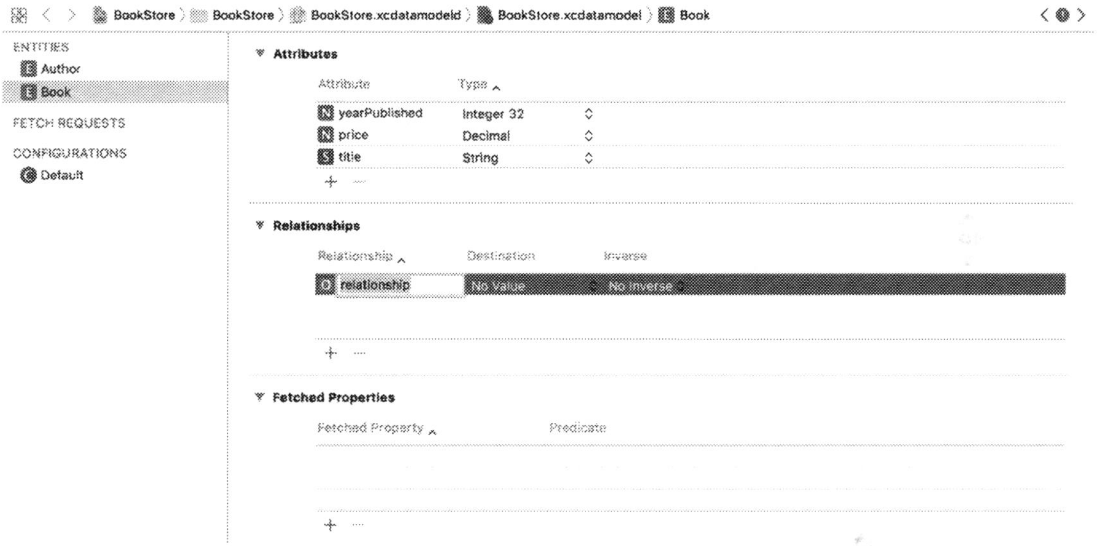

Figure 11-7. Adding a new relationship

2. You will be given the opportunity to name your relationship. You usually give a relationship the same name as the entity to which it derived from. Type in **author** as the name and select Author from the Destination drop-down menu.

3. You have created one half of your relationship. To create the other half, click the Author entity. Click the plus sign located at the bottom right of the screen and select **Add Relationship**. You will use the entity name that you are connecting to as the name of this relationship, so you will call it books. (You are adding an *s* to the relationship name because an author can have many books.) Under Destination, select **Book**, and under Inverse, select the

author relationship you made in the previous step. In the Utilities window on the right side of the screen, select the **Data Model Inspector**. Select **To Many** for the type of the relationship. Your model should now look like Figure 11-8.

Figure 11-8. *The final relationship*

Note   Sometimes in Xcode, when working with models, it is necessary to hit the Tab key for the names of entities, attributes, and relationships to update. This little quirk can be traced all the way back to WebObjects tools.

Core Data has two ways code can be generated for your entities. If you do not plan on customizing anything about the entity, Xcode can automatically generate the code for you. For this example, you will manually generate the code to see how Core Data is working. To do this, you need to tell Core Data not to automatically generate the code. Click the **Author** entity. On the right-hand side, set Codegen to **Manual/None**, as shown in Figure 11-9. Repeat this step for the **Book** entity.

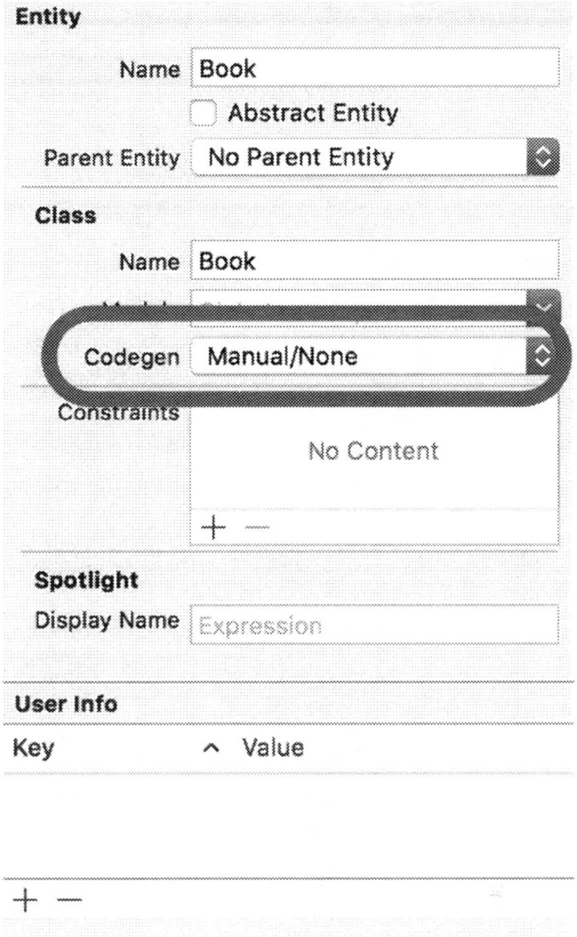

Figure 11-9. *Turning off codegen*

Now you need to tell your code about your new entity. To do this, hold down Shift and select both the Book entity and the Author entity and then select **Editor ➤ Create NSManagedObject Subclass** from the Application menu. Your screen should look like Figure 11-10.

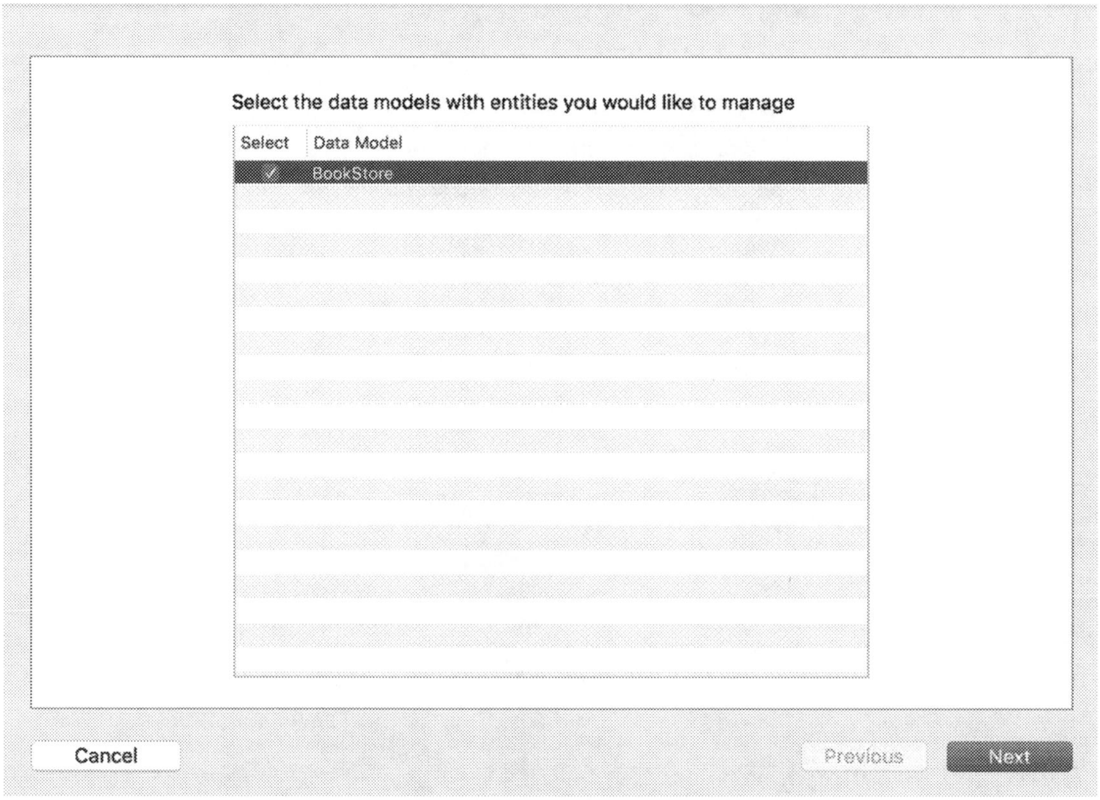

Figure 11-10. *Adding the managed objects to your project*

This screen allows you to select the data model you would like to create managed objects for. In this case, you have only a single data model. In some complicated applications, you may have more than one. Managed objects represent instances of an entity from your data model. Make sure the BookStore data model is checked and hit **Next**.

You will now be presented with a screen to select the entities to create managed objects, as shown in Figure 11-11. Make sure both are checked and click **Next**.

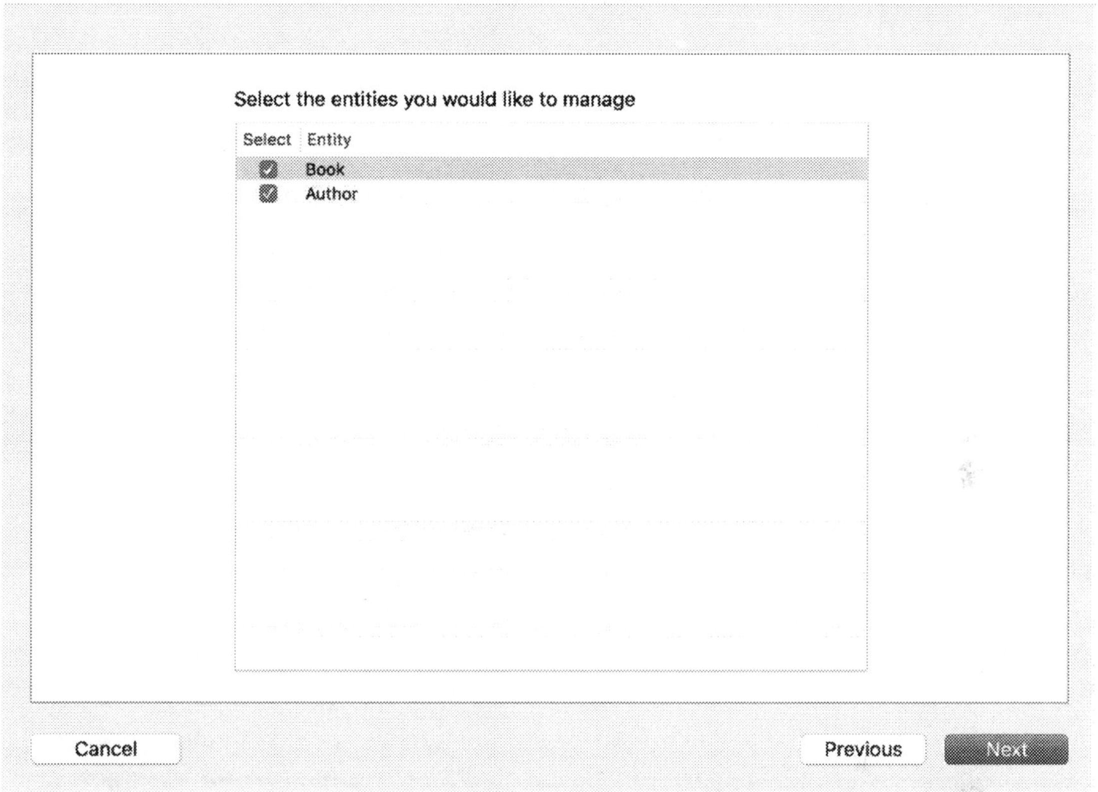

Select the entities you would like to manage

Select	Entity
☑	Book
☑	Author

Cancel   Previous   Next

Figure 11-11. *Selecting the entities to create managed objects*

Select the storage location and add it to your project. Then click **Create**. You will notice that eight files have been added to your project. Book+CoreDataProperties and Author+CoreDataProperties .h and .m files contain the information about your books and authors entities you just created. Book+CoreDataClass.h and Author+CoreDataClass.h will be used for logic relating to your new entities. These files will need to be used to access the entities and the attributes you added to your data model. These files are fairly simple because Core Data will do most of the work with them. You should also notice that if you go back to your model and click **Book**, it will have a new class in the Data Model Inspector. Instead of an NSManagedObject, it will have a Book class.

Let's look at some of the contents of Book+CoreDataProperties.h:

```
#import "Book+CoreDataClass.h"

NS_ASSUME_NONNULL_BEGIN

@interface Book (CoreDataProperties)

+ (NSFetchRequest<Book *> *)fetchRequest;

@property (nullable, nonatomic, copy) NSString *title;
@property (nullable, nonatomic, copy) NSDecimalNumber *price;
@property (nullable, nonatomic, copy) int32_t yearPublished;
@property (nullable, nonatomic, retain) Author *author;

@end

NS_ASSUME_NONNULL_END
```

You will see that the file starts by including Book+CoreDataClass.h, which includes the Core Data framework. This allows Core Data to manage your information. This file contains an extension to the Book class. An extension allows you to add new properties and functionality to an existing class. By creating the Book+CoreDataClass and the Book+CoreDataProperties extension files, Xcode allows the developer to separate the attributes from the basic logic. The superclass for the new Book object is NSManagedObject. NSManagedObject is an object that handles all of the Core Data database interaction. It provides the methods and properties you will be using in this example. Later in the file, you will see the three attributes and the one relationship you created.

Managed Object Context

You have created a managed object class called Book. The nice thing with Xcode is that it will generate the necessary code to manage these new data objects. In Core Data, every managed object should exist within a managed object context. The context is responsible for tracking changes to objects, carrying out undo operations, and writing the data to the database. This is helpful because you can now save a bunch of changes at once rather than saving each individual change. This speeds up the process of saving the records. As a developer, you do not need to track when an object has been changed. The managed object context will handle all of that for you.

Setting Up the Interface

The following steps will assist you in setting up your user interface:

1. In the BookStore folder in your project, you should have a Main.storyboard file. Click this file and Xcode will open it in the editing window, as shown in Figure 11-12.

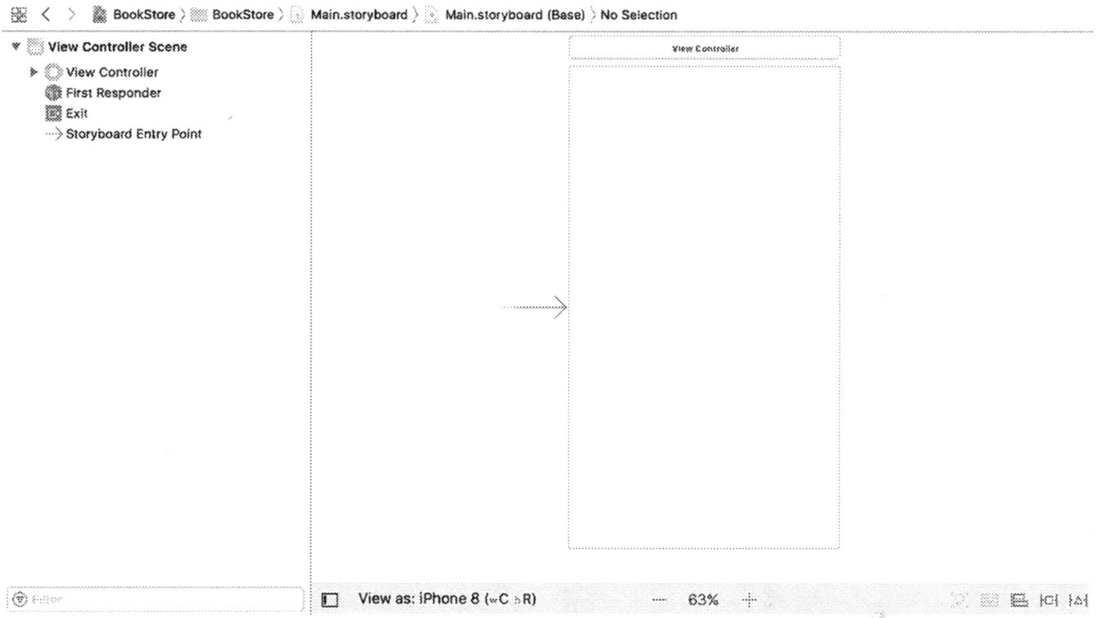

Figure 11-12. *Creating the interface*

2. There should be a blank view. To add some functionality to your
    app, you are going to need to add some objects from the Object
    Library. Type **table** into the search field on the bottom right of the
    screen. This should narrow the objects, and you should see Table
    View Controller and Table View. Drag the **Table View** to the scene,
    as shown in Figure 11-13. The Table View may need to be resized
    to fill the entire View.

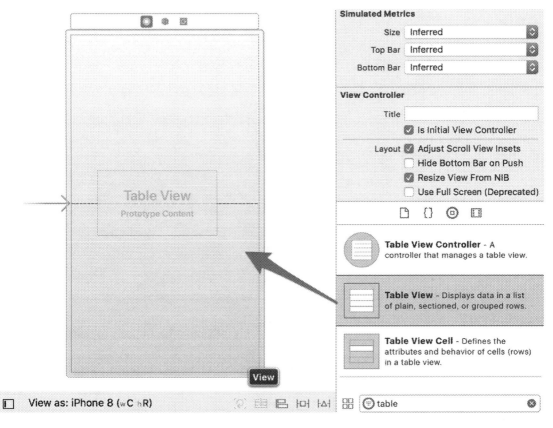

Figure 11-13. *Adding the Table View*

3.   You now have a Table View. To create cells in your Table View, you
     need to add a `Table View Cell`, search for the Table View Cell,
     and drag a Table View Cell to your table. You now have a table and
     a cell on your view, as shown in Figure 11-14.

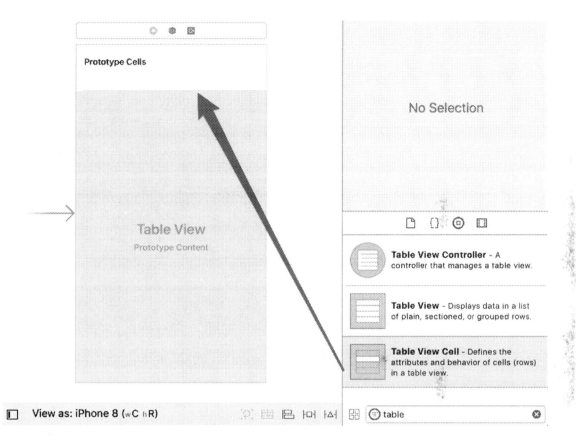

Figure 11-14.   *Adding the Table View Cell*

4. Select the cell, and in the Attributes Inspector on the right side, set Style to **Basic**. Also, set the Identifier to **Cell**. The identifier is used when your Table View contains multiple styles of cells. You will need to differentiate them with unique identifiers. For most of your projects, you can set this to Cell and not worry about it, as shown in Figure 11-15.

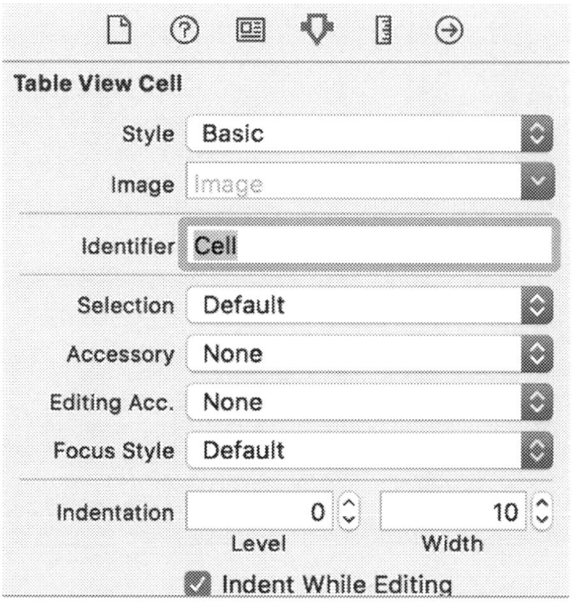

Figure 11-15. *Changing the style of the cell*

5. When using a Table View, it is usually a good idea to put it in a
    Navigation Controller. You will use the Navigation Controller to
    give you space to put an Add button on your Table View. To add
    a Navigation Controller, select your View Controller in the Scene
    box, which is the window to the left of your storyboard that shows
    your View Controllers (your View Controller will have a yellow
    icon next to it). From the Application menu, select **Editor ➤
    Embed In ➤ Navigation Controller**, as shown in Figure 11-16.

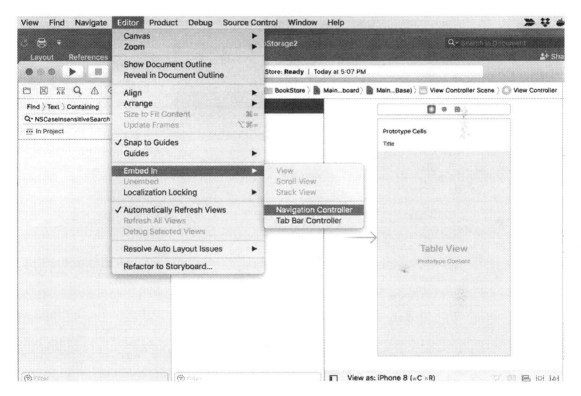

Figure 11-16. *Embedding in a Navigation Controller*

6. You will have a navigation bar at the top of your view. You will now add a button to the bar. This type of button is called a UIBarButtonItem. Search for *bar button* in your Object Library and drag a **Bar Button Item** to the top right of your view on the navigation bar, as shown in Figure 11-17.

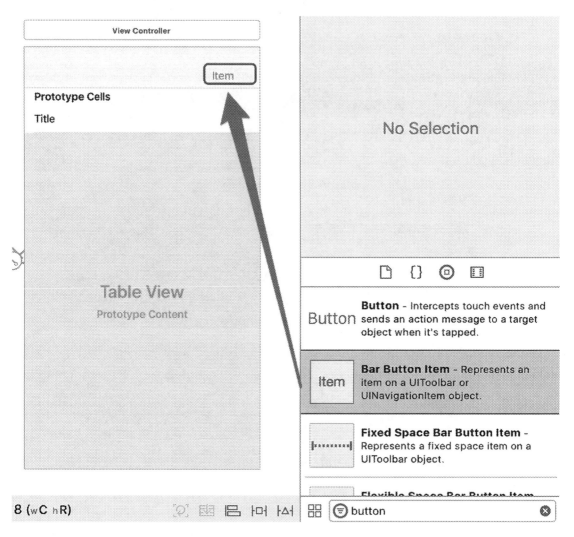

Figure 11-17. *Adding a Bar Button Item to the navigation bar*

7. Select the Bar Button Item and change the System Item from Custom to **Add** as shown in (Figure 11-18.). This will change the look of your Bar Button Item from the word *Item* to a plus icon.

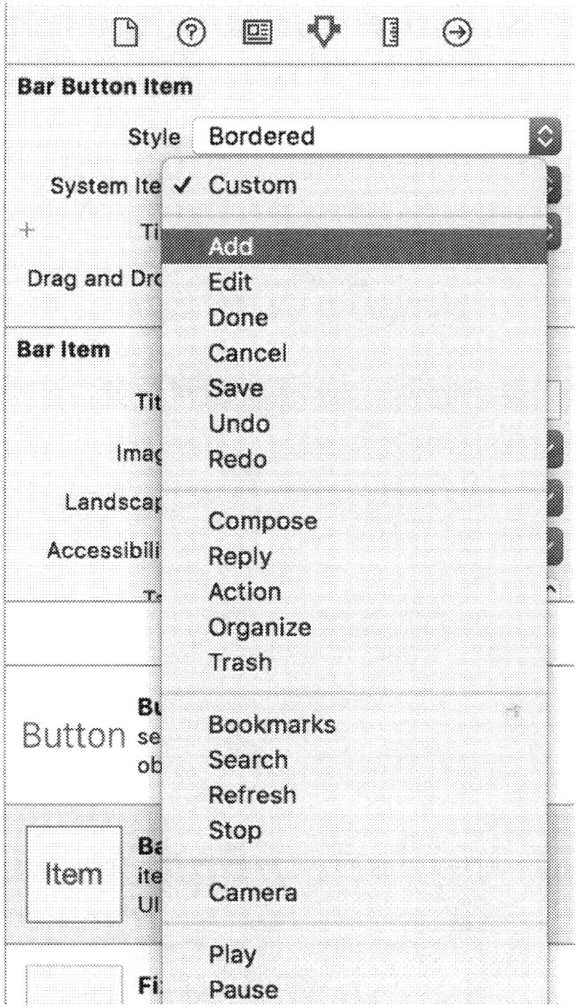

Figure 11-18. *Changing the Bar Button Item*

8.   Now that you have the interface created, you need to hook it up to your code. Hold down the Control key and drag your Table View to the View Controller in the Document Outline, as shown in Figure 11-19.

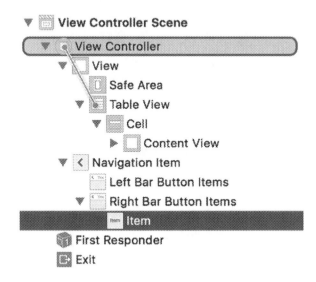

Figure 11-19. *Connecting the Table View*

9.   A pop-up will appear, allowing you to select either the dataSource or delegate outlet, as shown in Figure 11-20. You will need to assign both to the View Controller. The order in which you select the items does not matter, but you will have to Control-drag the Table View twice.

Figure 11-20. *Hooking up the Table View*

10. Now your Table View should be ready to go. You need to hook up your button to make it do something. In the top right of your Xcode window, click the **Assistant Editor icon** (it looks like two circles). This will open your code on the right side and your storyboard on the left side. Now Control-drag your **Add button** to the View Controller code on the right, as shown in Figure 11-21.

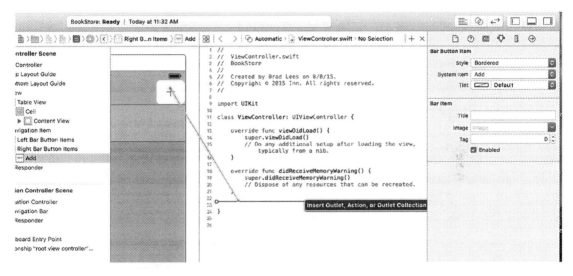

Figure 11-21. *Adding an action for your Button object*

11. It does not matter where you place the Add button in your code as long as it is within your class definition and outside of any methods. When you let go, you will be prompted for the type of connection you are creating. Set Connection to **Action**. Then add a name for your new method, such as **addNew**, as shown in Figure 11-22.

Connection	Action
Object	View Controller
Name	addNew
Type	id
Cancel	Connect

Figure 11-22. *Setting the type and name of the connection*

12.   The UITableView that was added previously will need to
      be accessible through code. To accomplish this, drag the
      UITableView from the left pane to the top of the code on the right
      and create an outlet named tableView. You will need to drag it to
      the class extension interface block.

The interface is complete now, but you still need to add the code to make
the interface do something. Go back to the Standard editor (click the list icon to
the left of the two circles icon in the top right of the Xcode toolbar) and select the
ViewController.h file from the file list on the left side. Because you now have a Table
View you have to worry about, you need to tell your class that it can handle a Table View.
Change your class declaration at the top of your file to the following:

```
@interface ViewController : UIViewController <UITableViewDataSource,
UITableViewDelegate>
```

You added UITableViewDelegate and UITableViewDataSource to your declaration.
This tells your controller that it can act as a Table View Delegate and Data Source. These
are called **protocols.** Protocols tell an object that they must implement certain methods
to interact with other objects. For example, to conform to the UITableViewDataSource
protocol, you need to implement the following method in the ViewController.m file:

```
- (NSInteger)tableView:(UITableView *)tableView
numberOfRowsInSection:(NSInteger)section;
```

Without this method, the Table View will not know how many rows to draw.
Before continuing, you need to tell your ViewController.h file about Core Data.
To do this, add the following line to the top of the file just under the #import <UIKit/
UIKit.h> statement:

```
#import <CoreData/CoreData.h>
```

You also need to add a managed object context to your ViewController class. Add
the following line right after the class ViewController line:

```
@interface ViewController : UIViewController <UITableViewDataSource,
UITableViewDelegate> {
    NSManagedObjectContext *managedObjectContext;
}
```

Notice that you also must add the curly braces. Now that you have a variable to hold your NSManagedObjectContext, you need to instantiate it so you can add objects to it. To do this, you need to add the following lines to your viewDidLoad method in the ViewController.m file:

```
AppDelegate *appDelegate = (AppDelegate *)[[UIApplication
sharedApplication] delegate];
managedObjectContext = appDelegate.persistentContainer.viewContext;
;
```

The first line creates a variable that points to your application delegate. The second line points your managedObjectContext variable to the application delegate's managedObjectContext. It is usually a good idea to use the same managed object context throughout your app. Also, at the top of ViewController.m, add the following line under the #import "ViewController.h" line:

```
#import "AppDelegate.h"
#import "Book+CoreDataClass.h"
```

The first new method you are going to add is one to query your database records. Call this method loadBooks.

```
32  - (NSArray *)loadBooks {
33       NSFetchRequest *fetchRequest = [[NSFetchRequest alloc]
initWithEntityName:@"Book"];
34       NSArray *bookArray = [[managedObjectContext executeFetchRequest:fet
chRequest error:nil] mutableCopy];
35
36       return bookArray;
37
38  }
```

This code is a little more complex than what you have seen before, so let's walk through it. Line 32 declares a new function called loadBooks, which returns an NSArray. This means you will receive an array that can contain any type of objects you want. In this case, the objects will be Books. You then return the array once you have it loaded.

You now need to add the data source methods for your Table View. These methods tell your Table View how many sections there are, how many rows are in each section, and what each cell should look like. Add the following code to your ViewController.m file:

```
41   - (NSInteger)numberOfSectionsInTableView:(UITableView *)tableView {
42        return 1;
43   }
44
45   - (NSInteger)tableView:(UITableView *)tableView numberOfRowsInSection:(
        NSInteger)section {
46
47        return [[self loadBooks] count] ;
48   }
49
50   - (UITableViewCell *)tableView:(UITableView *)tableView cellForRowAtInd
        exPath:(NSIndexPath *)indexPath {
51
52        UITableViewCell *cell = [tableView dequeueReusableCellWithIdentifie
          r:@"Cell"];
53        if (cell == nil) {
54            cell = [[UITableViewCell alloc] initWithStyle:UITableViewCellSty
              leDefault reuseIdentifier:@"Cell"];
55        }
56
57        Book *myBook = [[self loadBooks] objectAtIndex:indexPath.row];
58
59        cell.textLabel.text = myBook.title;
60
61        return cell;
62   }
```

In line 42, you tell your Table View that it will contain only a single section. In line 47, you call a count on your array of Books for the number of rows in your Table View. In lines 51 to 61, you create your cell and return it. Line 52 creates a cell for you to use. This is standard code for creating a cell. The identifier allows you to have more than one type of cell in a Table View, but that is more complex. Line 57 grabs your Book object from your loadBooks() array. Line 59 assigns the book title to your textLabel in the cell. The textLabel is the default label in the cell. This is all you need to do to be able to display the results of your loadBooks method in the table view. You still have one problem. You do not have any books in your database yet.

To fix this issue, you will add code to the addNew method you created earlier. Add the following code inside the addNew method you created:

```
66   - (IBAction)addNew:(id)sender {
67       Book *myBook = [NSEntityDescription insertNewObjectForEntityForName
         :@"Book" inManagedObjectContext:managedObjectContext];
68       myBook.title = [NSMutableString stringWithFormat:@"My Book%lu",
         (unsigned long)[self loadBooks].count];
69       [managedObjectContext save:nil];
70       [self.tableView reloadData];
71   }
```

Line 67 creates a new Book object for your book in the database from the entity name and inserts that object into the managedObjectContext you created before. Remember that once it is inserted into the managed object context, its changes are tracked, and it can be saved. Line 68 sets the book title to My Book and then sets the number of items in the array. Obviously, in real life, you would want to set this to a name either given by the user or from some other list. Line 69 saves the managed object context. Line 70 tells the UITableView to reload itself to display the newly added Book. Now build and run the application. Click the + button several times. You will add new Book objects to your object store, as shown in Figure 11-23. If you quit the app and relaunch it, you will notice that the data is still there.

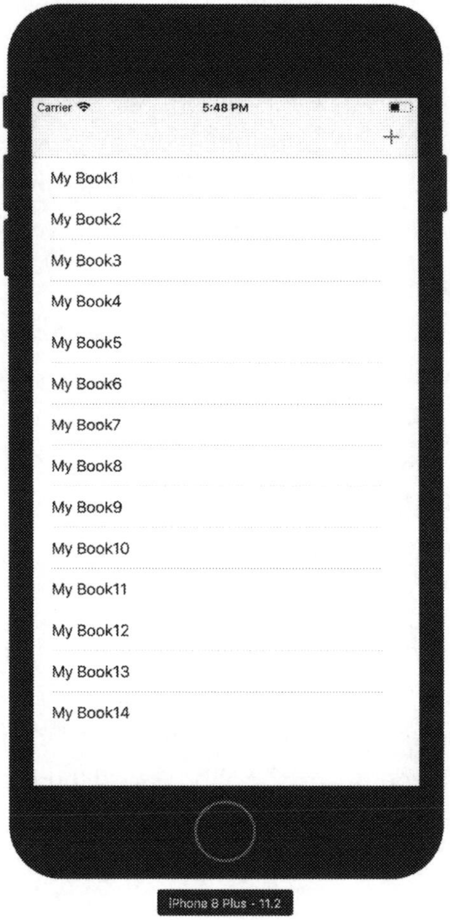

Figure 11-23. *The final app*

This was a cursory introduction to Core Data for iOS. Core Data is a powerful API, but it can also take a lot of time to master.

Summary

Here is a summary of the topics this chapter covered:

- *Preferences*: You learned to use NSUserDefaults to save and read preferences from a file, on both iOS and macOS.

- *Databases*: You learned what a database is and why using one can be preferable to saving information in a preferences file. You also learned about the database engine that Apple integrated into macOS and iOS and the advantages and limitations of this database engine.

- *Core Data*: Apple provides a framework for interfacing with the SQLite database. This framework makes the interface much easier to use.

- *Bookstore application*: You created a simple Core Data application. You used Xcode to create a data model for your bookstore. You learned how to create a relationship between two entities. You used Xcode to create a simple interface for your Core Data model.

Exercises

Perform the following tasks:

- Add a new view to the app for allowing the user to enter the name of a book.

- Provide a way to remove a book from the list.

- Create an Author object and add it to a Book object.

CHAPTER 12

Protocols and Delegates

Congratulations, you are acquiring the skills to become an iOS developer! However, there are two additional topics that iOS developers need to understand to be successful: protocols and delegates. It is not uncommon for new developers to get overwhelmed by these topics, so we thought it best to introduce the foundation topics of the Objective-C language first.

Multiple Inheritance

We discussed object inheritance in Chapter 1. In a nutshell, object inheritance means that a child can inherit all the characteristics of its parent. See Figure 12-1.

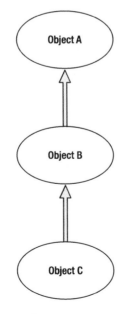

Figure 12-1. *Typical Objective-C inheritance*

© Stefan Kaczmarek, Brad Lees, Gary Bennett, Mitch Fisher 2018

S. Kaczmarek et al., *Objective-C for Absolute Beginners*, https://doi.org/10.1007/978-1-4842-3429-7_12

C++, Perl, and Python each have a feature called multiple inheritance. **Multiple inheritance** enables a class to inherit behaviors and features from more than one parent. See Figure 12-2.

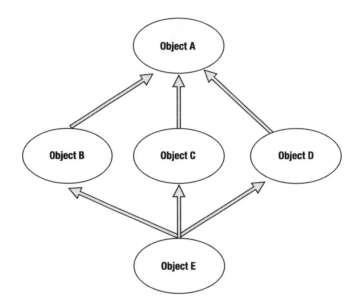

Figure 12-2. *Multiple inheritance*

However, problems can arise with multiple inheritance because it allows for ambiguities to occur. Because of this, Objective-C does not implement multiple inheritance. Instead, it implements something called a **protocol**.

Understanding Protocols

Apple defines a **protocol** simply as a list of method declarations, unattached to a class definition. A protocol is similar to a class interface with the exception that it does not define a particular class. For example, the methods that report user actions for the mouse on your Mac could be placed into a protocol.

Any class that wants to respond to mouse events could adopt the protocol and implement its methods. Protocols are easy to use since they are not related to the class hierarchy and any class can implement them.

Throughout the book, we have used the example of a bookstore. Previously, we discussed the fact that this bookstore may sell different types of media and how inheritance would help in that situation. For the purpose of explaining protocols, let's say that the bookstore also sells gum and candy. You would want to create a class for those items. Call it EdibleItem. It would not make sense to have Gum inherit the same methods as a Book or Magazine, but all of the items would need to be sold, and the inventory would need to be tracked. In this case, it would make sense to add the methods to a protocol that could be shared by each of the items.

Note   A protocol is much different than inheritance. When a class inherits from another class, it not only receives the method declarations, but it also receives the methods themselves. When using a protocol, the declarations are brought over, but the methods themselves need to be written.

Protocol Syntax

The interface example for a protocol is

```
@protocol InventoryItem
- (void)removeFromInventory;
- (void)addToInventory;
@end
```

The interface file for a class that implemented this protocol example would be:

```
@interface MyClass : SomeSuperClass <InventoryItem>
@end
```

Any class that wants to implement the InventoryItem protocol would include <InventoryItem> after the class definition.

For example, you could create this interface for the edible objects that you sell.

```
@interface Edible : NSObject <InventoryItem>
@end
```

It is not uncommon for iOS developers to have multiple protocols for their objects. This adds real power to your objects when needed. Additional protocols are placed after the first one followed by a comma, like so:

```
@interface EditbleItem : UITableViewController  <InventoryItem, SaleItem>
@end
```

This example illustrates the power of protocols. Class EditableItem now must implement all of the required method declarations from the InventoryItem and SaleItem protocols.

Understanding Delegates

Delegates are helper objects. They enable you to control the behavior of your objects. The methods listed in the delegate protocol become **helpers** to your class.

Note   The key to understanding delegates is to know that a delegate is a separate object consulted in order to augment the behavior of a host object. Thus, you can create an **application delegate** object that can affect the behavior of the iOS UIApplication object without subclassing or changing the UIApplication class. The object you create is the delegate object, and the messages that UIApplication will send your object are called **delegate methods**. These are typically defined in a protocol (UIApplicationDelegate) that your class must adopt. To work, a delegate object must be set as the delegate property of the host object.

You can now use these methods in your object. For example, implementing the CLLocationManagerDelegate protocol in your MyClass interface definition enables your object to be notified by the iPhone's GPS of your new location. The following example shows the method that you will include and define inside your object's implementation file:

```
- (void)locationManager:(CLLocationManager *)manager
didUpdateLocations:(NSArray<CLLocation *> *)locations
 {
......
}
```

The `locationManager` delegate method automatically gets called as your GPS location changes, allowing your code to process coordinates.

Next Steps

You will be well prepared to begin writing your own iOS apps. Don't take time off! Keep moving forward! The faster you begin using what you have learned, the better you will get. Whatever you do, don't stop now!

Summary

In this chapter, we covered why multiple inheritance is not used in Objective-C and how protocols and delegates work. There is still a lot to learn and know on your journey. Keep it up and help others along their way.

You should be familiar with the following terms:

- Multiple inheritance

- Protocol

- Delegate

Exercises

- Create a new iOS app project, and take a look at the `AppDelegate.h` file that is automatically generated for you. Note how the `AppDelegate` class implements the `UIApplicationDelegate` protocol.

- Add `NSLog` statements to each of the generated methods in the `AppDelegate.m` implementation file to monitor which methods are called when the application is launched in the simulator.

- Press the simulator's "Home" button while the app is running to see which methods are called as the app enters the background. This will give you a good understanding of how you can monitor how your app's state changes during its execution lifecycle.

CHAPTER 13

Introducing the Xcode Debugger

Xcode is fantastic! Not only is this tool provided free of charge from Apple, but it is actually really good. Aside from being able to create the next great Mac, iPhone, or iPad app, Xcode has a fantastic debugger built right into the tool.

So, what exactly is a debugger? First, let's get something straight: programs do *exactly* what they are written to do. Sometimes what is written isn't exactly what the program is really meant to do. Sometimes this means the program crashes or just doesn't do something that is expected. Whatever the case, when a program doesn't work as planned, the program is said to have **bugs**. The process of going through the code and fixing these problems is called **debugging**.

There is still some debate as to the real origin of the term "bug," but one well-documented case from 1947 involved the late Rear Admiral Grace Hopper, a Naval reservist and programmer at the time. Hopper and her team were trying to solve a problem with the Harvard Mark II computer. One team member found a moth in the circuitry that was causing the problem with one of the relays. Hooper was later quoted as saying, "From then on, when anything went wrong with a computer, we said it had bugs in it."[1]

Regardless of the origin, the term stuck, and programmers all over the world use debuggers, such as Xcode, to help find bugs in programs. People are the real debuggers; debugging tools merely help programmers locate problems. No debugger, whatever the name might imply, fixes problems all on its own.

---

[1]Michael Moritz, Alexander L. Taylor III, and Peter Stoler, "The Wizard Inside the Machine," *Time*, Vol.123, no. 16: pp. 56–63.

© Stefan Kaczmarek, Brad Lees, Gary Bennett, Mitch Fisher 2018
S. Kaczmarek et al., *Objective-C for Absolute Beginners*, https://doi.org/10.1007/978-1-4842-3429-7_13

This chapter will highlight some of the more important features of the Xcode debugger and will explain how to use them. Once you have finished this chapter, you should have a good enough understanding of the Xcode debugger and of the debugging process in general to allow you to search for and fix the majority of programming issues.

Getting Started with Debugging

If you've ever watched a movie in slow motion just so you can catch a detail you can't see when the movie is played at full speed, you've used a tool to do something a little like debugging. The idea that playing the movie frame by frame will reveal the detail you are looking for is the same sort of idea you apply when debugging a program. With a program, sometimes it becomes necessary to slow things down a bit to see what's happening. The debugger allows you to do this using two main features: setting a breakpoint and stepping through the program line by line (more on these two features in a bit). Let's first look at how to get to the debugger and what it looks like.

First, you need to load an existing program. The examples in this chapter use the MyBookstore project from Chapter 8, so open Xcode and load the **MyBookstore** project.

Second, a debug **device** needs to be selected. Xcode provides several device **simulators** for debugging purposes. So, it's possible to test the app on an iPad, iPhone 8, iPhone X, and so on—basically on whatever iOS device you want (Figure 13-1).

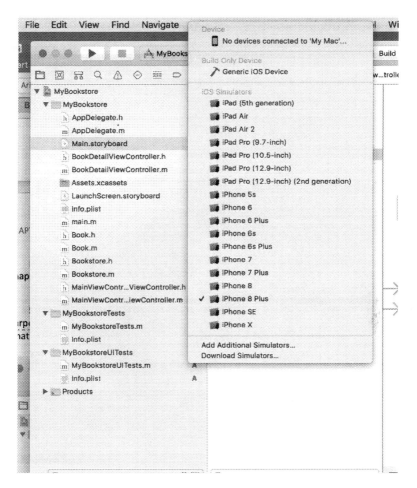

Figure 13-1. *Selecting the iOS simulator*

A simulator works just like the actual device and has the correct screen size based upon the chosen device. It's even possible to rotate and simulate a touch! The examples use the iPhone 8 Plus, but any iOS simulator can be used.

Setting Breakpoints

To see what's going on in a program, you need to make the program pause at certain points that you as a programmer are interested in. A **breakpoint** allows you to do this. Figure 13-2 shows a breakpoint set on line 22 of the MainViewControllerTableViewCont roller.m file. To do this, simply place the cursor over the line number (not the program text but the number 22 to the left of the program text) and click once.

If line numbers are not being displayed, simply choose **Xcode ➤ Preferences** from the main menu, click the **Text Editing** tab, and check the **Line Numbers** check box.

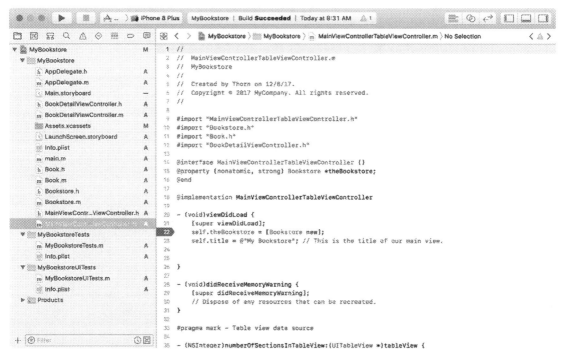

Figure 13-2. *Your first breakpoint*

You can also remove the breakpoint by simply dragging the breakpoint to the right of the line number column and then dropping it. In Figure 13-3, the breakpoint has been dragged to the right of the column and dropped. This will delete the breakpoint. Breakpoints can also be disabled by clicking the breakpoint once. The breakpoint will turn from dark blue (enabled) to light, translucent blue (disabled). Clicking again will reenable the breakpoint.

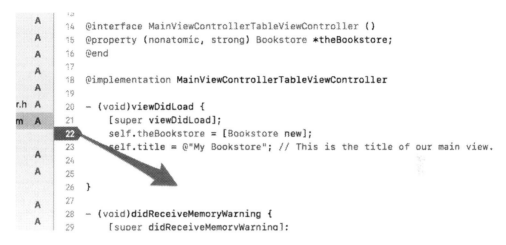

Figure 13-3. *Deleting a breakpoint*

Setting and deleting breakpoints are pretty straightforward tasks.

Using the Breakpoint Navigator

With small projects, knowing where all the breakpoints are isn't necessarily hard. However, once a project gets larger than, say, our small MyBookstore application, managing all the breakpoints could be a little more difficult. Fortunately, Xcode provides a simple method to list all the breakpoints in an application called the Breakpoint Navigator. This can be found by clicking the Breakpoint Navigator icon in the navigation selection bar, as shown in Figure 13-4.

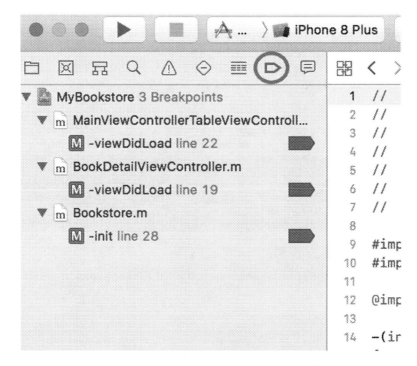

Figure 13-4. *Accessing the Breakpoint Navigator in Xcode*

Once clicked, it will list all the breakpoints currently defined in the application. From here, clicking a breakpoint will take you to the source file with the breakpoint. You can also easily delete and disable/enable breakpoints from here.

To disable/enable a breakpoint, simply click the blue breakpoint icon in the list (or wherever it appears). Don't click the line; it has to be the little blue icon, as shown in Figure 13-5.

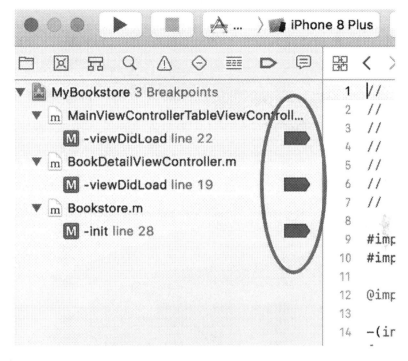

Figure 13-5. *Using the Breakpoint Navigator to enable/disable a breakpoint*

It is sometimes handy to disable a breakpoint instead of deleting it, especially if you plan to put the breakpoint back in the same place again. The debugger will not stop on these faded breakpoints, but they remain in place so they can be conveniently enabled and act as a marker to an important area in the code.

It's also possible to delete breakpoints from the Breakpoint Navigator. Simply select one or more breakpoints and press the **Delete** key. Make sure you select the correct breakpoints to delete since there is no undo feature.

It's also possible to select the file associated with the breakpoints. In this case, if you delete the file listed in the Breakpoint Navigator and press Delete, all breakpoints in that file will be deleted.

Please note that breakpoints are the lines with the small breakpoint icon, as shown in Figure 13-5. The file is outdented from the breakpoint; in Figure 13-5, the files are `MainViewTableViewController.m`, `BookDetailViewController.m`, and `Bookstore.m`. Figure 13-6 shows an example of what a file looks like with more than a single breakpoint.

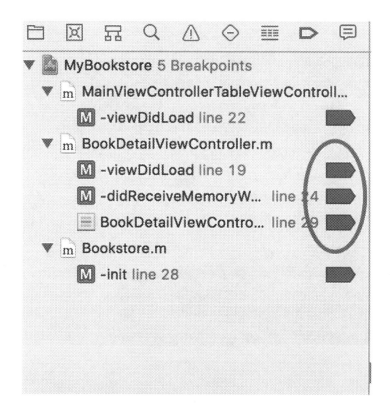

Figure 13-6. *A file with several breakpoints*

Debugging Basics

Set a breakpoint on the statement shown in Figure 13-2, line 22. Next, as shown in Figure 13-7, click the **Run** button to compile the project and start running it within the Xcode debugger.

Figure 13-7. *The Build and Debug buttons in the Xcode toolbar*

Once the project builds, the debugger will start; the screen will show the debugging windows, and the program will stop execution on the line statement, as shown in Figure 13-8.

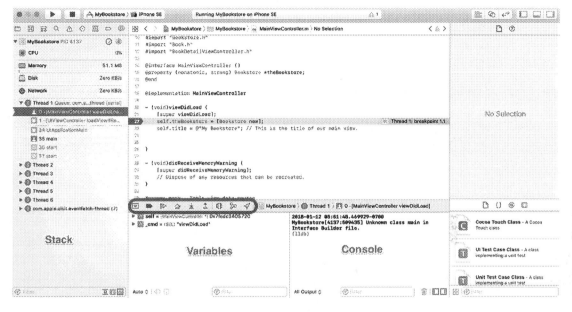

Figure 13-8. *The debugger view with execution*

The debugger view adds some additional windows. Let's go over the different parts of the debugger shown in Figure 13-8:

- *Debugger controls (highlighted within the red oval)*: The debugging controls can pause, continue, step over, step into, and step out of statements in the program. The stepping controls are used most often. The first button on the left is used to show or hide the Debug area. In Figure 13-8, the Debug area is shown.

- *Variables*: The Variables window displays the variables currently in scope. Clicking the little triangle just to the left of a variable name will expand it.

- *Console window*: The Output window will show useful information in the event of a crash or exception. Also, any NSLog output goes here.

- *Stack trace*: The stack shows the object stack as well as all the threads currently active in the program. The stack is a hierarchical view of what methods are being called. For example, main calls UIApplicationMain, and UIApplicationMain calls the UIViewController class. These method calls "stack" up until they finally return, which is where it gets its name.

Working with the Debugger Controls

As mentioned, once the debugger starts, the view will change. The debugging controls appear in Figure 13-8. The controls are fairly straightforward and are explained in Table 13-1.

Table 13-1. *Xcode Debugging Controls*

Control	Description
▶ ■	Clicking the **Stop** button will stop the execution of the program. Clicking the **Run** button starts debugging. If the application is currently in debug mode, clicking the **Run** button again will restart debugging the application from the beginning; it's like stopping and then starting again.
❙❙▷	Clicking the **Pause or Continue** button causes the program to pause or continue execution. The program will continue running until it ends, the **Stop** button is clicked, or the program runs into another breakpoint.

(Continued)

Table 13-1. (*Continued*)

Control	Description
	When the debugger stops on a breakpoint, clicking the **Step Over** button will cause the debugger to execute the current line of code and stop at the next line of code. If the debugger encounters a breakpoint while stepping over code, the debugger will go to the breakpoint instead of skipping over it (Figure 13-9). Clicking this icon will cause the debugger to go to the next line.
	Clicking the **Step Into** button will cause the debugger to go into the specified function or method (Figure 13-10). This is important if there is a need to follow code into specific methods or functions. Only methods for which the project has source code can be stepped into.
	The **Step Out** button will cause the current method to finish executing and the debugger will go back to the caller (Figure 13-10). For example, if you were to step into a line and then immediately click **Step Out**, the `init` method would finish executing, and the debugger would then go back to the original line, effectively finishing the current method (`init`) and stepping back out.

Using the Step Controls

To practice using the step controls, let's step into a function. As the name implies, the **Step Into** button follows program execution into the method that is highlighted. Make sure there is a breakpoint set on the line statement shown in Figure 13-8 (line 22 of the example; yours may be different) of the MainViewControllerTableViewController.m file and click the **Run** button. Your screen should look similar to Figure 13-9.

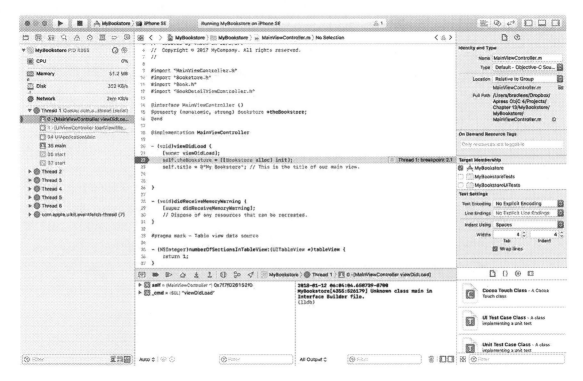

***Figure 13-9.** The debugger stopped on line 22*

Click the **Step Into** button ; this will cause the debugger to go into the property definition of the Bookstore object. The screen should look like Figure 13-10.

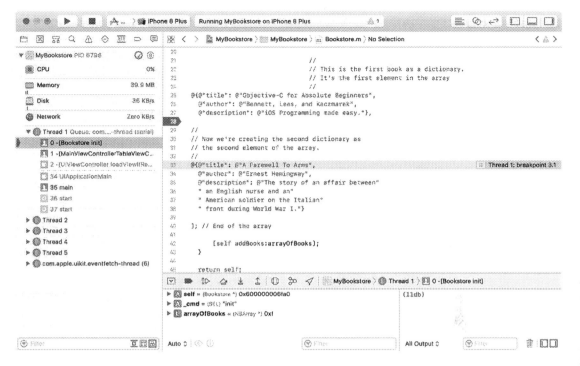

Figure 13-10. *Stepping into the init method of the Bookstore object*

It's important to note that not only is the debugger in the Bookstore object, but the debugger has also moved to the Bookstore.m file (it used to be in the MainViewControll erTableViewController.m file).

The **Step Over control** ⌂ continues execution of the program but doesn't go into a method. It simply executes the method and continues to the next line. The **Step Out** control ⌃ is a little like the opposite of **Step Into**. If the **Step Out** button is clicked, the current method continues execution until it finishes. The debugger then returns to the line before **Step Into** was clicked. For example, if the **Step Into** button is clicked on the line shown in Figure 13-9 and then the **Step Out** button is clicked, the debugger will return to the MainViewControllerTableViewController.m file on the statement shown in Figure 13-9 (line 23 in the example), the line where the **Step Into** was made.

Looking at the Thread Window and Call Stack

As mentioned, the Thread window displays the current thread (there is only one in the example program). However, it also displays the **call stack**. If you look at the difference between Figures 13-9 and 13-10 as far as the Thread window goes, you can see that Figure 13-10 now has the [Bookstore init] method listed because [MainViewControllerTableViewController viewDidLoad] calls the [Bookstore init] method.

Now, the call stack is not simply a list of functions that **have** been called; rather, it's a list of functions that are currently **being** called. That's an important distinction. Once the init method is finished and returns (line 22), [Bookstore init] will no longer appear in the call stack. You can think of a call stack almost like a breadcrumb trail. The trail shows you how to get back to where you started.

Debugging Variables

It is possible to view information about a variable by hovering over the variable as well as by viewing it in the variables section. Let's do this by starting from scratch. To do this, click the **Stop** icon to stop debugging the app and then clear all breakpoints by going to the Breakpoint Navigator (see Figure 13-11), highlighting the project, and then pressing the **Delete** button on the keyboard. (Note that you may not see as many breakpoints; we added more to demonstrate how it would look in a real project.)

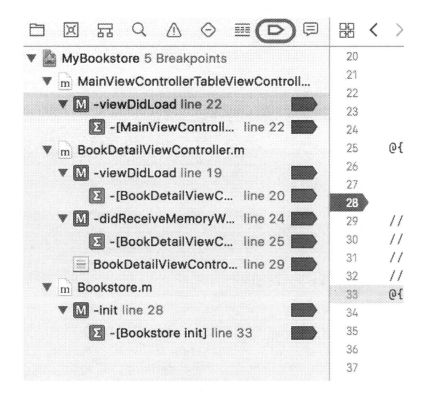

Figure 13-11. *Deleting all breakpoints*

So, now let's add a new breakpoint so you can see some variables. Change to the Project Navigator by clicking the **Folder** icon. Select the Bookstore.m file and set the breakpoint on line 42, as shown in Figure 13-12.

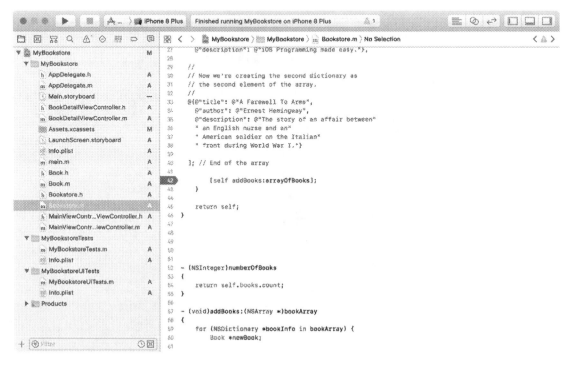

Figure 13-12. *Setting the new breakpoint*

Next, run the application. When the debugger stops on line 42, hover the mouse over arrayOfBooks in the code. There will be a small pop-up, as shown in Figure 13-13.

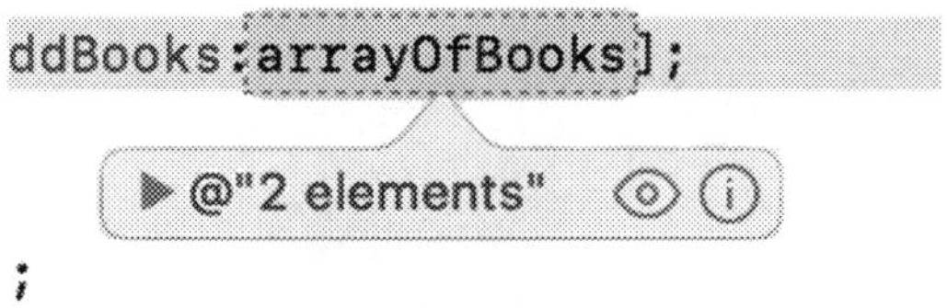

Figure 13-13. *Initial variable pop-up. You need to expand this!*

Next, click the disclosure arrow (the arrow in Figure 13-13). The two items contained in the array will be shown. Click each of the book's disclosure arrows again. What will be displayed are the variables associated with the Books stored in the array, as shown in Figure 13-14.

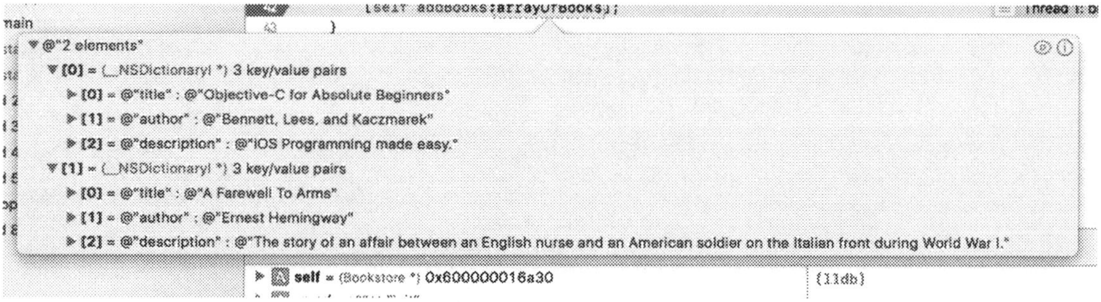

Figure 13-14. *List of Book properties*

Dealing with Code Errors and Warnings

While coding errors and warnings aren't really part of the Xcode debugger, fixing them is part of the entire debugging process. Before a program can be run (with or without the debugger), all errors must be fixed. Warnings won't stop a program from building, but they could cause issues during program execution. It's best not to have any warnings at all.

Let's take a look at a couple of different types of warnings/errors. To start, let's add an error to your code. On line 22 of the MainViewControllerTableViewController.m file, change

```
self.theBookstore = [Bookstore new];
```

to

```
self.theBookstore = [Bookstore newBookStore];
```

Xcode will display a small red exclamation point (stop sign) indicating that there is an error on that line. Next, click the exclamation point to see the error, as shown in Figure 13-15.

```
19
20  - (void)viewDidLoad {
21        [super viewDidLoad];
22        self.theBookstore = [Bookstore newBookStore];          ❶ No known class method for selector 'newBookStore'
23        self.title = @"My Bookstore"; // This is the title of our main view.
24
25
```

Figure 13-15. *Viewing the error in Xcode*

Generally, the error points to the real problem. In the previous case, the BookStore object doesn't know about a method called newBookStore.

Tip   Encountering this error when building a project generally means the method name is misspelled or perhaps the proper header file hasn't been included to let the compiler know about this method. If you know the method exists, then check to see whether the header is included. Otherwise, it might just be a typo.

Let's fix the error by changing the word newBookStore back to new on line 22. Xcode will remove the error, and it will look fine again.

Warnings

Warnings indicate potential problems with the program. As mentioned, warnings won't stop a program from building but may cause issues during program execution. It's outside the scope of this book to cover those warnings that may or may not cause problems during program execution; however, it's good practice to eliminate all warnings from a program.

Let's pick on line 22 again. This time, remove [Bookstore new]; altogether and replace it with just a @""; as shown in Figure 13-16. This time, instead of a red exclamation point, you now see a warning triangle. When clicked, the warning is displayed, just like it did for the error.

```
19
20   - (void)viewDidLoad {
21       [super viewDidLoad];
22       self.theBookstore = @"";          ⚠ Incompatible pointer types assigning to 'Bookstore *' from 'NSString *'
23       self.title = @"My Bookstore"; // This is the title of our main view.
24
25
26   }
```

Figure 13-16. *Viewing an Xcode warning*

It may not be convenient to always click an error or warning in this way. A more convenient way is to view all the errors and warnings across the entire app. To do this, you use the Issue Navigator. To get to the Issue Navigator, just choose the triangle from the Navigator panel. Figure 13-17 is an example of viewing all the errors and warnings.

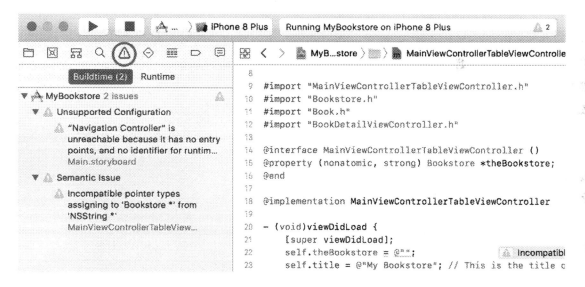

Figure 13-17. *Errors and warnings in the Issue Navigator*

Clicking each line in the Issue Navigator will go to the file and location of the error or warning. This is a fast and easy way to find and navigate to all the errors in the build.

Now, just either undo all of these changes or go back and fix these issue so there are no longer any warnings or errors. Now, play around with running the app; setting breakpoints; and stepping over, into, and out of code. Just have fun. Xcode definitely provides a lot of features to help debug a program and make finding warnings and errors easy to do.

Summary

In this chapter, we covered the high-level features of the free Apple Xcode debugger. Regardless of price, Xcode is an excellent debugger. Specifically, in this chapter, you learned the following:

- The origins of the term "bug" and what a debugger is
- The high-level features of the Xcode debugger
    - Breakpoints
    - Stepping through a program
- How to use the debugging controls
    - Restart and continue (pause)
    - Step over
    - Step into
    - Step out
- Working with the various debugger views
    - Variables
    - Console
- Looking at program variables
- Dealing with errors and warnings

Exercise

Perform the following task:

- Change the Device Type field from iPhone 8 Plus to something else. Just have fun playing around with the different simulator sizes.

Index

Get the eBook for only $5!

Why limit yourself?

With most of our titles available in both PDF and ePUB format, you can access your content wherever and however you wish—on your PC, phone, tablet, or reader.

Since you've purchased this print book, we are happy to offer you the eBook for just $5.

To learn more, go to http://www.apress.com/companion or contact support@apress.com.

Printed in the United States
By Bookmasters